THE ART OF REASONING IS NOTHING MORE THAN A LANGUAGE WELL ARRANGED.

ÉTIENNE BONNOT DE CONDILLAC, 1790

THE VALIDITY OF ALL THE INDUCTIVE METHODS DEPENDS ON THE ASSUMPTION

THAT EVERY EVENT, OR THE BEGINNING OF EVERY PHENOMENON, MUST HAVE

SOME CAUSE; SOME ANTECEDENT, UPON THE EXISTENCE OF WHICH IT IS

INVARIABLY AND UNCONDITIONALLY CONSEQUENT.

JOHN STUART MILL, 1911

I CAN'T BE AS CONFIDENT ABOUT COMPUTER SCIENCE AS I CAN ABOUT BIOL-

OGY. BIOLOGY EASILY HAS 500 YEARS OF EXCITING PROBLEMS TO WORK ON.

IT'S AT THAT LEVEL.

DONALD KNUTH, 1993

SHAWN T. O'NEIL

BIO/RECURSION

AN EXPLORATION IN R

PUBLISHED BY —

SHAWNTONEIL.COM

First printing, February 2018

Contents

Dedicated to:

Dr. Andrew A. Poe

a.k.a. "Captain Recursion"

1 *Programming in R*

The desire to economize time and mental effort in arithmetical computations, and to eliminate human liability to error is probably as old as the science of arithmetic itself.

Howard Aiken, 1937

While the contents of this book may be implemented in almost any programming language, we'll be implementing them in R. R (a derivative of an earlier language called S) was originally designed for statistical computing: producing linear models, analyses of variance, that sort of thing. As we'll see though, R supports a full complement of programming techniques. It also includes some additional easy-to-use features for visualization (via the `ggplot2` and `TurtleGraphics` libraries) which will be useful for this material. In this chapter we'll briefly introduce the R language and some basic programming concepts; not enough to be considered a thorough introduction to R specifically, or programming generally, but enough for our own purposes.

For those with an existing background in programming, R can be described as a *dynamically typed, pass-by-value, multi-paradigm (but largely functional)*, and *vectorized* language.[1]

- *Dynamically typed:* Variables holding data in R can change their data (and the type of data they hold) over time; a `<- 5` sets a to be a "numeric" type, later a line like `a <- "XB"` can set it to a "character" type (similar to "strings" in other languages). Further, there is no need to indicate a variable's type when it is first created. This can be contrasted with Java's `int a = 5; String b = "XB";` where a is forever destined to hold an integer and b can only hold strings.

- *Pass-by-value:* Parameters given to functions effectively become *copies* during the function call, meaning that changes made inside

[1] For those without extensive programming experience, don't let these technical definitions intimidate you. Feel free to read them for their terminological value and focus on the code samples later in this chapter.

the function call are not saved after the call ends. If we consider lines such as letters <- c("A", "b", "C") and answer <- tolower(letters), then letters will still hold c("A", "b", "C") while answer will hold c("a", "b", "c"). This is unsurprising–the point is that the tolower() function couldn't modify the original letters data *even if it wanted to*. This is in contrast to "pass-by-reference" languages like Python and Java, where functions are free to modify the data underlying the parameters so that those changes persist after the function ends.[2] For example, it is possible to write a Python function where answer = tolower(letters) results in letters being changed to ["a", "b", "c"] and answer holding the number of changes made (2 in this case).

[2] The terms "pass-by-value" and "pass-by-reference" are historically laden and indicate fairly specific behavior. In attempts to avoid confusion, the Python community uses the term "pass-by-name" and some Java programmers use the tortured "pass-by-value-of-the-reference" to specify what amounts to slight variations on the basic principle.

- *Multi-paradigm (but largely functional):* Although R supports most of the major programming paradigms, including object-oriented (where collections of data and functions form "objects" meant to represent real-world entities) and procedural (meaning we specify how the computer should perform tasks in step-by-step terms), its functional aspects edge out the others in typical usage. This means that functions are assigned to variables like any other type of data, and functions are free to take functions as parameters and return functions as answers. (R also supports other advanced functional concepts such as closures.) Because this book focuses on recursion but also loop-based techniques, we'll have a unique opportunity to explore the transition points between traditional procedural and more "functional" techniques.

- *Vectorized:* As a statistical language, R enforces vectorized operations as opposed to single-datapoint operations, a feature shared with only a few other languages (e.g. MATLAB). For example, a <- c(1, 2, 3, 4) stores in a a vector of four numbers, as does b <- c(2, 4, 1, 7). The operation a * b returns the vector c(2, 8, 3, 28), while a < b returns the vector of logical values c(TRUE, TRUE, FALSE, TRUE). In fact, even a <- 5 stores a vector in a, where the vector contains only a single numeric element. We'll be making some use of this; given a vector like chars <- c("A", "T", "G", "C"), we can get a subvector holding all but the last element as subchars <- chars[1:(length(chars) - 1)], which reduces to chars[1:3], returning the vector c("A", "T", "G"). This example highlights another difference between R and many other languages–indices in R start at 1 rather than 0 (so chars[1] holds "A", and there is no chars[0]).

R is a large language, and unfortunately one with many special cases–although R functions are by default pass-by-value, it is *possible* to pass some data by reference. As such, these definitions and the rest of this chapter constitute more of a rough field-guide to R than a definitive reference.

1.1   Installing R

The most straightforward way to write and execute R programs is to first download and install the R interpreter[3] itself from `http://r-project.org`, and then download the RStudio Integrated Development Environment (IDE) from `http://rstudio.org`. While R itself handles the execution of R code, RStudio provides a text editor aware of R's specialized syntax and facilitates sending R code to the R interpreter for execution.

[3] Interpreter: a program designed to interpret, or read and execute lines of code. This is in contrast to compiled languages, meaning the code is translated into machine code readable directly by the CPU.

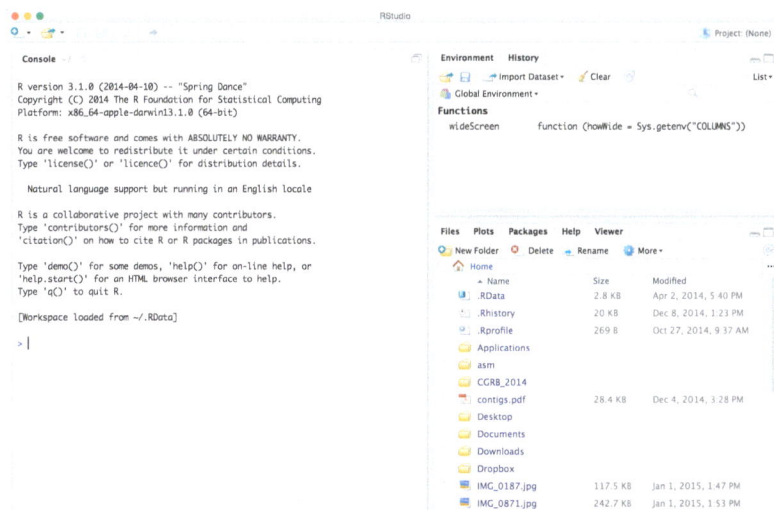

Figure 1.1: RStudio after initial installation.

When first opened, RStudio presents three panes (Figure 1.1). On the left is the R interpreter itself–here we can type a line of R code like `print("Hello World")` followed by the Enter key and that line will be executed. The upper-right pane shows some of the variables currently stored by the R interpreter; executing a line like `a <- c(1, 2, 3, 4)` will cause `a` to appear here. Later, a line like `print(a)` will print the stored contents of `a`. The lower-right pane shows a file browser, tab for help information, and a plots tab for the output of graphical function calls.

None of these panes, however, are where we'll be primarily working. Rather than executing lines of R code one at a time, we want to write R programs, or *scripts*: files containing many lines of code that can be executed as a batch. To edit such a file, we can select File → New File → R Script. This creates a new pane in the upper-left portion of the window with a text editor for writing the script (Figure 1.2).[4]

To execute lines in a script, we can either 1) highlight them (with the mouse) and click the Run button, which sends them to the

[4] Actually, it is a good idea to create a "Project" in RStudio, which is a simply a folder that might contain multiple R scripts and other files. RStudio also supports the creation of "R Markdown" files: documents containing human-readable text interleaved with chunks of code and their output, which can later be exported as reports in PDF or HTML format.

Figure 1.2: Writing an R script. The Source button will execute all the lines in the file, while individual lines can be executed by highlighting them and click Run.

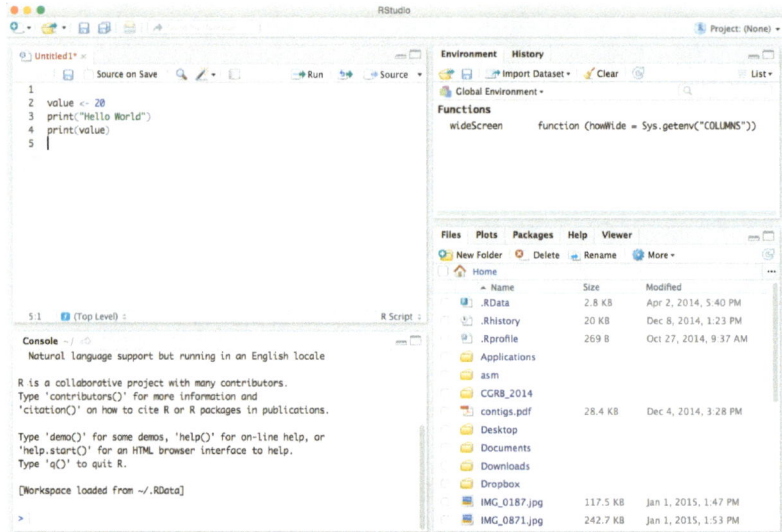

R interpreter below for execution, or 2) click the Source button, which sends all lines in the file to the interpreter for execution. It is worth noting that the former "highlight-and-run" method allows us to execute lines out of order. Naturally, computer programs are sensitive to the order of execution, so we suggest focusing on the Source button to execute the script as a whole each time.

1.2 Data Types, Variable Assignment

R supports a number of data types, and we'll augment these with some provided by packages later. The most basic type of data in R are vectors: of integers, character strings, numerics,[5] or logicals (TRUE or FALSE values, also known as boolean values in other languages). Anything after a # is ignored by the R interpreter, allowing us to add "comments" to scripts (Figure 1.3). Single []s can be used to index, or access, an individual vector element, and indices start at 1.

As with many languages, R uses an evaluate-then-assign strategy, and we can reuse variable names (Figure 1.4).

Because vectors are the most basic type, operations are *vectorized*, or performed element-by-element. If one vector is shorter, it will be "recycled" as needed (Figure 1.5). We'll only occasionally make use of the vectorized features of R in this book. One handy function we'll see is seq(), which returns a sequence of numbers as a vector (seq(1, 4) returns the vector c(1, 2, 3, 4)).

The character type might better be described as a vector of strings: in the v5 variable of Figure 1.3, "Mary" can be found at v5[2].[6] In later chapters we'll prefer to work with DNA sequences as vectors like c("A", "C", "T", "G") rather than c("ACTG") so that we can access individual letters (also called "bases" in molecular bi-

---

[5] Numerics are "general" (possibly non-integer) numbers, like 4.2, though by default even numbers like 4 become a numeric 4.0 and are stored as a numeric, unless they are explicitly converted to integers.

[6] Again, since vectors are the most basic type, v5[2] returns "Mary", which is itself a vector of length one. In fact, v5[c(2, 3)] will return the vector c("Mary", "Jim").

```
# vector of numerics
v1 <- c(1, 4, 5, 8, 7)
lenv1 <- length(v1)
print(lenv1)            # prints 5
print(v1[4])            # prints 8

# single elements are actually vectors of length 1
v2 <- 215.6
# same as:
v2 <- c(215.6)
print(length(v2))       # prints 1

# vectors of logicals and character strings
v3 <- c(TRUE, TRUE, FALSE, TRUE)
v4 <- FALSE             # same as v4 <- c(FALSE)
v5 <- c("Joe", "Mary", "Jim")
v6 <- "Bridget"         # same as v6 <- c("Bridget")
```

Figure 1.3: The simplest data type in R is the vector, though there are different types of vectors.

```
value <- 5
value <- value + 3      # value + 3 assigned to value
print(value)            # prints 8
```

Figure 1.4: Variables may be reassigned based on the results of computations.

ology). In Chapter 6 we'll write helper functions to convert between these two representations. The c() function can be used to concatenate two or more vectors, producing another: c(c(2, 4), c(8, 10)) returns the vector c(2, 4, 8, 10), and c(c(1, 2, 3), 10) returns c(1, 2, 3, 10).

R vectors are simple–they can only hold so-called "atomic" elements (e.g. numbers and character strings). Notably, vectors cannot contain vectors; an expression like c(c(1, 2), c(3, 4)) produces not a vector of two vectors, but the deconstructed vector c(1, 2, 3, 4). Further, vectors must hold all the same type of elements. The line values <- c(4, TRUE, "Joe") will result in values holding all character strings (in this case, "4", "TRUE", and "Joe") due to R's enforcement of this rule.

WHILE VECTORS ARE THE SIMPLEST DATATYPE IN R, the *list* is much more flexible. A list can hold any number of elements of different types, including vectors and other lists. In Figure 1.6 we've created a list of three elements: two lists (each themselves containing two vectors of length one) and a numeric vector.

Now, one may be forgiven for thinking that info[3] will return the vector in the third position of the info list (holding just c(9.6, 4.2)), but just as []-syntax applied to a vector always returns a vector, []-*syntax* applied to a list always returns a *list*. So, something like val <- info[3] is equivalent to val <- list(c(9.6, 4.2)), namely a list of length one (containing a vector of length two). So, an alternative syntax is needed, and that is the [[]]-extractor: val <-

Figure 1.5: Most operations are vectorized, with shorter vectors being recycled if needed.

```
nums <- c(1, 2, 3, 4)
mult <- c(10, -10, 1, -1)
result <- nums * mult
print(result)              # prints 10 -20 3 -4

mult2 <- c(10, -10)
result <- nums * mult2     # recycles mult2
print(result)              # prints 10 -20 30 -40

mult3 <- 10                # same as mult3 <- c(10)
result <- nums * mult3     # recycles mult3
print(result)              # prints 10 20 30 40
```

Figure 1.6: Lists can contain any number of different types of elements, including vectors and other lists.

```
info <- list(list("Kim", 27), list("Joe", 42), c(9.6, 4.2))
print(length(info))        # prints 3
print(info[[3]])           # prints c(9.6, 4.2)
```

`info[[3]]` extracts the element itself (the vector) at the third position (and is equivalent to `val <- c(9.6, 4.2)` in this case). Similarly, `info[2]` is equivalent to `list(list("Joe", 42))`, while `info[[2]]` returns the inner list itself (just `list("Joe", 42)`).

Though we won't do so often, we can assign to elements of lists (and vectors) by specifying the slot, even if it doesn't exist. Because lists can be arbitrarily complex, an alternative to `print()`, `str()`, is sometimes used to print a summary of a list's structure (Figures 1.7 and 1.8).

Figure 1.7: New elements can be inserted into lists, and while `print()` can print the contents of a list, the `str()` function is often used to examine a list's structure.

```
info[[4]] <- list("Bob", 19)
str(info)                  # print a structure summary
```

Elements of lists (and most R data types) can have "names," allowing us to access elements by name as opposed to index number. Figure 1.9 shows an example of using `catalog[["people"]]` as opposed to `catalog[[1]]`. There is also a `names()` function that returns the names of a list (or other type) as a character vector.[7]

Because accessing list elements by name is so common, a shortcut syntax exists for it: `info$people` is converted to `catalog[["people"]]`, so something like `print(catalog$people)` also prints the vector containing `"Kim"` and `"Joe"`. Similarly, new elements can be concatenated to the ends of lists by name via a direct assignment; `catalog$heights <- c(4.7, 5.1)` would add a new third element to the `catalog` list, accessible later as `catalog$heights`, `catalog[["heights"]]`, or `catalog[[3]]`.

```
List of 4
 $ :List of 2
  ..$ : chr "Kim"
  ..$ : num 27
 $ :List of 2
  ..$ : chr "Joe"
  ..$ : num 42
 $ : num [1:2] 9.6 4.2
 $ :List of 2
  ..$ : chr "Bob"
  ..$ : num 19
```

Figure 1.8: Output for code in Figure 1.7.

If you find R lists and vectors confusing, remember that vectors are the simplest datatype and can only hold similar collections of items (but not vectors or other sub-collections), whereas lists can hold any number of different elements, including vectors and other lists. When in doubt, the `class()` function can be used to

[7] Figure 1.9 also reveals that long expressions can be broken over multiple lines, provided that the line to continue ends with a character letting the R interpreter know that the expression isn't finished (common choices are the comma , and operators like +). You may also notice that within a function call we use = to assign parameters by name, rather than <-, which is used to assign data to variables.

determine a variable's type: `print(class(catalog))` will print
`"list"` while `print(class(catalog$people))` will print `"character"`
(the most common vector types are `"character"`, `"numeric"`, and
`"logical"`). Finally, don't forget that syntax like `some_list[[2]]`,
`some_list[["some_name"]]`, or `some_list$some_name` can be used to
access individual list elements by index and name (if the elements
are named).

```
catalog <- list(people = c("Kim", "Joe"),
                ages = c(27, 42))
print(catalog[["people"]])  # prints "Kim" "Joe"
print(names(catalog))       # prints "people" "ages"
```

Figure 1.9: List elements can be accessed by name.

Although lists are rarely considered in normal (statistical) usage
of R, we'll be using them quite a bit. We'll also find we need to
convert other data types–like vectors–to and from lists. The function
`as.list()` coerces its input into a list. For example, if `a <- c(4,
5, 6)`, then `a_as_list <- as.list(a)` converts the vector `a` into
a list of single-element vectors. The `unlist()` function does the
opposite: given a list, it extracts the elements and returns a vector
(here `unlist(a_as_list)` returns the same vector as `a`). Occasionally,
we'll even want to convert more exotic data types into a vector,
but we'll have to use an intermediate list representation, as in
`unlist(as.list(some_exotic_type))`.[8]

[8] R includes many other "as." functions, including `as.character()` which coerces its input into a character vector, `as.integer()` which coerces to an integer vector (elements rounded down), and `as.data.frame()` (coerces to a data frame, covered next).

DATA FRAMES are used to represent tables of data in R. In practice,
they are lists with each element (usually a vector) representing a
column of the table. The `catalog` list generated above is much like
a data frame with two columns (one for people and one for ages).
True data frames, though, enforce the rule that each column must
have the same length. Thus, if a new column is added, it is filled out
to the correct length (Figure 1.10).

```
catalog_df <- data.frame(people = c("Kim", "Joe"),
                         ages = c(27, 42))
catalog_df$heights <- c(4.7, 5.1)      # add a new column
catalog_df$registered <- TRUE          # add another new column
print(catalog_df)
```

Figure 1.10: Data frames are like lists, where each element represents a column of a table. Data frames enforce that all columns are the same length.

Since data frames are essentially lists, we can access an individual column by name, as in `print(catalog_df$people)` or
`print(catalog_df[["people"]])`, and `length(catalog_df)` returns
the number of columns. There are also `nrow()` and `ncol()` functions
that return the number of rows and columns of a data frame (or
matrix, discussed below). While data frames are one of the most
important types for normal (statistical) uses of R, in this book lists
will play a more central role so we won't cover other features of data
frames at this time.

	people	ages	heights	registered
1	Kim	27	4.7	TRUE
2	Joe	42	5.1	TRUE

Figure 1.11: Output for code in Figure 1.10.

WHILE DATA FRAMES ARE A TYPE of 2-dimensional data store, we'll also occasionally have a need for simpler 2-dimensional stores called matrices. These can be created by specifying the cell data (as a vector), as well as the number of rows and columns (Figure 1.12).

```
m <- matrix(c(1, 2, 3, 4, 5, 6), nrow = 2, ncol = 3)
print(m)
print("Printing element at 2,3:")
print(m[2, 3])                        # prints 6
```

Figure 1.12: Matrices are effectively 2-dimensional vectors.

```
     [,1] [,2] [,3]
[1,]    1    3    5
[2,]    2    4    6
[1] "Printing element at 2,3:"
[1] 6
```

Figure 1.13: Output for code in Figure 1.12.

Elements of a matrix can be access via [row, col] syntax, e.g. print(m[2,3]) prints 6 (since 6 is the value in row 2, column 3). As the output in Figure 1.13 hints, we can also extract an entire row or column as a vector by leaving the row or column number missing: m[1,] returns the vector c(1, 3, 5) (the first row) and m[, 2] returns the vector c(3, 4) (the second column).

Matrices can also have row as well as column names, and if only one element is given to initialize the cells it will be reused. Figure 1.14 shows the creation of a 2×3 matrix of zeros with row names "A" and "B", and column names "X", "Y", and "Z". The last line sets one of the cells to 30.

Just as with named lists, matrix elements can be accessed by name, as in print(m2["A", "Y"]) and m2["B", "Y"] <- 30; whole rows and columns can be accessed with syntax like m2["A",] and m2[, "Y"]. Like vectors, matrices are restricted to holding only the same type of data (e.g. character, numeric, or logical). In fact, while a data frame is supported by a list underneath, a matrix is supported by a vector.

Figure 1.14: Matrix rows and columns can be named, and cells and rows can be accessed by name.

```
m2 <- matrix(0, nrow = 2, ncol = 3,
             dimnames = list(c("A", "B"),
                             c("X", "Y", "Z")))
m2["B", "Y"] <- 30           # set cell B,Y to 30
print(m2)
```

```
  X  Y Z
A 0  0 0
B 0 30 0
```

Figure 1.15: Output for code in Figure 1.14.

BESIDES VECTORS, LISTS, DATA FRAMES, AND MATRICES, R includes some special types of data. The value NA can be used to indicate "missing" or "unknown" values in vectors, for example ages <- c(44, NA, 31) indicates that the second age is unknown. The function is.na() returns a logical vector: is.na(ages) in this case would return the logical vector c(FALSE, TRUE, FALSE).[9]

Another potential value is NULL, as in a variable that is "unset" (semantically different than "unknown"). For example, val <- NULL is a valid line of code, and later is.null(val) will return the length-one logical vector TRUE. Lists can hold NULL as well, as in info <- list(people = c("Kim", "Joe"), ages = NULL). In this case is.null(info) will return FALSE, but is.null(info$ages) will

[9] In R the . character has no special meaning and is often found in variable and function names. This is sometimes confusing for those coming from other languages where the . character is an operator of some kind. Generally we'll stick to using underscores when creating our own variable and function names.

return TRUE. Note that while is.na() can return a logical vector of any length, is.null() always returns a logical vector of length one.

As we can see, R supports a rich and often confusing set of data types, and we've covered but a sampling. Still, these should serve as a sufficient introduction for the chapters to come.

1.3 Control Structures

Control structures are used to alter the flow of code execution from the standard top-to-bottom order. The basic control structures we'll cover include while-loops, if/else if/else blocks, for-loops, and most importantly functions.

While-loops execute a *block* of code (lines enclosed in a pair of {}-braces) so long as a logical conditional or variable evaluates to TRUE. A simple example is shown in Figure 1.16. When executed, this code will print 1, 2, 3, and "done!". Any expression that produces a logical vector can be used for the check, including function calls like is.null(val). Owing to R's vectorized nature, an expression might return a long logical vector. What would happen if the first line in Figure 1.16 was var <- c(1,100)? In this case val < 4 would return the logical vector c(TRUE, FALSE), and only the *first* logical value will be used for the check (and a warning message will be produced).

```
val <- 1
while(val < 4) {
 print(val)
 val <- val + 1
}
print("done!")
```

Figure 1.16: A while-loop. This example prints 1, 2, 3, and then "done!".

Logical statements can be combined with operators like & (and), | (or), and ! (not). For example, if val <- 1 then val < 4 & val == 2 would be FALSE, since val < 4 is true but val == 2 is not (== tests for equality, != tests for inequality). Similarly, !val < 4 results in FALSE (the negation of TRUE).[10]

[10] For those unfamiliar with & and |, whereas the & operator is straightforward, the | operator might be better read as "and/or," since a | b will be true if a is true, b is true, or both. For those familiar with these operators in other languages, note that R uses & and | rather than the more commonly seen && and ||.

IF/ELSE IF/ELSE STATEMENTS conditionally execute a block of code. An example can be found in Figure 1.17.

Here, exactly one of the blocks will be executed, depending on the contents of age. If age holds 20 the opening "checking" message will print, the second block will execute, and then the "done" message will print. If age is 30, then only the last block will execute.

While an if/else if/else block must have exactly one if()-controlled block, it may have zero or more else if()-controlled blocks (i.e., they are optional) and then an optional else-controlled block. Figures 1.18 and 1.19 show examples of simpler constructs.

Figure 1.17: An if/else if/else statement. Which of the four blocks will run depends on the contents of age.

```
print("checking U.S. age restrictions")

if(age < 18) {
 print("too young to vote")
} else if(age < 21) {
 print("old enough to vote")
 print("too young to drink")
} else if(age < 25) {
 print("old enough to vote and drink")
 print("too young to rent a car")
} else {
 print("old enough to vote, drink, rent cars...")
 print("... and old enough to know better than do all at once!")
}

print("done checking age")
```

Figure 1.18: An if/else if/else statement utilizing only an if()-controlled and an else-controlled block.

```
print("checking U.S. drinking age")

if(age < 21) {
 print("you can't drink!")
} else {
 print("have one on me")
}

print("done checking age")
```

In contrast to some other languages with similar-looking syntax, due to the way else and if() statements are implemented in R, else if() and else statements should occur on the same line as the previous block's closing }, as in the examples shown.

All of the control structures can be nested to powerful effect. To drive an example, %% is the modulus operator (remainder after long division), so a line like val %% 2 == 0 returns TRUE if val is even and FALSE if it is odd. Figure 1.20 shows a while-loop that prints all even numbers between 0 and 100. When nesting structures like this, we increase the indentation level for each nesting level. This makes it easy to visualize the logical structure of code.

FOR-LOOPS SET A VARIABLE to each element of a vector or list, and execute a block of code with that setting. Figure 1.21 illustrates printing three different names (contained in a vector) and the number of characters in each (using the nchar() function). Here person is the variable that is set to every element of the people vector in turn–we could have used any name for this auto-changing variable.

The output of Figure 1.21 are lines "Kim", 3, "Joseph", 6, "Jake", and 4. Often, the seq() function is used to generate a vector of numbers to loop over.[11] Figure 1.22 illustrates using this technique

[11] Readers with experience in other languages might recognize R's for loop as a "foreach" loop; R has no equivalent to C and Java's traditional-style for-loops (for(i = 1; i < 10; i++) {...}).

```
print("checking U.S. presidential age")

if(age > 35) {
 print("Hey, you can run for president!")
}

print("done checking age")
```

Figure 1.19: An if/else if/else statement utilizing only an if()-controlled block.

```
val <- 0
while(val <= 100) {
  if(val %% 2 == 0) {     # val is even
    print(val)
  }
  val <- val + 1          # increment val
}
```

Figure 1.20: An if statement nested inside of a while-loop.

to print even-numbered rows of a matrix m.

It is worth noting that for these simple examples of while and for loops, there are vectorized solutions usually considered preferable by the R community. To print all even rows of a matrix m, for example, we could use print(m[seq(1, nrow(m), 2),]), since seq() can take a third "step" parameter and row selection with [,]-syntax is itself vectorized. However, many of the the techniques used in this book will use loops in ways that aren't easy to vectorize.

There is a myth that for- and while-loops in R are particularly slow. While vectorized operations are generally faster than loop-based ones in R, loops are not egregiously slow *except* when they are used to iteratively lengthen a vector or list (or matrix or data frame). Figure 1.23 gives an example where a vector of even numbers between 0 and 10,000 is built using a loop–this is quite slow for reasons to be discussed in Chapter 2. In Chapter 4 we'll discuss data types that can be iteratively lengthened efficiently (stacks and queues).

FUNCTIONS ARE THE LAST AND MOST IMPORTANT control structure we'll cover. They allow us to define a block of code that can be executed later by name–they often take a number of inputs called *parameters* and return an output value. Figure 1.24 shows an example of a simple function definition and use.

When the interpreter reads the lines defining the function, it stores it in add_two_nums much like any other data is stored in a variable. But, these lines are not *executed* until the function is later *called*, taking the x and y data as parameters and returning the value to be then stored in answer. Note that in this function we've specified the parameters by position; we could also specify them by name (as in answer <- add_two_nums(a = x, b = y)) or by both position and name (as in answer <- add_two_nums(x, b = y)).[12]

[12] By the way, when return() is called inside the function, the function execution ends; if there were any other lines after return() in the function block, they would not be executed.

Figure 1.21: An example for loop; the output here is "Kim", 3, "Joseph", 6, "Jake", and 4.

```
people <- c("Kim", "Joseph", "Jake")

for(person in people) {
 print(person)
 print(nchar(person))
}
```

Figure 1.22: Using a for loop to iterate over a vector of numbers (seq(1, nrow(m))).

```
m <- matrix(0, nrow = 20, ncol = 5)  # 20x5 matrix of 0s

for(i in seq(1, nrow(m))) {
 if(i %% 2 == 0) {                    # if i is even
   print(m[i, ])                      # print row i
 }
}
```

[13] This is the "pass-by-value" property mentioned earlier in this chapter. Actually, R does not copy data (a slow operation) unless it absolutely needs to using what is known as a "copy-on-write" strategy. Still, we needn't worry about how these lower-level details are implemented and can instead focus on the effects.

Of crucial importance, the parameters names used by the function block (a and b) need not correspond to any variable names used outside the function, including those given to the function when called (x and y). In effect, the data underlying x is copied into a for use by the function, similarly the data in y is copied into b.[13] These parameters (e.g. a and b), as well as any variable created by the function call with <- (e.g. result) are *local* to the function call. This means they are removed when the function call ends, and they "shadow" any other variables that happen to have the same name at the time of the function call. The formal name for these are *local variables*.

The upshot is that functions that work only with their parameters (and create their own variables with <-) generally can't 'step on' other existing data. Figure 1.25 modifies Figure 1.24 to demonstrate this fact. Here, after the function returns a and result contain their original "outside" values defined before the function call, and no b exists.

In a sense, then, a function call can only affect the "outside world" by returning a value, which can then be assigned to a variable (e.g. answer).[14] Usually, this is exactly what we want: to encapsulate a block of code as a function and use it as a black box. By doing so we can organize even huge programs as small, manageable functions calling other small, manageable functions (and yes, a custom function can call other custom functions, provided they are defined at the point they are called).

[14] This is one of the primary tenets of the "functional programming" paradigm. A function which always returns the same value for the same inputs, and has no other side-effects, is called a *pure* function.

On the other hand, occasionally, and especially in later chapters of this book, we do want a function to modify some existing data without having to use return(). For this we can use *global* variables–those that persist beyond function calls and are readable and writable at any time. We can create and write to global variables in R by using the <<- assigner (they can be read from just like

```
val <- 0
evens <- c()                           # empty vector

while(val <= 10000) {
 if(val %% 2 == 0) {                   # if val is even
   evens <- c(evens, val)              # append val to evens (slow!)
 }
 val <- val + 1
}

print(evens)
```

Figure 1.23: While for and while loops are not particularly slow, lengthening an R vector or list iteratively (a common operation in loops) is a slow operation.

```
add_two_nums <- function(a, b) {
 result <- a + b
 return(result)
}

x <- 4
y <- 7
answer <- add_two_nums(x, y)
print(answer)                          # prints 11
```

Figure 1.24: A simple function. The function is defined first, but the lines it contains are not executed until it is called on the second-to-last line. Note that the parameter names (a and b) need not relate to variable names used in the function call (x and y).

any other variable, unless a local variable of the same name shadows them).[15] Figure 1.26 illustrates a modification to Figure 1.24 using a global variable called CALL_COUNTER to keep track of how many times the function has been called.

We must remember to use <<- when assigning to a global variable (otherwise a shadowing local variable is created causing confusing bugs), and we are using capital letters for their names simply as a visual reminder of their special nature.

BY DEFAULT, VALUES IN R THAT ARE NOT ASSIGNED TO VARIABLES are printed. This can be easily seen by just printing a variable name at the interpreter prompt (Figure 1.27).

Another consequence of this is that function return values are printed if the function is called but the result is not stored. As an example, consider Figure 1.28: here we have a function which prints a message, but if the given value is small, we want the function to do *nothing*, so we simply have it return.[16]

In R however, calling return() doesn't simply stop the execution of the function, it does indeed return a value, and that value is NULL. Thus the call check_val(5) results in a printout of NULL. To prevent this and make our function act more like it is simply stopping, we can make the returned NULL invisible (not printed by default), with return(invisible()).

[15] Technically, there is a hierarchy of "globalness" in R, and <<- assigns to variables "up" in the hierarchy. Since we are initially assigning these at the topmost level though (not inside any function), they are truly global.

[16] This is not a pattern generally seen in functional programming, but is common otherwise.

Figure 1.25: Parameters and variables created inside functions with <- are local variables; they shadow existing variables of the same name and are removed when the function call ends.

```
add_two_nums <- function(a, b) {
  result <- a + b
  return(result)
}

a <- "test a"
result <- "test result"
x <- 4
y <- 7
answer <- add_two_nums(x, y)
print(answer)                          # prints 11
print(a)                               # prints "test a"
print(result)                          # prints "test result"
print(b)                               # Error: object 'b' not found
```

Figure 1.26: Global variables may be read as any other (unless they are shadowed by a local variable) and are written to with <<-. Here we're using capital letters only as a reminder that they are global.

```
add_two_nums <- function(a, b) {
  CALL_COUNTER <<- CALL_COUNTER + 1
  result <- a + b
  return(result)
}

CALL_COUNTER <<- 0                      # initialize global
answer <- add_two_nums(2, 4)
print(CALL_COUNTER)                     # prints 1
answer <- add_two_nums(6, 5)
print(CALL_COUNTER)                     # prints 2
```

1.4   Packages

R packages are downloadable add-ons providing additional functions. Most packages are stored in an online repository called the Comprehensive R Archive Network, or CRAN. Installing a package from CRAN is straightforward (assuming an active internet connection is available). For example, to install the stringr package, in the interpreter window (at the > prompt, *not* in the script), run install.packages("stringr"). You may be you prompted via a popup window to select the nearest download location.

Once the process is complete, there are two ways to utilize functions provided by the package in a script. The first is to prefix the function name with the package name and ::, as in greeting <- stringr::str_c("hi", "there"). This line runs the str_c() function from stringr (which concatenates character vectors). Alternatively, one may first "load" the functions in a package by calling library(); in this example we would first run library(stringr) and then greeting <- str_c("hi", "there"). Usually these calls to library() are located at the top of the script.

Throughout this book we will use functions from several packages. Rather than describe these functions and packages in detail

```
> a <- c(4, 5, 6)
> a
[1] 4 5 6
```

Figure 1.27: Values or variables that are not assigned are printed by default.

```
check_val <- function(val) {
  if(val < 10) {
    return()
  }
  print("Given value is at least 10.")
}

check_val(5)        # prints NULL
```

Figure 1.28: A function which should do nothing if a small value is given.

here, we'll just summarize them and note on which pages they are first introduced. Also, rather than prefix the function names, we will assume all scripts load these libraries at the top (Figure 1.29).

```
library(stringr)
library(rstackdeque)
library(hash)
library(TurtleGraphics)
library(ggplot2)

# Code below
# ...
```

Figure 1.29: Loading libraries needed for scripts.

- stringr: This package provides a number of functions for working with character vectors and their elements. Many of these functions have "regular" R equivalents–for example, str_c() from stringr is very similar to the built-in paste()–but the functions in stringr are more consistent in names and parameters. Functions from stringr we'll use include str_sub(), str_length(), str_c(), and str_detect(); these are described on page 39.

- rstackdeque: While the various data structures built into R (data frames, lists, matrices, etc.) are powerful, there are a couple we'll need that are not provided. The first are "stacks" (page 59) rstackdeque provides these with functions rstack(), insert_top(), without_top(), peek_top(), and empty(), as well as helper conversion functions as.list() and as.data.frame(). Other structures provided by this package are queues, through functions rpqueue(), insert_back(), without_front() and peek_front(). The functions provided by rstackdeque are described on page 69.

- hash: Another data structure we'll make heavy use of is the hash table. The hash package provides these through functions hash(), has.key(), keys(), and values() (page 72).

- TurtleGraphics: The TurtleGraphics package provides a simple interface for programmatic, line-based drawing. We'll use this only in the last chapter, where we'll learn how some of the techniques in other parts of the book can be visualized in beautiful ways. Functions provided by TurtleGraphics include turtle_init(), turtle_forward(), turtle_turn(), and several others described on page 133.

- ggplot2: This package provides a powerful toolset for plotting data stored in data frames. The main function provided by this package is ggplot(), which works in coordination with others like geom_line() and geom_tile(). Unfortunately, the ggplot2 package is large and a useful tutorial for it would be outside the scope of this book, so we'll present and use ggplot2 code without explanation. Excellent resources abound, including the official website http://docs.ggplot2.org, books such as *ggplot2: Elegant Graphics for Data Analysis* by Hadley Wickham, and *A Primer for Computational Biology* by Shawn T. O'Neil (yours truly) available as an open-access resource and in print.

1.5   *Getting Help*

Because of R's size and complexity, the official documentation and other unofficial resources are extremely helpful. The most important too in this is the help() function: when run at the interactive > prompt it will show a help page on a given function name. For example, help("length") will show information on the length() function.[17]. To get help on an installed package like stringr, try help(package = "stringr")

There also exist a number of excellent books and online resources. For readers new to programming and R, I would recommend (naturally) my own *A Primer for Computational Biology*, though many other books recently on the market are good as well. For beginner to intermediate programmers, I like *The Art of R Programming* by Norm Matloff. For a deeper look at R, *Advanced R* by Hadley Wickham is enlightening.

[17] A shortcut for help() is ?; so ?length is a shortcut for help("length").

2 Recursive Structures

Let's consider a simple R list, as shown in Figure 2.1. Organizing data into lists is one of the most common features of programming, and R lists allow us to store any type of data in sequential order.

```
nums <- list(3, 5, 12)
```

Figure 2.1: A simple list of numbers.

How might a list like this be stored in the computer's memory? It might be stored simply as a contiguous sequence of binary numbers; in this case if the numbers were stored in an 8-bit representation, this could simply be 000000110000010100001100 (where 00000011 is 3, and so on).

Unfortunately, a strategy like this won't work for more general types of data. What if we wanted to store a list of more complicated objects, as in names <- list("Mary", "Joe", "Allison")? In this case, what might be stored is again a series of integers, but this time those integers indicate the "address" or location of the data in memory. Thus, a list like 100111000010110100101101 would indicate that "Mary" exists at ad-

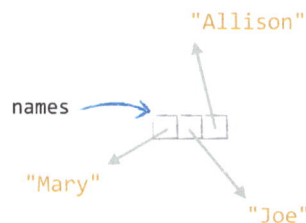

Figure 2.2: Visualizing the "address" model for lists. Here we are indicating that individual data element may occur anywhere in memory by distributing them visually in the figure.

dress 156 (10011100), "Joe" at address 45 (00101101), and so on (Figure 2.2).[1] These address elements are sometimes known as "references" (though references also often keep track of the type of data at the given address). The primary advantage of a system like this is that data elements of arbitrary size can be "referenced" by the list elements.

Now, what if we desire to append a new element, say "Katie", to the list? This would require creating the new data element for

[1] Most modern computers use 64 bits to store a simple integer; some programming languages like R define their own representation using many more to allow for much larger numbers. Using more bits for addresses also allows the computer to reference more places in memory; this is one of the primary advantages of using a 64-bit processor over a 32-bit processor.

"Katie" (which gets stored in memory anywhere it will fit by the interpreter working in conjunction with the operating system), and *appending* to the list the new address for it.[2] Let's assume it is fairly easy for the system find a sufficiently large chunk of memory, somewhere, for the new data element. But what about appending the new address? If the next few bits of memory (after the current list of addresses) are unused, then they can simply be written at the end of the current list and some bookkeeping updated to indicate the new length of the list. Frequently, however, we run into a situation where the next few bits of memory are already being used for some other important data!

Figure 2.3: An example layout of memory. In this case, we can't easily append to the names list because not enough unused space exists at the end of it.

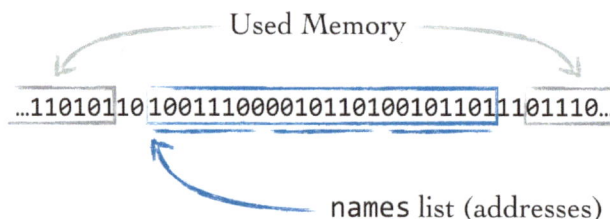

In this situation, there are a few options. First, lists (even lists of addresses) could be allowed to stretch over non-contiguous segments of memory, which would also require extra bookkeeping to manage where each portion of a list resides and how long it is. Second, the system might look for a new, larger segment of unused memory, and simply copy all of the addresses to that location so the append can be completed.[3]

As programmers, we can help the system out by considering a third, rather unusual option. Rather than keep lots of bookkeeping for lists split over arbitrary-sized pieces, or copy data when we run out of room, we can simply *restrict* lists to be of a given size, say two. If we know that a list will never have more than two elements, we can avoid the problem altogether![4]

Perhaps you are thinking, "how can lists restricted to holding only two elements possibly be of any use?" The answer involves the addressing strategy described above, which allows lists to hold data of arbitrary size and type (including other lists!) as elements. Thus, we can represent a list of "A", "B", "C", and "D" as shown in Figure 2.4.

[3] This copy-when-out-of-room strategy is used by R vectors, which can result in obnoxious amounts of copying for vectors that are appended to frequently. In general, it is not a good idea to "grow" native R types like vectors, lists, matrices, and data frames via many append operations for this reason.

[4] Although the examples in this section all consider data as simple strings like "Mary" and "A", they could very well be more important data elements like DNA strings (e.g. "CTAGAC") or even collections of multiple pieces of information (e.g. list("CTAGAC", 6, 0.23)).

Figure 2.4: Storing an arbitrary number of elements in lists restricted to length two.

```
chars <- list("A", list("B", list("C", list("D", NULL))))
```

In this example, we are using nested lists in a "element, rest" structure: the first element of the list is the first data element, and the second element stores the "rest" of the list. We use the special data type NULL for the rest to indicate a list which has no elements (Figure 2.5). We're following our "rule" just fine: each list in the nested structure above has exactly two elements. For some generality, we'll represent an empty list with something like chars <- NULL; thus a list either a "element, rest" pair, or NULL (empty).

Now, for the interpreter and operating system, appending a new piece of data like "E" simply requires finding some free space for a two-element list (list("E", NULL)) and modifying the address of the innermost NULL to address it instead.

Accessing a given element of this structure directly can be quite tedious. For example, we can access the third element as chars[[2]][[2]][[1]]. Soon we'll see more elegant ways to access individual elements. But first, what if we wanted to print all of the data elements in order? The first straightforward method is shown in Figure 2.6. In this strategy, we create a "working copy" of the data in a variable called data. In a loop, we'll print the first element of data, and then *set* data *to the second element of* data (so that it then contains the rest of the list). The output of this bit of code reliably prints "A", "B", "C", and "D" (not shown).

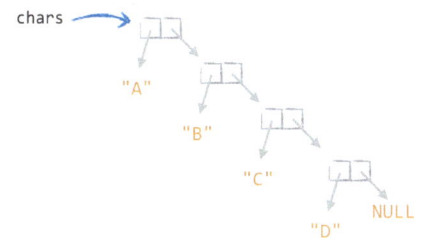

Figure 2.5: An "element, rest" list containing four data elements.

```
data <- chars
while(!is.null(data)) {
  el <- data[[1]]
  print(el)
  data <- data[[2]]
}
```

Figure 2.6: Printing a nested-list structure with a loop.

Figure 2.7 shows a more sophisticated strategy that uses a function to accomplish the same task.

```
print_list <- function(data) {
  if(is.null(data)) {
    return(invisible())
  }
  el <- data[[1]]
  rest <- data[[2]]
  print(el)
  print_list(rest)
}
```

Figure 2.7: Recursive method for printing the elements of a nested list in order.

Now this function is a bit trickier. In analyzing how it works, we should remember that the input to the function should be any list of the right "structure;" data could be list("A", NULL), or list("A", list("B", NULL)), or even just NULL. First, it checks to see if the input list is NULL (representing an empty list). If so, no work needs to be done at all, and the function can simply return(invisible()), ending the function execution. Otherwise, it extracts the first element as el and the rest list; it prints el and then calls print_list(rest)!

This works because data is a *local variable* in the function, meaning each execution of the function works with its own data as passed to it, independent of any other data that might exist for other

What would happen if print_list(rest) was called *before* print(el)? Could the behavior be replicated easily using a looping strategy as above?

```
print_list: ("A" ("B" ("C" ("D" NULL))))
  prints "A" and calls:

   print_list: ("B" ("C" ("D" NULL)))
     prints "B" and calls:

      print_list: ("C" ("D" NULL))
        prints "C" and calls:

         print_list: ("D" NULL)
           prints "D" and calls:

            print_list: NULL
                does nothing; returns
```

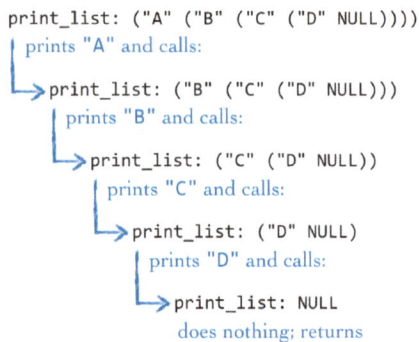

Figure 2.8: Calls for the recursive method of printing nested lists.

calls (see page 20). When we call `print_list(chars)`, a local data will contain `list("A", list("B", list("C", list("D", NULL))))`; this call will in turn call `print_list(rest)`; *this* call will have its own data containing `list("B", list("C", list("D", NULL)))`, and so on. Eventually, somewhere deep inside the nested function calls, a data will contain only `NULL`, in which case no further calls will be required (Figure 2.8).

This strategy–a function that calls itself–is known as *recursion*. If we aren't careful, a function that calls itself might do so forever. But in this case, the inputs are always getting smaller: the size of the input list is decreasing for each sub-call, and eventually the size is small enough that no sub-call is needed. In a recursive function, this is known as the base case. Proper recursive functions thus have:

- One or more *base cases*, representing the easiest versions of the problem requiring minimal computational work.

- One or more *recursive cases*, calling the same function but with parameters that are "closer to" the base case.

Revisiting the earlier frustrating line of code that returns the third element, `chars[[2]][[2]][[1]]`, let's write a function that returns the ith element from a nested list of this type (Figure 2.9). As before, we have base, or "easy" cases, and a recursive case.

Figure 2.9: Recursive method for returning the ith element from a nested list.

```
get_ith <- function(data, i) {
  if(is.null(data)) {
    return(NA)
  }
  if(i == 1) {
    return(data[[1]])
  } else {
    rest <- data[[2]]
    answer <- get_ith(rest, i - 1)
    return(answer)
  }
}
```

In this function there are actually two base cases. First, if data is `NULL`, then the list is empty and there is no i^{th} element, so we return `NA` (the standard "missing data" value in R). Second, if $i = 1$, then we simply need to return the first data element (which is guaranteed to exist, since lists of the right structure are either `NULL` or a "data, rest" list). Otherwise, for the recursive case, the answer is defined as getting item $i - 1$ from rest. Note that this function has the built-in property that asking for an i larger than the number of elements returns `NA`. (Can you see why?)

This function is slightly different from `print_list()` in that each call uses the return value of the sub-call as the answer to return; all

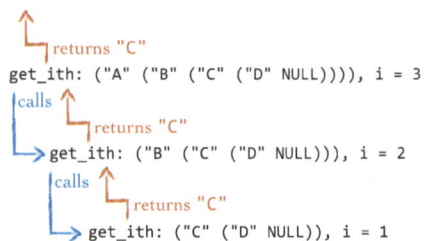

```
  returns "C"
get_ith: ("A" ("B" ("C" ("D" NULL)))), i = 3
 calls

     returns "C"
   get_ith: ("B" ("C" ("D" NULL))), i = 2
   calls

       returns "C"
     get_ith: ("C" ("D" NULL)), i = 1
```

Figure 2.10: Call structure for the recursive method of get_ith() for i = 3.

but the last call waits on a series of sub-calls. This actually happens for the print_list() function as well, but there the return value isn't used. For get_ith(), the *depth* of the recursion equals i (Figure 2.10).

An interesting exercise is to compare extracting the ith element this way and extracting the ith element from a contiguous list of addresses in memory (as at the beginning of this chapter). The former requires i steps (at least one per function call), while the latter can simply access the memory location at "the location of the start of the list plus i (times the number of bits per address)". Said another way, the former bounces from memory location to memory location as the chain of addresses are followed, whereas in the latter case the correct memory location can be directly accessed via some simple addition. In terms of time, accessing the ith element of a nested list such as this requires i computational steps, while doing so from a long list of addresses requires only one computational step. Another potential disadvantage of recursion is that in many languages, R included, there is a limit to how deep a recursive process can go. We'll explore this more in Chapter 4.

THIS RECURSIVE PARADIGM supports a huge variety of operations–indeed, every computational operation we can think of can, in theory, be implemented as a recursive procedure. We'll cover just two more here before expanding into more sophisticated data structures.

First, how might we tackle our original problem of appending an item to the end of the list? We'd like to be able to say something like chars2 <- append_end(chars, "E"). Again, a recursive solution works well (Figure 2.11).

```
append_end <- function(data, new_el) {
  if(is.null(data)) {
    return(list(new_el, NULL))
  }
  el <- data[[1]]
  rest <- data[[2]]
  new_rest <- append_end(rest, new_el)
  return(list(el, new_rest))
}
```

Figure 2.11: Recursive method for appending an element to the end of a nested list.

This function perhaps best illustrates the "trust" that often accompanies designing recursive methods. In the base case (in which the list we are appending to is empty, or just NULL), we simply return a new list consisting of new_el, NULL. Otherwise, we generate a new_rest by recursing, assuming that the answer will be correct! With that done, all that needs to be done is to return a new list consisting of the current first element and the new_rest.

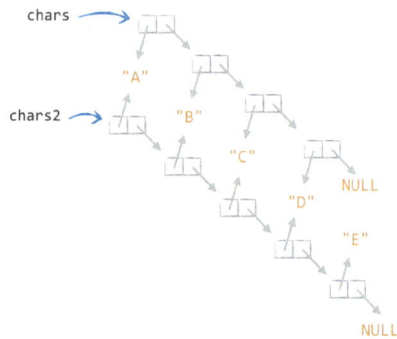

Figure 2.12: Memory structure after calling chars2 <- append_end(chars, "E").

AN ADVANCED ASIDE: This type of list is known as a *linked list*, and designing them this way has the interesting property of producing structures that are *persistent*. By this we mean that, after a line like chars2 <- append_end(chars, "E"), the chars list contains the same data it did as before the append. The "history" of the list can thus be tracked. This is primarily related to the fact that the append_end() function is pure, or side-effect-free: it does not modify any data (lists) passed to it, and indeed only creates new lists (a new list is created in memory when the list() function is called).

If we wanted to implement an append_end() that was not persistent, we would have to have our function find and *modify* the address referring to the NULL element to instead point to a new two-element list (containing the new data item and NULL). This is how linked-lists are normally described in languages like C, Python, and Java. These languages frequently make use of "impure" functions (those that can modify the data underlying their parameters), while R and similar languages like Scheme, Lisp, ML, and Haskell emphasize the use of pure functions (those that can only create new local variables and data and return them), and consequently persistent data structures.

There is a downside to the additional feature of persistence: it uses more memory. Indeed, every time list() is called in R, a new segment of memory is allocated to store its contents. This means that appending to the end in this way results in creating n new lists to store the data, where n is the length of the list being appended to (notice that list() is called exactly once by any call of append_end(), and the depth of the recursion is also n.) This is hardly much better than the appending solution proposed at the beginning of this chapter, where if there isn't enough room in the memory block, the entire list is copied (requiring n copy operations)! While the data stored in the lists may be shared (because of the addressing scheme for list storage), the structure of the list itself must be copied (Figure 2.12).

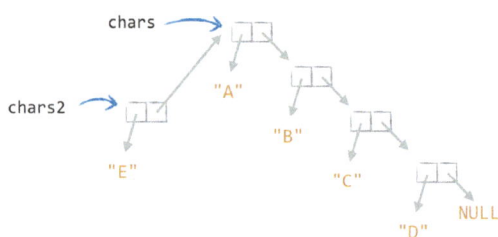

Figure 2.13: Memory structure after calling chars2 <- append_front(chars, "E").

On the other hand, consider the problem of appending to the *beginning* of a nested list. This requires constructing only one new list: to hold the new data element (in the first index) and the rest of the data (in the second element). In fact, append_front() wouldn't even be a recursive function. This is still a persistent structure, as the original variable still accesses the rest of the data. In this case both lists "share" a majority of their structure (Figure 2.13). For a comprehensive discussion of persistent data structures and structure-sharing, see *Purely Functional Data Structures* by Chris Okasaki.

FOR A LAST THOUGHT ON RECURSIVELY OPERATING ON NESTED LISTS, let's consider R's `lapply()` function. For those familiar, `lapply()` is a "higher-order" function. It takes two parameters: first, an R list to operate on, and second, a *function* to apply to each element of that list. The result is another R list collecting the results of the function call on each element. As an example, consider the "tolower()" function, which takes a character vector and returns a lower-case version of it; `print(tolower("C"))` returns "c".

```
names <- list("Bob", "Mary", "Joe")
lower_names <- lapply(names, tolower)
print(lower_names)            # prints "bob" "mary" "joe"
```

Figure 2.14: Example of using `lapply()` to apply a function on each element of an R list.

Can we implement a `nested_lapply()` that does the same thing with our own nested lists? Indeed we can–given a nested list and a function, it should return a nested list resulting from applying the function to each data element (Figure 2.15).

```
nested_lapply <- function(data, func) {
  if(is.null(data)) {
    return(NULL)
  }
  el <- data[[1]]
  rest <- data[[2]]
  new_el <- func(el)
  new_rest <- nested_lapply(rest, func)
  return(list(new_el, new_rest))
}
```

Figure 2.15: Recursive method for applying a function to each element of a nested list.

Figure 2.16 contains a summary utilizing our various functions.

```
chars <- NULL
chars <- append_end(chars, "W")
chars <- append_end(chars, "X")
chars <- append_end(chars, "Y")
chars <- append_end(chars, "Z")

print_list(chars)         # prints "W", "X", "Y", "Z"
print(get_ith(chars, 3)) # prints "Y"

lchars <- nested_lapply(chars, tolower)
print_list(lchars)        # prints "w", "x", "y", "z"
```

Figure 2.16: Overview of creating and using a nested list structure.

Exercises

1. Write a function that uses a while-loop instead of recursion for `get_ith()`.

2. Write a side-effect-free function called `append_front()` that appends an element to the *front* of a given nested list. Try using a

loop to generate two 200-element lists, one generated by appending only to the front, and one generated by only appending to the end. Which is faster? Why?

3. Do you run into trouble using one method or the other for the previous question to create 2,000-element nested list? Why do you think that might be?

4. Write a side-effect-free function called without_front() that returns a nested list without its first element. Does this function require any recursive calls?

5. Write a function called to_nested_list() that converts an R list to a nested list, using either append_front() or append_end() from above. The order of elements should be preserved.

6. Write a recursive function called get_els() that returns a range of elements from a nested list. As an example, if chars <- list("A", list("B", list("C", list("D", list("E", NULL))))), then get_els(chars, 2, 4) should return the nested list containing "B", "C", and "D".

7. Implement a recursive insert_at_ith() function, which inserts a new element into a nested list so that it occurs at the ith spot in the list. For example, if chars <- list("A", list("B", list("C", list("D", list("E", NULL))))), then insert_at_ith(chars, "X", 3) should return a nested list with data "A", "B", "X", "C", "D", and "E". How deep does the recursion go, in terms of either i or the number of elements in the nested input list?

8. Write a pure recursive function to reverse a nested list.

2.1   Trees

As much fun as these nested lists are, they are just a run-up to more sophisticated and interesting data structures known as trees. There are many applications for trees; one of the most common is simply to keep data in sorted order efficiently. Why might we want to keep data in sorted order? Usually, it's because we want to find some information quickly–consider trying to find a given page in a book with pages ordered, versus one with pages in random order!

Hypothetically, we could keep an ordered dataset as a native R list or as a nested list; in either case we'd simply have to ensure that new elements are added to the correct location based on the data order (exercise 7 in the previous section asked you to do just this).

Rather, let's extend our concept of a nested list in a seemingly innocuous way. Previously we restricted our lists to holding exactly two elements. Now, we'll suppose that they can hold exactly *three*.

To represent a single data element "C", we'll put it in the second index with NULL in the other two indices: char <- list(NULL, "C", NULL). We could use any of the three indices for storing the data element, but it will be clearer to use the second because the first and third will be reserved for lists, which instead of calling *rest* we'll call *left* and *right*. For example, to represent the data elements "A", "C", and "E", we could organize the lists as in Figure 2.17, where every list has exactly three elements.

```
chars <- list(list(NULL, "A", NULL), "C", list(NULL, "E", NULL))
```

Figure 2.17: Storing three elements in a nested list with "left" and "right" sublists.

To help keep the data in sorted order, we're going to impose the following rule: all elements and sub-elements of the left list must be smaller than the middle data element, and all elements and sub-elements of the right list must be greater than (or equal to) the middle data element. Thus, while linked lists were of the form "element, rest," these trees are of the form "smaller rest, element, larger (or equal to) rest."

With this organization and rule, we have options in how we might structure the lists. For example, another possibility is shown in Figure 2.18.

```
chars <- list(NULL, "A", list(NULL, "C", list(NULL, "E", NULL)))
```

Figure 2.18: Alternative structure for storing "A", "C", and "E", where each list has three elements and the ordering rule is enforced.

With three elements, the number of possible structures is 5, with four elements, the number jumps to 14. It also becomes quickly unwieldy to represent them serially as above. Consider the structure chars <- list(list(NULL, "A", NULL), "C", list(list(NULL, "D", NULL), "F", NULL)); it represents only four elements, but is certainly very difficult to read. In fact, the easiest way to visualize a structure like this is by using the addressing scheme representation first introduced in Figure 2.2, visualized with all addresses pointing "downward" as in Figure 2.19.

This structure is known as a *binary search tree*. Traditionally, trees (of the mathematical kind) are drawn upside-down (the cover image for this book hints at this), with each sublist representing a *node* in the tree. The top-most node is called the *root*, and the bottom-most nodes are called *leaves*. Leaves do not have *children* nodes, though other *internal* nodes do. All nodes, except the root, have one *parent*.

Printing the elements in order can be accomplished with a recursive function, similar to print_list() used for printing nesting lists (Figure 2.20).

Here there are *two* recursive calls, with print(el) sandwiched in between. The first causes the left sub-tree to be printed; once that is done the element itself is printed, and finally the second recursive

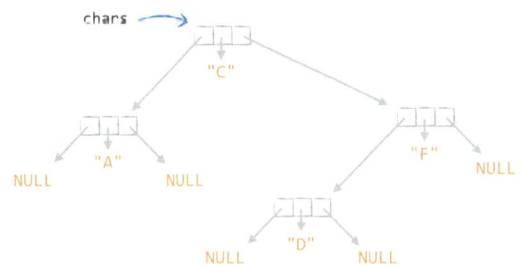

Figure 2.19: Graphical representation for a binary search tree with four elements.

Figure 2.20: Recursive method for printing a binary search tree in order.

```r
print_tree <- function(data) {
  if(is.null(data)) {
    return(invisible())
  } else {
    left <- data[[1]]
    el <- data[[2]]
    right <- data[[3]]

    print_tree(left)
    print(el)
    print_tree(right)
  }
}

chars <- list(list(NULL, "A", NULL),
              "C",
              list(list(NULL, "D", NULL), "F", NULL))
print_tree(chars)      # prints "A", "C", "D", "F"
```

call causes the right sub-tree to be printed. Based on the rule that smaller data elements go left, this will cause the items to be printed in order.

Now: given a tree of the correct structure, how can we insert an element new_el into it such that the ordering rule is preserved? It turns out that the rule that smaller elements go left make it easy: if new_el is less than the middle, it goes somewhere in the left sub-tree. Otherwise, it goes somewhere in the right sub-tree. What do we mean by "goes somewhere in the left sub-tree?" We mean: if the left sub-tree is NULL, then we can replace the left sub-tree by a list(NULL, new_el, NULL); otherwise, we can recursively compute a new left sub-tree (Figure 2.21).

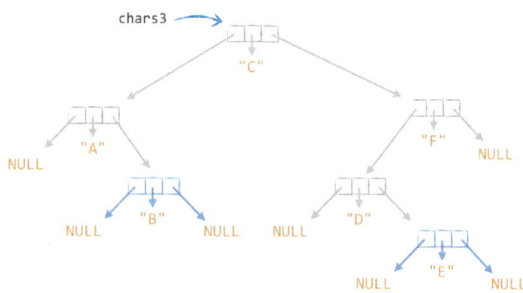

This function might seem complex, but in reality it is quite like the append_end() function for nested lists. In this case though we have to two cases to consider (left or right). Example usage is shown in Figure 2.23. Note that new data nodes always appear as "leaves" of the returned tree.

So far, the same data is being used for both ordering and storage. However, we can make them more general if the elements stored are themselves lists, with the first item being the "key" to order the data by, and the second being any additional data "value" that should be stored with the key (as in Figure 2.24).

This adjustment requires a few small modifications to our tree functions. First, the print function should print both the key and the value; in Figure 2.20 we can can modify the line print(el) to instead read print(str_c(el[[1]], el[[2]])). Next, our insert_tree() function needs to use the key for the comparison,

Figure 2.22: Structure of chars3 after inserting "B" and "E".

```
insert_tree <- function(data, new_el) {
  if(is.null(data)) {
    return(list(NULL, new_el, NULL))
  } else {
    left <- data[[1]]
    el <- data[[2]]
    right <- data[[3]]

    if(new_el < el) {                    # create new left
      new_left <- insert_tree(left, new_el)
      return(list(new_left, el, right))
    } else if(new_el == el) {        # update middle
      return(list(left, new_el, right))
    } else {
      new_right <- insert_tree(right, new_el)
      return(list(left, el, new_right))
    }
  }
}
```

Figure 2.21: Method for inserting a new element into a binary search tree.

```
chars2 <- insert_tree(chars, "B")
print_tree(chars2)    # prints "A" "B" "C" "D" "F"
chars3 <- insert_tree(chars2, "E")
print_tree(chars3)    # prints "A" "B" "C" "D" "E" "F"
```

Figure 2.23: Using the insert_tree() function.

rather than the element itself. This is as simple as changing the if(new_el < el) to if(new_el[[1]] < el[[1]]) in Figure 2.21. We can then use the tree by adding more complex elements (Figure 2.25 and 2.26).

Figure 2.24: Storing an ordering "key" and corresponding "value" in a tree.

```
simple_tree <- list(NULL, list("C", 4.7), NULL)
```

Figure 2.25: Using a key/value tree, ordered by keys.

```
simple_tree <- list(NULL, list("C", 4.7), NULL)
simple_tree <- insert_tree(simple_tree, list("A", 9.2))
simple_tree <- insert_tree(simple_tree, list("D", 5.6))
print_tree(simple_tree)
```

Now, why are structures of this type known as binary *search* trees? Primarily because we can efficiently search for data by key (an operation also supported by hash tables, discussed in later chapters).

Figure 2.27: Retrieving a value by key.

```
get_value <- function(data, key) {
  if(is.null(data)) {
    return(NA)                          # not present
  }

  left <- data[[1]]
  el <- data[[2]]
  right <- data[[3]]

  if(key == el[[1]]) {                  # found it!
    return(el[[2]])                     # return the value
  }

  if(key < el[[1]]) {
    answer <- get_value(left, key)      # look left
    return(answer)
  } else {
    answer <- get_value(right, key)     # look right
    return(answer)
  }
}

print(get_value(simple_tree, "C"))      # prints 4.7
print(get_value(simple_tree, "Q"))      # prints NA
```

```
[1] "A 9.2"
[1] "C 4.7"
[1] "D 5.6"
```

Figure 2.26: Output for code in Figure 2.25.

In Figure 2.27, get_value() is a recursive function that returns the value associated with a given tree. It operates similarly to the insert_tree() function, but with an extra case. First, it checks to see if the tree being searched in is empty; if so, it can simply return NA, the standard value for "unknown" in R. Otherwise, it extracts the left, el, and right; if the key being searched for is the key being held in el at this node in the tree, it can simply return the value. If el is not the right value, the function can recurse left, *or* right, depending on whether the key being searched for is less than the central element or not.

Of particular interest is how quickly we can retrieve a value this way from very large tree. The number of steps is equal to the number of recursive calls, which is at most the largest *depth* of the tree, since recursive calls are mode on left or right nodes (but not both) at each level (Figure 2.28). If we are lucky, our tree will be very wide and not very deep. What is the smallest depth we can hope for? Consider a "full" tree, where all leaf nodes are at the same depth and every node has two children (Figure 2.29).

Surely such a tree can't be made less deep. In this case, at every level the size of the sub-tree in consideration is reduced by approximately half; if at the start the number of nodes in consideration for the search is n, at the next level it is $n/2$, then $n/4$, and so on. How many times can a number be divided in half until 1 is reached? The answer is $\log_2(n)$, which grows much slower then n itself (Figure 2.30).

Note that essentially the same search process occurs for inserting an element, except in this case the search always goes to a leaf, and so for a "full" tree the time to insert an element is also approximately $\log_2(n)$.

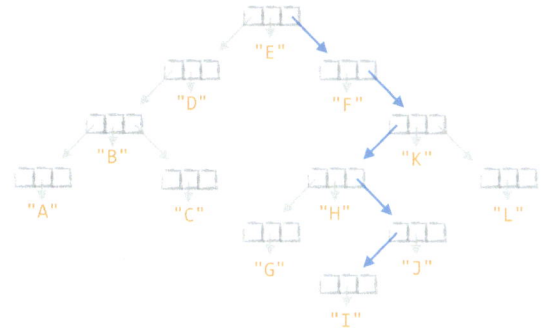

Figure 2.28: A tree of depth 6; data and arrows pointing to NULL have been removed for clarity. The search path to "I" is highlighted in blue: "E" is less than "I", so the call is made on `right`, then "F" is less than "I", so the call is made on `right` again, and so on.

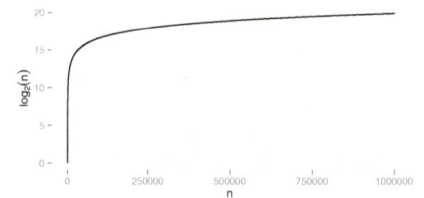

Figure 2.30: A plot of $\log_2(n)$. For even very large values of n the value of $\log_2(n)$ is small.

Unfortunately, not all trees are full. If elements are inserted more or less randomly, the resulting tree will be quite likely to be close to full. But if elements are inserted in order, then they will stack up along the right (Figure 2.31, top). This can result in insertions or lookups to run in time much slower than $\log_2(n)$. More sophisticated tree types ensure that after every insertion or removal the tree stays "balanced," for example AVL trees may "rotate" triplets of nodes to ensure balance (Figure 2.31 bottom). There are a number of tree types that ensure balance and thus guarantee $\log_2(n)$-behavior, with names like 2-3 trees, red-black trees, and the aforementioned AVL trees.

Exercises

1. Write a recursive function that returns the number of elements in a binary search tree.

2. Write a function that computes the depth of a tree, defined as the length of the longest path from the root to a leaf.

3. One problem with the key/value binary search tree we've imple-

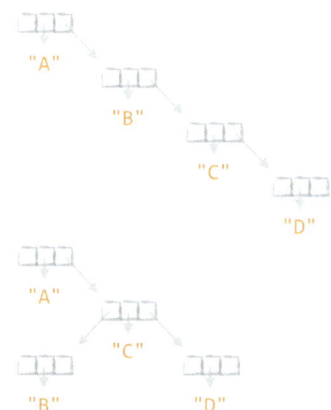

Figure 2.31: Top: an unbalanced tree resulting from elements being inserted in order. Bottom: the result of re-balancing the right sub-tree via rotation.

mented is that it allows duplicate keys to be stored in the tree, even if they are associated with different values. If duplicate keys are added, which entry will be returned by a search? Write a function that checks to see if a tree contains duplicate keys; it should return TRUE if it does, and FALSE if not. (You might first want to also implement min_item() and max_item() functions that return the smallest (resp. largest) items stored in a tree.)

4. Modify the insert_tree() function such that it refuses to insert a duplicate value and prints a warning if the user tries to do so.

5. The binary search trees discussed here are *persistent*, just like the nested linked lists of the last section. When performing an insertion, how many new nodes are created for the new tree, and how many are shared with the old version? You may want to draw a picture of node relationships before and after insertion, as in Figure 2.12 or Figure 2.13.

3   *Searching and Sorting*

One essential object is to
choose that arrangement
which shall tend to reduce to a
minimum the time necessary
for completing the calculation.

Ada Lovelace, 1843

To ground the discussion from the last chapters a bit, let's consider a common problem in bioinformatics, the *substring search* problem: given a long string (such as the DNA sequence for a chromosome, perhaps around 100 million letters), find matching locations of a short string (such as a DNA "read" produced from a sequencing machine, usually on the order of 100 letters).

Long sequence:
>   AGAGCCTAGAGCGAGAGTCCGTGAGACGACGAGAGACCCTGGACGAGACCG

Short sequence:
>   ACGA

Problem: find all locations where the short sequence matches the long sequence.

Figure 3.1: A small instance of the substring search problem.

To tackle this problem in R, we'll need to know about a few functions for working with character data, many of which are available in the `stringr` package. First, it's important to recall that in R the elements of a "character" vector are strings; if `names <- c("Johnny", "Marilyn")`, then `names[1]` returns the string `"John"`. Often, we'll be interested in vectors of a single string and working with substrings of it. The `str_sub()` function returns substrings of all elements of the vector: `str_sub(names, 2, 5)` returns the vector `c("ohnn", "aril")`, and if `name <- "Marilyn"` (which is just a character vector of length one) then `str_sub(name, 2, 5)` returns `"aril"` (another length-one vector).[1]

[1] Recall from Chapter 1 that the simplest form of data in R is the vector, and most functions take and return vectors.

Other useful functions in `stringr` include `str_length()` which returns the number of characters in a string, for example `str_length("Mary")` returns 4. The `str_c()` function concatenates strings using a given separator: `str_c("Mary", "O'Connor", sep = "_")` returns `"Mary_O'Connor"` while `str_c("Mary", "O'Connor")` returns `"MaryO'Connor"`.

The `str_detect()` function returns TRUE if a pattern is found in a string, and FALSE otherwise; to detect a pattern at the start or end of a string, we can use the regular expression patterns `^` and `$`. `str_detect("abracadabra", "^cad")` returns FALSE because "cad" does not occur at the start of "abracadabra", while `str_detect("abracadabra", "abra$")` returns TRUE since "abra" occurs in the string at the end.[2]

[2] Regular expressions are a specialized and powerful syntax for finding patterns in strings. We'll be using only `^` and `$` from this syntax.

RETURNING TO SUBSTRING SEARCH, a straightforward way to solve this problem is to simply scan along the long sequence looking for matches with the shorter (or even using something like `str_detect()`). But this would be relatively slow, as it requires scanning over the entire longer string. For matching a single short sequence this might not be bad, but in practice we often have millions of short sequences (produced by the sequencing machine) that we wish to match against the chromosome. Better would be to "index" the large sequence in some way, potentially spending extra time up front to make each search go faster.

We'll start by indexing our chromosome via a binary search tree. Suppose we know that we'll never want to search for short sequences longer than, say, 10 characters. (In real life the number would be larger; we'll also use the 50 character sequence shown in Figure 3.1 as our genome.) Thus, we'll consider every 10-character substring of the genome, and store it in the binary tree as a key, along with the location of that substring as the value (Figure 3.2).

Figure 3.2: Adding substrings of the genome to a binary search tree.

```
genome <- "AGAGCCTAGAGCGAGAGTCCGTGAGACGACGAGAGACCCTGGACGAGACCG"

tree <- NULL

for(index in seq(1:str_length(genome))) {
  subseq <- str_sub(genome, index, index+9)
  element <- list(subseq, index)
  tree <- insert_tree(tree, element)
}

print_tree(tree)
```

```
[1] "ACCCTGGACG 36"
[1] "ACCG 48"
[1] "ACGACGAGAG 26"
[1] "ACGAGACCG 43"
[1] "ACGAGAGACC 29"
[1] "AGACCCTGGA 34"
[1] "AGACCG 46"
[1] "AGACGACGAG 24"
[1] "AGAGACCCTG 32"
[1] "AGAGCCTAGA 1"
[1] "AGAGCGAGAG 8"
[1] "AGAGTCCGTG 14"
```

Figure 3.3: Partial output for code shown in Figure 3.2.

Figure 3.3 shows the printed output, where entries are printed in dictionary order according to the sequences, along with the locations of those sub-sequences in the longer genome sequence. (Sub-sequences near the end are truncated to an appropriate length automatically by the `str_sub()` function, saving us from having to consider those as special cases.)

Given this tree, how can we find all locations where the short sequence "ACGA" occurs? Well, consider a tree (or sub-tree) with a root node holding the key "AGAGCCTAGA" and value 1 (Figure 3.4).

This sequence does not start with "ACGA", so "ACGA" does not occur at position 1 of the original sequence. Furthermore, "ACGA" is *less* than "AGAGCCTAGA" ("ACGA" < "AGAGCCTAGA" returns TRUE), and so if any nodes are to start with "ACGA" then they must be somewhere in the left sub-tree. (The same rules apply for query sequences greater, which would be found in the right sub-tree).

```
print_subseq_matches <- function(data, subseq) {
  if(is.null(data)) {
    return(invisible())
  }

  left <- data[[1]]
  el <- data[[2]]
  right <- data[[3]]
  pattern <- str_c("^", subseq)  # for str_detect at start of key

  if(!str_detect(el[[1]], pattern)) {      # no match
    if(subseq < el[[1]]) {                 # continue search right
      print_subseq_matches(left, subseq)
    } else {              # continue search left
      print_subseq_matches(right, subseq) # continue search left
    }
  } else {                                 # match!
    print(str_c(el[[1]], el[[2]], sep = " "))
    print_subseq_matches(left, subseq)   # continue search left
    print_subseq_matches(right, subseq)  # AND right
  }
}

print_subseq_matches(tree, "ACGA")
```

Figure 3.5: Finding matches for short sequences in the tree-index genome sequence.

On the other hand, if the sequence *did* start with "ACGA", then the value needs to be printed since "ACGA" occurs at that location. Further, in this case more matches might be found in both the left and right sub-trees, so the search must continue in both directions. Of course, if the tree is empty (NULL) then nothing needs to be done at all (Figure 3.5). This code will reliably indicate that "ACGA" occurs at positions 26, 29, and 43 of the original sequence.

Now, the most important question is, how much work is required to find these matches? This recursive function is not nearly as simple as the previous ones we've seen, which always branch left or right–this function sometimes branches left or right, and sometimes branches both ways. This means the amount of work could be larger. As an extreme example, consider a tree built from the sequence "AAAAAAAAAAAAA" and the search sequence "A". Here the query will match at every node, and the branching will always be to both sides; every node will be visited

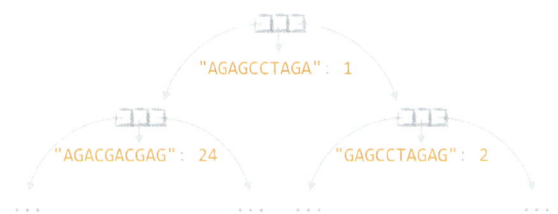

Figure 3.4: A key/value binary search tree, with subsequences of a long string indexing their locations within the string.

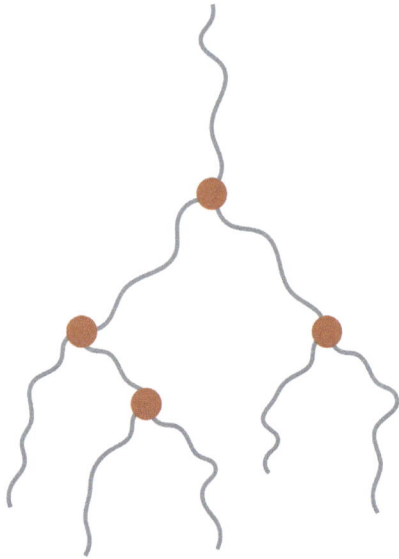

Figure 3.6: Potential search path for matching sequences; matching, "branching" nodes are shown in red, other, non-matching but still searched nodes occur along the black paths.

for a run time of n, rather than the depth of the tree. On the other hand, if there are no matches anywhere, then the search path will simply run a single path down to a leaf, visiting very few nodes.

Consider this, however: up until the search finds a matching node, there is only one search path. When the matching node is reached, the number of search paths that are in consideration increases by one. This happens at every matching node, so the total number of search paths is $m + 1$, where m is the number of matching locations (see Figure 3.6). Thus, the total search size–the total amount of work completed–is *at most* $m + 1$ times the depth of the tree. In the case of a nicely balanced tree (which could be guaranteed by using a red-black or AVL tree, rather than our simple search tree), this is approximately $m \log(n)$, where n is the number of nodes, which is approximately the length of the long genome sequence we are searching in. This is much better than the amount of work to do a simple scan, n, unless of course the query sequence matches every location in which case they are the same.

3.1   Order Notation

We've been making heavy use of terms like "at most" and "approximately" while simultaneously attaching to these words exact quantities, like n and $m \log(n)$. We might acknowledge that the equation is really more like $(m + 1) \log(n) = m \log(n) + \log(n)$. We might even go so far as to compute the amount of CPU steps running an if-statement requires, resulting in something like $6m \log(n) + 3 \log(n)$. In reality though, we don't need to know about the 6, or the 3, or the +1, to understand how the function behaves–the major terms affecting the run of the function are n and m, and everything else is just peanuts.

Even smaller terms in a polynomial don't much matter. Consider a runtime like $n^3 + n + \log(n)$. The first term dominates the equation so much that it's needlessly tedious to even list the others. More importantly, how we compare the runtimes for algorithms depends on these concepts. Consider a runtime for a potential alternative function, $0.5n^{3.1} - 100n$. Which algorithm would be faster? At first blush, the first terms seem pretty similar, but the second terms give a clear advantage to the latter. However, for a large enough input size n, the first is actually smaller, which can be seen by solving $n^3 + n + \log(n) < 0.5n^{3.1} - 100n$ for n. (And, after all, if we only cared about small input sizes, we wouldn't need computers!) In this sense, it turns out the largest term in a polynomial will always dominate. Computer scientists use a concept called "order notation" to capture these concepts in a mathematical way.

Formally, a function $f(n)$ of an input size n, is said to be $O(g(n))$

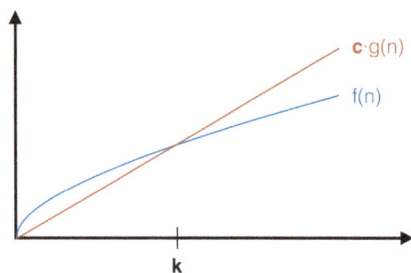

Figure 3.7: The function $f(n)$ is $O(g(n))$ if, not counting constant multipliers, $f(n)$ is always less than or equal to $g(n)$ after some point (i.e., there exists a c and k such that $f(n) \leq cg(n)$ for $n \geq k$).

($f(n)$ is "order of" or "big-oh" of $g(n)$), if there exist some numbers c and k such that $f(n) \leq cg(n)$ for all $n \geq k$. Which is to say, not counting constant multipliers not related to n, $f(n)$ is smaller than or equal to $g(n)$ for sufficiently large n.

Thus, $2n^2 + n$ is $O(n^2)$, and $3n$ is $O(n)$. (Technically n is also $O(3n)$. When both directions are true, we can use the Greek letter theta, as in $3n$ is $\Theta(n)$. This is more rarely seen as usually we're interested in placing an *upper* limit on the runtime of an algorithm, rather than a tight bound.) As a rule of thumb, when computing order notation constants and lower terms are dropped; thus $0.5m \log(n) - 100m$ is $O(m \log(n))$. We include m as it is not a constant, but rather a parameter of the function which can change depending on the input. In some cases, it is not possible to remove a term, for example $m + \log(n)$ is $O(m + \log(n))$ since either term could be larger. We say that methods that take a constant amount of time no matter the input size run in time $O(1)$, or "constant time."

In general, if the run time of a function is $O(f(n))$ *times* $O(g(n))$, then the runtime is just $O(f(n)g(n))$. (The same goes for addition.) We applied this rule for the search process above: if we had used a balanced tree, the depth would be $O(\log(n))$, and the number of search paths is $O(m)$. Since the total runtime is at most the number of search paths times the length, it is $O(m \log(n))$.

Finally, note that big-O notation describes a guaranteed less-than-or-equal to relationship, in the worst case (not counting small terms and constants). Thus, just because a function like get_value() *might* find the answer right away without recursing doesn't make its runtime $O(1)$.

Exercises

1. Modify the find_subseq() function to not print the matching locations, but rather return them as a tree containing only those elements.

2. Write a function called lca() (short for "lowest common ancestor") that takes two keys and returns the highest element in the tree of which both keys are ancestors. (You can assume that both keys are in the tree, and that the first parameter is smaller than the second). For example, in the tree of Figure 2.22, lca(tree, "G", "L") should return "K", and lca(tree, "C", "F") should return "E". What is the runtime of your algorithm in order notation?

3. A "range query" involves identifying all of the elements in a range. Write a function print_range() that prints all elements between two queries, for example print_range(tree, "AACT",

"CACT") should print all entries greater than (or equal to) "AACT" and less than (or equal to) "CACT". What is the runtime of this algorithm in order notation?

4. In order notation, what is the runtime of the append_end() function of Figure 2.11?

5. Is $\log_2(n)$ $O(\log_4(n))$? Is $\log_4(n)$ $O(\log_2(n))$? You may want to look up the rules for transforming logarithms into a common base to answer this question.

3.2   Faster Search

The simplest strategy for the substring search problem would use $O(n)$ time, by simply scanning each potential position of the genome for a match. Our tree-based strategy above would use $O(m \log_2(n))$, where m is the number of matches, if the tree constructed was sufficiently balanced (this could be guaranteed by using a self-balancing tree). It turns out that neither of these strategies are used in real life, for a couple of important reasons. First, $O(m \log_2(n))$ is fast, but better speed can still be achieved. Second, the tree we've constructed uses a considerable amount of storage– storing 10 letters at each node for $O(n)$ nodes, we're looking at storing approximately 10 times the size of the genome in data; storing 100 letters for searching for longer substrings would require 100 times as much, and so on. These are all $O(n)$ if we consider 10 and 100 to be constants, but in reality we'll quickly run out of memory if we are working with large genomes.

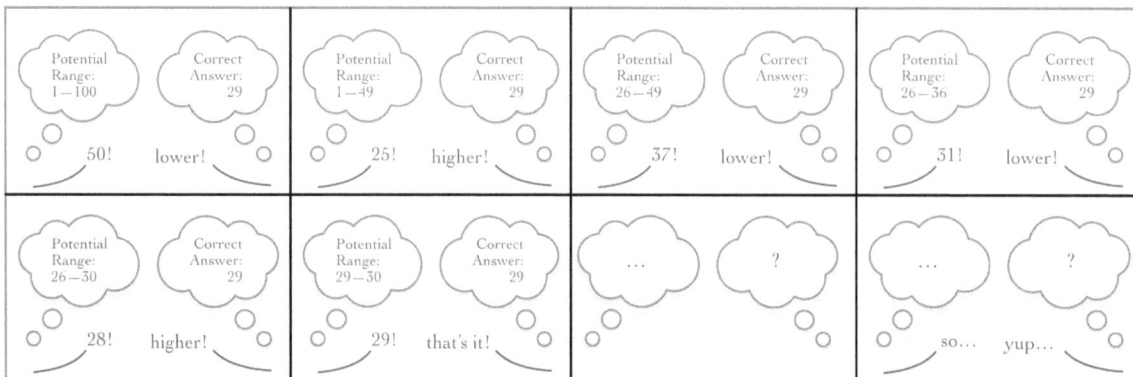

Figure 3.8: Searching an ordered set of potential answers for the correct answer, given information about whether the "middle guess" is too low or too high.

An alternative strategy works similarly, but utilizes a list or table (such as a data frame) as opposed to a tree. Before we discuss it, let's consider the common children's game of "I'm thinking of a number between 1 and 100," wherein the guesser guesses a number, and is told "higher" or "lower" after each guess. Intuitively, the right strategy is to guess in the middle of the current potential range–50. If "lower" is the result, we guess again in the middle of the remaining potential range at 25, and so on (Figure 3.8). How many steps will it take to get to the right answer? Why, $O(\log_2(n))$ of course, where n is the size of the initial range.

With that in mind, let's consider a table of all of the *suffixes* (ending strings) of the long sequence, along with information about the position where that suffix starts (Figure 3.9).

To create a table like this in R, we can start by writing a short function get_suffix() that returns a suffix of a given string given an index. We can then create a data frame of the right "size" by initializing the index column to the list of valid indices, and the suffix column to be filled with NA values initially. Then, we can use a for-loop to fill in each entry of the suffix column (Figure 3.10; we don't want our character vectors automatically converted into a "factor" data type, so we specify stringsAsFactors = FALSE).

Index	Suffix
1	AGAGCCTAGAGCGAGAGTCC...
2	GAGCCTAGAGCGAGAGTCC...
3	AGCCTAGAGCGAGAGTCC...
4	GCCTAGAGCGAGAGTCC...
5	CCTAGAGCGAGAGTCC...
6	CTAGAGCGAGAGTCC...
7	TAGAGCGAGAGTCC...
	...
48	ACCG
49	CCG
50	CG
51	G

Figure 3.9: A table of suffixes of the long genome sequence, along with the start position of each suffix.

```
get_suffix <- function(index, str) {
  return(str_sub(str, index, str_length(str)))
}

# data frame without suffixes filled in
suffix_df = data.frame(index = seq(1, str_length(genome)),
                       suffix = NA,
                       stringsAsFactors = FALSE)

# fill in suffixes
for(index in seq(1, str_length(genome))) {
  suffix_df$suffix[index] <- get_suffix(index, genome)
}
```

Figure 3.10: Generating a table of suffixes and corresponding indices using lapply().

Alternatively, we can create this table using a more functional style. We start by creating a list of indices (from 1 to the length of the genome), and use lapply() to apply our get_suffix() function to each index we want. Finally, we can unlist() the suffixes and index column to create the data frame columns (Figure 3.11).

```
indices <- as.list(seq(1,str_length(genome)))
suffixes <- lapply(indices, get_suffix, str = genome)

suffix_df <- data.frame(index = unlist(indices),
                        suffix = unlist(suffixes),
                        stringsAsFactors = FALSE)
```

Figure 3.11: Generating a table of suffixes and corresponding indices using lapply().

Now, we want to search for a query string like ACGA amongst the starts of suffixes in this table. This is very similar to the search we did in our tree earlier. When we find a suffix that starts with the query sequence, we know that the query occurs at that index. Rather than having to scan each suffix, though, let's *sort* the table

```
Index      Suffix
36     ACCCGAGACGAGACCG
48     ACCG
26     ACGACGAGAGACCCGAGACG...
43     ACGAGACCG
29     ACGAGAGACCCGAGACGAGACCG
34     AGACCCGAGACGAGACCG
46     AGACCG
       . . .
18     TCCGTGAGACGACGAGAGAC...
22     TGAGACGACGAGAGACCCTG...
40     TGGACGAGACCG
```

Suffix Array

Figure 3.12: A table of suffixes of the long genome sequence, along with the start position of each suffix, sorted by the suffixes. Note that given any index, the suffix sequence can easily be generated as-needed from the original genome sequence, thus the column of numbers in are all that is required and all that really constitute the "suffix array."

Figure 3.13: Ordering the suffix table by suffixes.

[3] Figure 3.13 uses some rather dense R code. The syntax df[a, b] selects rows from df defined by a and columns defined by b. Since we've left b off it selects all columns. The order() function returns a vector indicating which indices are necessary to order a vector; for example order(c("B", "C", "A")) returns c(3, 1, 2). Thus, suffix_df[order(suffix_df$suffix),] selects all columns and rows from suffix_df, ordered by the suffix column.

[4] Cheating in this way–not recursing as far as possible–is known as "arm's-length recursion." It is generally frowned upon because it tends to over-complicate code.

by the suffixes, producing what is known as a "suffix array" (Figure 3.12).

This table contains quite a lot of data, but note that after the column of indexes has been generated in the correct order, the column of suffixes is no longer needed: at any time we can call get_suffix() to regenerate any one of them. Nevertheless, for this example we'll store the entire data frame, re-ordering it by the suffix column (Figure 3.13).[3]

Finding a row that starts with ACGA now works very similarly to the children's game described above. We start with a range of rows (1 to 50) and guess the middle (the 25th row); the suffix there is CGAGAG..., and so we note that by ordering, the query sequence, if it matches the start of some suffix, must do so at a row above the 25th. So the potential range is now 1 to 25, and we check in the middle again at row 12, which has suffix AGAGTC.... Again we note that we need to look in the top half of this table. This process continues until we've found a row where the suffix matches our query of ACGA at the start, or we run out of table to search (indicating no matches).

This method is inherently recursive–at each step, we are asking the exact same question on a smaller (by half) data set. This pattern of searching for an element of a sorted table or list, removing half of it from consideration on each iteration, is known as *binary search* (Figure 3.14).

```
suffix_df <- suffix_df[order(suffix_df$suffix), ]
```

Despite the overall simplicity of the method, implementing a binary search can be tricky. The reason is the number of ways dividing integers in half might turn out: if the range is sufficiently large, then we can easily divide the range in half with something like middle_range <- rangeL + as.integer((rangeU - rangeL)/2) (ensuring that each sub-range is smaller than the original). But if the range is small, we can get into a situation where this simple splitting doesn't result in a smaller range, leading to infinite recursion. (Consider what would happen if rangeL = 5 and rangeU = 6). Rather than check for many different cases, we'll simply cheat a bit and say that the base case of the recursion is any case with two or fewer rows in the range, resulting in multiple sub-cases within the base case.[4]

Once we've found a single row number that matches the query sequence, by the nature of the order of the table other suffixes that match *must occur right next to that row*. Thus, to find all matches, we can start with a "seed" match and scan the table up and down for all the other matches (Figures 3.12 and 3.15), printing the indices that match the sequence as 26, 43, and 29.

Once the sorted suffix table has been produced, how much time

```r
search_table <- function(table, subseq, rangeL, rangeU) {
  pattern <- str_c("^", subseq)
  range_size <- rangeU - rangeL + 1

  # base case: range in question is one or two rows
  # search directly
  if(range_size <= 2) {
    if(str_detect(table$suffix[rangeL], pattern)) {
      return(rangeL)
    } else if(str_detect(table$suffix[rangeU], pattern)) {
      return(rangeU)
    } else {
      return(NA)
    }
  }

  ## recursive case: split range in half
  middle_range <- rangeL + as.integer((rangeU - rangeL)/2)
  middle_suffix <- table$suffix[middle_range]
  if(subseq < middle_suffix) {
    answer <- search_table(table, subseq, rangeL, middle_range)
    return(answer)
  } else {
    answer <- search_table(table, subseq, middle_range, rangeU)
    return(answer)
  }
}

found_row <- search_table(suffix_df, "ACGA", 1, nrow(suffix_df))
print(found_row)                           # prints 3
```

Figure 3.14: Utilizing a recursive binary search procedure to find a suffix that starts with the subsequence ACGA.

does the search procedure take for a single query suffix? The binary search itself takes $O(\log_2(n))$ (where n is the number of suffixes/-size of the table/genome size) as discussed for the children's game. Once a matching row has been identified, the scanning procedure looks only at that row and neighboring rows that match, for a total time of $O(m)$, where m is the number of matching locations. Thus, the total runtime is $O(m + \log_2(n))$, a significant improvement on the $O(m \log_2(n))$ tree-based method of the last section if m is large!

3.3   Sorting

In the suffix-array solution above, after we had produced a table of suffixes and indexes, we needed to *sort* it.[5] Sorting data is an important problem in much of computing, and it serves as entry point into the study of algorithms for many computer science students. It is also a problem that is best solved by recursion.

Before we consider the recursive methods for sorting though, let's first consider how we might sort a list of numbers (or any elements

[5] This isn't quite true. In practice, methods that use suffix arrays do not generate them in the way that we did by creating a table of suffixes. It turns out that the suffix array (the index column) can be generated in $O(n)$ time using another recursive method described in 2005 by Juha Kärkkäinen, Peter Sanders, and Stefan Burkhardt. Additionally, the search procedure can be improved from $O(\log_2(n))$ to $O(w)$, where w is the length of the query string, using a recursive method that exploits certain properties of the list of first letters of the suffixes after sorting (known as the "Burrows-Wheeler Transform"). For details on these sophisticated methods we refer the reader to "Fast and accurate short read alignment with Burrows-Wheeler transform" by Heng Li and Richard Durban, *Bioinformatics* 25(14), 2009.

Figure 3.15: Scanning neighboring rows for matches after binary searching for a matching suffix.

```r
scan_matches_from <- function(table, rownum, subseq) {
  suffix <- table$suffix[rownum]
  pattern <- str_c("^", subseq)

  # scan back to start of matching rows
  while(str_detect(suffix, pattern)) {
    print(table[rownum, ])
    rownum <- rownum - 1
    suffix <- table$suffix[rownum]
  }
  rownum <- rownum + 1
  suffix <- table$suffix[rownum]

  # scan forward through matching rows, printing
  while(str_detect(suffix, pattern)) {
    print(table$index[rownum])
    rownum <- rownum + 1
    suffix <- table$suffix[rownum]
  }
}

if(!is.na(found_row)) {
  scan_matches_from(suffix_df, found_row, "ACGA")
}.
```

that can be ordered) using a naïve strategy: look for elements that are out of order, and swap them. In fact, to start let's write a function that will sort a vector called `naive_sort()`. It will use a loop to consider adjacent pairs of elements, and swaps those pairs that are out of order (Figure 3.16).

Figure 3.16: An initial start toward a naïve sorting method. This function uses a loop to compare neighboring pairs of elements, and swaps them if they are out of order.

```r
naive_sort <- function(vec) {
  for(index in seq(1,length(vec) - 1)) {
    el_a <- vec[index]
    el_b <- vec[index + 1]
    if(el_b < el_a) {
      vec[index] <- el_b
      vec[index + 1] <- el_a
    }
  }

  return(vec)
}

sorted <- naive_sort(c(9,5,8,6,1,2,0,3,4,7))
```

This function will correct a few out-of-order elements, but certainly won't fully sort the input vector. Still, consider what will happen with the 9 at the start: after the first loop, it will have been swapped with the 5. After the second loop, it will have been swapped with the 8, and so on, until at the end it will be swapped up to the last position. In a sense, the largest number has "bubbled" to the correct position.

What if we ran the whole process a second time? It should be easy to see that the second largest number, 8, will be bubbled to its correct place in the second-to-last position. In fact, all we need to do to ensure the entire vector is sorted is to repeat this loop n times, where n is the number of elements. This process is known as a "bubblesort" because on its bubbly nature (Figure 3.17).

Figure 3.17: Bubblesort.

```
bubble_sort <- function(vec) {
  for(counter in seq(1,length(vec))) {
    for(index in seq(1,length(vec) - 1)) {
      el_a <- vec[index]
      el_b <- vec[index + 1]
      if(el_b < el_a) {
        vec[index] <- el_b
        vec[index + 1] <- el_a
      }
    }
  }
  return(vec)
}

sorted <- bubble_sort(c(9,5,8,6,1,2,0,3,4,7))
```

How fast is this sorting routine? Each inner loop examines all n elements, and so runs in $O(n)$ time. But this loop is run n times, so the total runtime is $O(n^2)$. This is a commonly-found runtime for methods that have nested loops of the same "size," and sadly, it's not particularly fast (Figure 3.18). One might attempt to optimize this procedure, by noticing that since after the first loop the largest element is in place, the second loop need only look at the first $n-1$ elements. The third loop similarly needs to only look a the the first $n-2$ elements, and so on. But, this is a "small optimization" because $n + (n-1) + (n-2) + \cdots + 2 + 1 = n(n+1)/2$, which is $O(n^2)$ anyway.

RATHER THAN USING BUBBLESORT, let's devise the recursive solution mentioned earlier. Being a recursive algorithm, we have a base case to consider, and a recursive case. The base case will simply be if the length of the input vector is 1 or 0–if so, it is already sorted and can just be returned. On the other hand, if the length of the vector is greater than one, we need a scheme:

1. First, we'll pick a random element from the list to use as a "pivot."

2. Second, we'll generate three vectors: those that are less than the pivot called lessthan, those that are equal to the pivot (equalto),

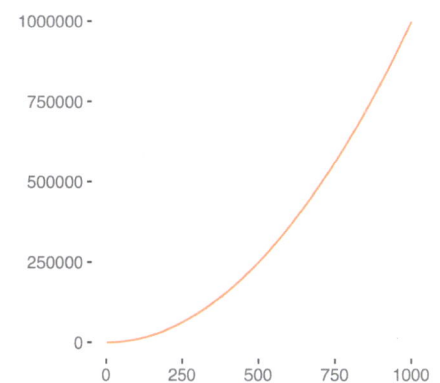

Figure 3.18: Plotting n vs. the quickly-growing n^2.

and those that are greater than the pivot (greaterthan).

3. Third, we'll sort the lessthan and greaterthan vectors (recursively!) to produce lessthan_sorted and greaterthan_sorted.

4. Finally, the concatenation of lessthan_sorted, equalto, and greaterthan_sorted is the fully-sorted answer, which can be returned.

Step 3 above is clearly the most important. In particular, we need to argue that lessthan and greaterthan are *smaller* than the original input. If they aren't, the recursive cases will never approach the base case and infinite recursion (error) will result. But of course this is true–at least one element must equal the pivot, so both lessthan and greaterthan must be smaller than the input vec. The code is illustrated in Figure 3.19, in a function called quicksort.

Figure 3.19: Quicksort, a recursive sorting method. In this code we are using R's vectorized syntax to extract subsets of elements, as in lessthan <- vec[vec < pivot].

```
quicksort <- function(vec) {
  if(length(vec) <= 1) {
    return(vec)
  }

  pivot <- sample(vec, 1)

  lessthan <- vec[vec < pivot]
  equalto <- vec[vec == pivot]
  greaterthan <- vec[vec > pivot]

  lessthan_sorted <- quicksort(lessthan)
  greaterthan_sorted <- quicksort(greaterthan)

  answer <- c(lessthan_sorted, equalto, greaterthan_sorted)
  return(answer)
}

sorted <- quicksort(c(9,5,8,6,1,2,0,3,4,7))
```

The name of the method is quicksort. How quick is it? Analyzing the runtime of this algorithm is no easy task, partially because it makes not one, but *two* recursive calls, and also because it utilizes randomness as it runs. For the latter, we'll temporarily make the simplifying assumption that the sample chooses the median element of the list, resulting in lessthan and greaterthan being of equal size; if length(vec) is n, we'll suppose that lessthan and greaterthan have approximately $n/2$ elements each.

One way to analyze a recursive algorithm like this is to write an equation that describes its runtime, in terms of itself. Such an equation is known as an *recurrence relation*. Suppose $T(n)$ is the runtime of the algorithm with n inputs (under the "pivot is median" assumption above). If $n = 1$, then $T(n)$ is $O(1)$: no real work is done. But what about if $n > 1$? The run time depends on how long it takes to perform the steps listed above. First, in step one, a random element is selected; presented without argument, R uses $O(1)$ time for this simple operation. In step 2, elements are extracted in comparison with the pivot. This requires comparing each element with the pivot, and so this step takes $O(n)$ time. The third step performs two recursive calls, on vectors of size (by simplifying assumption) $n/2$. Since we don't have any way to describe this runtime other than via $T()$, we'll say this is $2T(n/2)$. Finally, the three sub-lists must be concatenated; R performs this in $O(n)$ time since each element must be included in the answer. Thus, the total time in the recursive case is $O(1) + O(n) + 2T(n) + O(n)$, or just $2T(n/2) + O(n)$.

$$T(n) = \begin{cases} 2T(n/2) + O(n), & \text{if } n > 1, \\ O(1), & \text{otherwise.} \end{cases}$$

It is possible to come up with a simple solution for recurrence relations like this, using a process not too dissimilar from recursion. First, we start by replacing $T(n/2)$ according to the definition $T(n/2) = 2T(n/4) + O(n/2)$:

$$\begin{aligned} T(n) &= 2T(n/2) + O(n) \\ &= 2\left(2T(n/4) + O(n/2)\right) + O(n) \\ &= 4T(n/4) + 2O(n/2) + O(n) \\ &= 4T(n/4) + O(n) + O(n). \end{aligned}$$

Similarly, we can replace $T(n/4)$ with $2T(n/8) + O(n)$, and with some rearrangement obtain

$$T(n) = 8T(n/8) + O(n) + O(n) + O(n).$$

This process will continue, until we get an equation like $xT(n/x) + O(n) + O(n) + \cdots + O(n)$. How many steps can we do this, until n/x is approximately 1 (wherein $T(n) = O(1)$ will apply)? Since x is being doubled at each iteration, the number of steps is $\log_2(n)$, thus there will be $O(\log_2(n))$ terms of $O(n)$ in the entire series.

$$T(n) = O(1) + \underbrace{O(n) + O(n) + \cdots + O(n)}_{O(\log_2(n)) \text{ terms}}.$$

Thus, the total runtime for the algorithm under the given assumptions is $T(n) = O(n\log_2(n))$, significantly better than the $O(n^2)$ of bubblesort (Figure 3.20).[6]

ANOTHER INTERESTING WAY to get a handle on the runtime of this function is with a visual diagram (Figure 3.21). We can illustrate the function calls as nodes in a "tree," wherein each node is sized

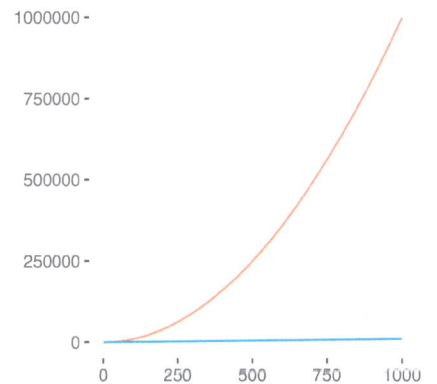

Figure 3.20: A plot of n^2 (red) and $n\log_2(n)$ (green) for values of n from 1 to 1,000.

[6] We are taking some liberties in notation here, particularly in simplifying expressions like $2O(n/2)$ to $O(n)$. A more rigorous approach would not use order notation, but use variables for constants as in

$$T(n) = \begin{cases} 2T(n/2) + c_1 n + c_2, & \text{if } n > 1, \\ c_3, & \text{otherwise.} \end{cases}$$

You might try solving this recurrence yourself to verify it results in the same solution.

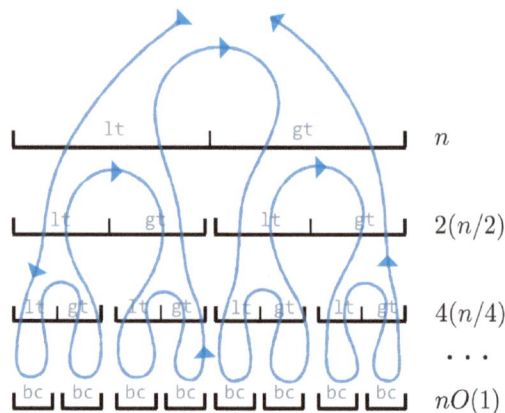

Figure 3.21: A "weighted call tree" for quicksort, under the assumption that every pivot splits lessthan and greaterthan (here represented by lt and gt, bc stands for "base case") into two roughly-equal halves. The blue line traces the path of execution: in any node a local greaterthan and lessthan are created, then lessthan is sorted recursively followed by greaterthan before the answer is concatenated and returned. In this path, going down a level represents a call, and going up a level represents a return.

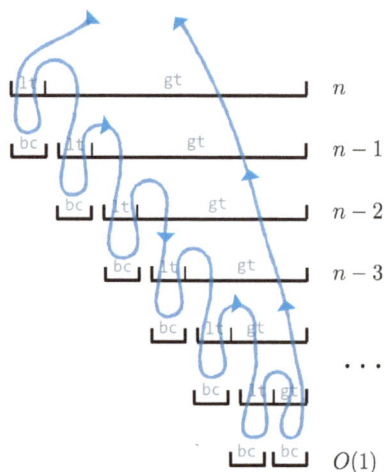

Figure 3.22: A "call tree" for quicksort, where the pivot is always the smallest or nearly the smallest element.

according to the amount of work done at that call (not counting the work done in recursive calls). Thus, the top node represents the $O(n)$ work done by the initial call, and this node calls two sub-nodes representing $O(n/2)$ work each; each of these make calls representing $O(n/4)$ work, and so on. But, at the level where each node requires $O(n/4)$ work, there are 4 such nodes; a similar argument applies to every level. The main question then is, how many levels are there? Notice the similarity to a balanced binary tree: there are $O(\log_2(n))$ levels, for a total amount of work of $O(n \log_2(n))$.

We've made a pretty big assumption here, which is that the randomly-chosen pivot is the median and always divides the input vector exactly in half. This will be true on average, but what happens if we get unlucky? Let's consider the case where the pivot always happens to be the smallest (or perhaps second-smallest) element of the list. In this case, lessthan will always be empty (and so sorting it will be an instance of the base case), and greaterthan will have $n - 1$ elements. The recurrence relation for this case is

$$T(n) = \begin{cases} T(n-1) + O(n), & \text{if } n > 1, \\ O(1), & \text{otherwise.} \end{cases}$$

The corresponding graphical call-tree representation is shown in Figure 3.22. Now the amount of work at each level decreases incrementally, so it takes many more levels to reach the bottom. The total amount of work is $n + (n - 1) + (n - 2) + \cdots + 1 = n(n + 1)/2$, which is $O(n^2)$ indicating that in the worst case quicksort, despite its name, can be as slow as bubblesort.

As we said, on average a randomly selected pivot will split the vector in half, and indeed it has been shown that with very high probability quicksort will run in $O(n \log_2(n))$ time. It is notable that quicksort does use random choices to guarantee this no matter the order of the input: any deterministic rule could result in $O(n^2)$ runtime if the data are "stacked against the rule." (For example, if the data are already sorted, always using the first element as the pivot is equivalent to being unlucky enough to always choosing the smallest element.)

Much as there are self-balancing binary trees that give strong guarantees on $O(\log_2(n))$ operations, there are other recursive sorting methods that guarantee $O(n \log_2(n))$ runtime without using randomization. Examples include mergesort and treesort (when using a balanced binary tree), which will be covered in the exercises.

Exercises

1. Mergesort operates in a similar fashion as quicksort: the input
   vector is split into two equal-sized sub-vectors, these are sorted
   recursively, and then the answers are combined into the final
   answer. The main difference is in how the list is split in half.

   Mergesort requires a small auxiliary function called merge()
   which takes two sorted vectors and returns a single sorted vector
   with all of the elements. Write this function and argue that in
   runs in $O(n)$ time.

   With the merge() function written, mergesort() is simple: the
   base case is the same as for quicksort(), but otherwise split
   the input vector in two pieces called first_half (containing
   the first $\approx n/2$ elements) and second_half (containing the rest).
   Recursively call mergesort() on these halves, and use merge() to
   merge the sorted sub-vectors into a single answer to return. Since
   this method guarantees an equal split, its runtime is a guaranteed
   $O(n \log_2(n))$.

2. Treesort simply inserts all the elements of a vector into a binary
   search tree, and uses a recursive method to re-extract them to
   a vector (or list) in order. Argue that for a balanced binary tree,
   the runtime for treesort is also $O(n \log_2(n))$, and implement a
   treesort using the binary search trees discussed earlier.

3. A colleague thinks that if splitting the input vector into two parts
   works well for mergesort, then splitting into three (and recursing
   three times) must be even better. What would be the runtime of
   this modified sort? Is it in principle better, worse than, or equal
   to regular split-in-half version? Why? (It will help to have solved
   problem 5 on page 44.)

4 Induction and Stacks

I have deeply regretted that I did not proceed far enough at least to understand something of the great leading principles of mathematics, for men thus endowed seem to have an extra sense.

Charles Darwin, 1876

BEES have an interesting biology. As you may know, a single female, the queen, lays eggs producing most of the male worker bees in a hive. These males have no father and are clones of the queen. Female (queen) bees on the other hand are rarer, and have both a mother and a father. The family tree for a male bee is illustrated in Figure 4.1. If we consider the number of ancestors of the bee at each generation (including himself as his "first" generation, as we'll count generations backward through time) then the sequence goes 1, 1, 2, 3, 5, 8, 13, and so on. You might recognize this as the famous Fibonacci sequence, after the 11th century mathematician who studied it. (Leonardo Fibonacci was also largely responsible for moving Europe away from the Roman Numeral counting system to the Arabic system we use today.) Apparently, the number of bees at a given generation n, which we'll call $bees(n)$ (and is often annotated as $fib(n)$, since the same equation describes the Fibonacci sequence), is the sum of the number of bees of the previous two generations ($1 + 1 = 2, 1 + 2 = 3, 2 + 3 = 5$, and so on):

$$bees(n) = \begin{cases} 1, & \text{if } n = 1, \\ 1, & \text{if } n = 2, \\ bees(n-1) + bees(n-2), & \text{otherwise.} \end{cases}$$

Figure 4.1: The family tree of a male bee.

But, is it enough to simply assert this relationship? That the number of bees at a given generation is equal to the sum of the previous generations? Perhaps not. We've based this only on observation of a small number of cases, and we could envision an obstinate observer

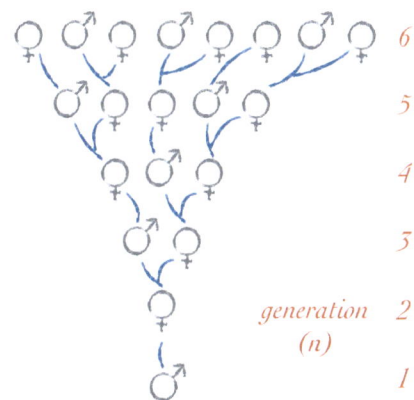

$bees(n - 1)$

$\parallel$

$males(n - 1) + females(n - 1)$

$\parallel$

$bees(n) = females(n) + males(n)$

$\parallel$

$females(n - 1)$

$\parallel$

$bees(n - 2)$

Similar argument

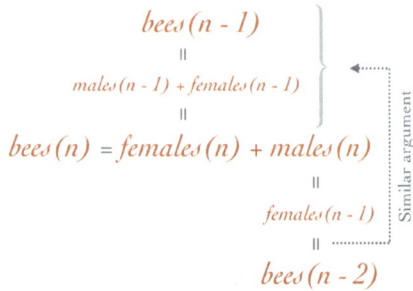

Figure 4.2: A sketch of the proof for $bees(n) = bees(n - 1) + bees(n - 2)$. The logic for $females(n - 1)$ uses the same argumentation as for $females(n)$.

who might not agree that $bees(36) = bees(35) + bees(34)$ without a ridiculous extension of the drawing (there would be over 14 million bees in the figure at the 36th generation!) Rather, we should argue the relationship analytically by producing a proof.

Proof. Based on simple observation, we can argue conclusively that $bees(1) = 1$ and $bees(2) = 1$.

For any other n, let's *assume*, for the moment, that $bees(n - 1)$ gives the correct number of ancestors at generation $n - 1$ according to the formula, as does $bees(n - 2)$ for generation $n - 2$. If these facts are true (see discussion below), then all we need show is that $bees(n - 1) + bees(n - 2)$ gives the correct answer for generation n (since this is equated to $bees(n)$).

1. First, $bees(n) = females(n) + males(n)$, the number of females and males at generation n, respectively.

2. Consider $females(n)$: in the family tree, every bee (male and female) has exactly one mother. Further, every female in the tree gives birth to exactly one bee in the tree. Thus, the very rules of bee biology dictate that $females(n) = males(n - 1) + females(n - 1)$, which in turn equals $bees(n - 1)$.

3. Now consider $males(n)$. Every male at generation n in the tree mates to contribute to exactly one female offspring at generation $n - 1$ (in this family tree at least). Further, every female at generation $n - 1$ has exactly one male parent at generation n. Thus, $males(n) = females(n - 1)$.

4. By the same logic as step 2 above, $females(n - 1) = bees(n - 1)$.

Finally, we have that:

$$
\begin{aligned}
bees(n) &= females(n) + males(n) & \text{(step 1)} \\
&= bees(n - 1) + males(n) & \text{(step 2)} \\
&= bees(n - 1) + females(n - 1) & \text{(step 3)} \\
&= bees(n - 1) + bees(n - 2) & \text{(step 4)} .
\end{aligned}
$$

$\square$

THE STEPS ABOVE WILL WORK FINE for any given n, so long as we can actually *assume* that the formula produces good numbers for $bees(n - 1)$ and $bees(n - 2)$ as we did. Our simple observations showed that this is true for the first two generations, which means that the proof must hold for $n = 3$; that is, that $bees(3) = bees(2) + bees(1)$ $(2 = 1 + 1)$. This shows that the formula is further correct for $bees(3)$, and thus that the proof holds for $n = 4$ as well ($bees(4) =$

$bees(3) + bees(2))$. In a sense, our "proof" is an infinite series of sub-proofs, each relying on the correctness of the previous two (Figure 4.3).

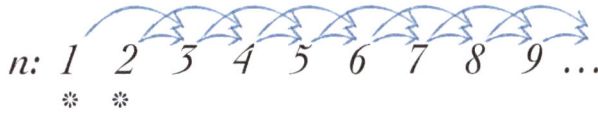

$$n: 1 \quad 2 \quad 3 \quad 4 \quad 5 \quad 6 \quad 7 \quad 8 \quad 9 \ldots$$

Figure 4.3: Dependency of sub-proofs. We show the truth of $n = 1$ and $n = 2$ by observation, and these imply the truth of $n = 3$ by argumentation. Similarly, $n = 2$ and $n = 3$ imply the truth of $n = 4$, and so on.

This strategy of proving a "cascade of correctness" is known as *induction*. You might remember mathematical induction from a class in mathematics, for example to prove an identity like $1 + 2 + \cdots + n = n(n+1)/2$ (Figure 4.4). In simple mathematical induction, there is a base case where the identity is shown for a small value, and an inductive case where the cascade is described mathematically.

In the case of our bees, we're reasoning more generally about structures that exist in nature (or computer programs). We still have a base case (or cases), and we still have an inductive case (or cases). But we call this more general form of proof *structural induction*, as it relies on more than mere manipulation of formulae.

Base Case, $n = 1$:

$$1 = \frac{1(1+1)}{2} = \frac{2}{2} \overset{\checkmark}{=} 1$$

Inductive Case, $n > 1$:

$$\underbrace{1 + 2 + \cdots + (n-1)}_{\substack{\text{Assuming true} \\ \text{for } n-1:}} + n = \frac{n(n+1)}{2}$$

$$\underbrace{\frac{(n-1)((n-1)+1)}{2}}_{\text{Rearrangment:}}$$

$$\frac{n(n+1)}{2} \qquad \overset{\checkmark}{=} \frac{n(n+1)}{2}$$

Figure 4.4: A sketch of the proof for $1 + 2 + \cdots + n = n(n+1)/2$ by mathematical induction.

4.1 Computing the Fibonacci Sequence

At this point, rather than using $bees(n)$, let's switch to $fib(n)$ to emphasize that the sequence of numbers we're describing is indeed the Fibonacci sequence. How might we write a program to compute the nth Fibonacci number? We can use recursion, and the code itself nearly mirrors the definition. Indeed, the contents of the `else` block in Figure 4.5 could simply be `return(fib(n-1) + fib(n-2))`.

```
fib <- function(n) {
  if(n == 1) {
    return(1)
  } else if(n == 2) {
    return(1)
  } else {
    a <- fib(n - 1)
    b <- fib(n - 2)
    answer <- a + b
    return(answer)
    # or simply: return(fib(n - 1) + fib(n - 2))
  }
}

print(fib(8))                    # prints 21
```

Figure 4.5: A function for computing the nth Fibonacci number.

The reason this code produces correct answers is due to the way functions and local variables work, as in the recursive functions from previous chapters. Here, we called `fib(8)`, an instance of the

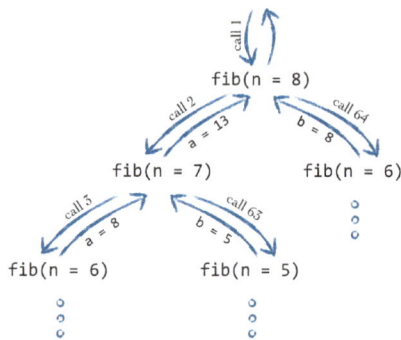

Figure 4.6: Call tree for `fib(8)`.

call that had a local variable n equaling 8. In turn, that call called `fib(7)`, which in turn had its own local n equal to 7, independent of all other variables named n. This call called `fib(6)`, and so on; eventually the answer to `fib(7)` (13) was returned and stored as a. Next, `fib(6)` was computed (in a recursive manner) and stored in b, and finally the sum of these was returned (see Figure 4.6). Just like the other recursive functions we've studied, this function has:

- Base cases, representing the easiest versions of the problem requiring minimal computational work, and

- Recursive cases, calling the same function but with parameters that approach the base case.

What do recursion and induction have to do with each other? The fact that the base cases for the recursive function and the base cases of the inductive proof are identical is no accident. Most notably, induction is an excellent way to prove the correctness of a recursive method.

Proof that `fib(n)` *computes the* n^{th} *Fibonacci number for any n.* Base case: if $n = 1$ or $n = 2$, `fib(n)` directly returns the correct answer.
Inductive case: For any other n, we assume by induction that `fib(n-1)` (stored in a) and `fib(n-2)` (stored in b) are computed correctly. The return value, a + b, equals `fib(n)` by the definition of the Fibonacci sequence. □

Although this proof is so simple as to be unnecessary, we'll see the technique used in other situations.

Exercises

1. In Chapter 1 we created a CALL_COUNTER global variable that recorded how many times a particular function is called. Modify the `fib()` function to do the same, such that each time `fib()` is called it increments CALL_COUNTER by 1. Produce a table with the following columns for n from 1 through 15. (Reset CALL_COUNTER to 0 for each n before calling `fib()`.) Do you notice any pattern? You may want to plot the results.

Table 4.1: Fill in the values in this table for n from to 1 to 15.

n	fib(n)	CALL_COUNTER
1		
2		
3		
...		

2. Write a recursive function (don't use a loop) that computes a factorial: $factorial(n) = 1 \cdot 2 \cdot \ldots \cdot n$.

3. Predator/prey models can be described as a pair of equations that are recursively defined (also known as difference equations). For example, the following equations have been used, where $x(n)$ describes the density of prey at time point n, $y(n)$ the density of predators, and r, b, c, and d are parameters of the model.

$$x(n) = (r+1) \cdot x(n-1) - r \cdot x(n-1)^2 - b \cdot x(n-1) \cdot y(n-1) ,$$
$$y(n) = c \cdot x(n-1) \cdot y(n-1) + (1-d) \cdot y(n-1) .$$

Write a pair of recursive functions[1] to compute the number of predators and prey for a given n, with the following parameters: $x(1) = 0.3$, $y(1) = 0.8$, $r = 0.25$, $b = 1.1$, $c = 0.95$, and $d = 0.55$. See if you can plot the density of predators and prey as n varies from 1 to 20.

[1] The x() function should call itself and y(), and y() should call itself and x().

4. Try drawing a call tree for x(4) from the predator/prey model above.

5. Use structural induction to prove that insert_tree() (page 34) returns a properly formed binary search tree, assuming the parameter data is a properly formed binary search tree.

6. Determine an equation that relates fib() with the value of CALL_COUNTER in Exercise 1 in terms of n. Use structural induction to prove that your equation holds for all n. (Hint: there is a relationship between CALL_COUNTER for n and fib(n-1).)

4.2   Stacks

Hopefully we're already familiar with the basic data types provided by R like vectors, data frames, and especially lists (review Chapter 1 if not). Here we're going to learn about a new data structure called a stack, which provides limited but very efficient access to some of the data elements it holds.

Stacks, also known as Last-In First-Out (LIFO) queues, hold data elements in the order in which they are first inserted. Usually we think of the new elements as being placed at the "top" of the stack. Stacks support the following operations in constant time ($O(1)$), no matter the number of elements already in the stack: push, to add a new element to the top of the stack, pop, to remove the element at the top, and peek, to access the element at the top without removing it. While stacks are very efficient for these three operations, most other operations are slower. For example, determining if a given element is present in a stack requires searching the entire stack (an $O(n)$ operation).[2]

R does not by default include support for stacks, but the package rstackdeque provides this functionality (Figure 4.8).

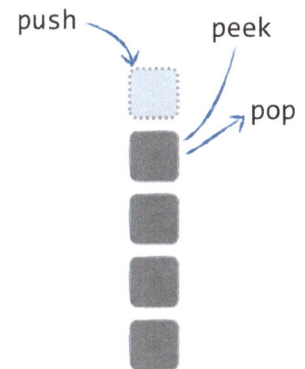

Figure 4.7: A stack. Dark squares are existing items; a "pop" would remove the top item, "peek" accesses the top item, and new items can be added to the top with "push."

[2] The nested list structures described in Chapter 2 implement stacks, with insert_front() serving as "push."

Figure 4.8: Basic operations with an rstack.

```
s <- rstack()
print(empty(s))       # prints TRUE
s <- insert_top(s, "A")
print(empty(s))       # prints FALSE
s <- insert_top(s, "B")
s <- insert_top(s, "C")

print(s)              # prints summary of s: "C", "B", and "A"
print(peek_top(s))    # prints "C"
s <- without_top(s)
print(s)              # prints summary of s: "B" and "A"
print(peek_top(s))    # prints "B"
```

Stacks implemented in this package can be created (initially empty) with a line like s <- rstack(). Elements may be inserted via insert_top(s, element) and removed via without_top(s); each of these returns a modified copy of the stack. Peeking is accomplished with peek_top(s), which returns the top element but does not modify s. The empty() function will return TRUE if the given stack has no elements, and FALSE if it does.

Some measure of R-specific functionality is included with rstacks. For example, it is possible to "unstackify" an rstack, returning the elements as a list by running as.list() on it (an $O(n)$ operation, Figure 4.9).

Figure 4.9: Converting an rstack to a list.

```
s_list <- as.list(s)  # list containing "A" and "B"
```

Any R data type can be an element of an rstack, including data frames, lists, and matrices. Like R lists, rstacks may hold different types of data elements. If the elements of an rstack are lists, and each internal list has the same names in the same order, then as.data.frame() will treat each element as a row when converting the stack to a data frame (Figure 4.10).[3]

Figure 4.10: Converting an rstack to a data frame.

```
rows <- rstack()
rows <- insert_top(rows, list(name = "Bob", age = 24))
rows <- insert_top(rows, list(name = "Mary", age = 21))

df <- as.data.frame(rows)
print(df)
```

The output can be found in Figure 4.11. These functions are "side-effect-free," meaning that they have no effect on the data given to them as parameters. For example, s2 <- insert_top(s, "X") results in the s2 stack holding the contents of the s stack as well as an "X", while the s stack remains unchanged (does not include "X").

Together, these features can be used to investigate the behavior of functions like fib(). Consider Figure 4.12, which plots the number of calls required to compute fib(n) for n from 1 to 15. The output

[3] The powerful purrr package also includes a number of functions for mapping lists to other lists, data frames, and vectors. In some cases we'll be using rstacks as intermediary data structures because unlike R lists and data frames, we can efficiently add to them in an element-by-element fashion (see Chapter 2).

```
  name age
1 Mary  21
2 Bob   24
```

Figure 4.11: Output for code in Figure 4.10.

(Figures 4.13 and 4.14) reveals the relationship between the nth Fibonacci number and the number of function calls required to compute it via recursion.

```r
fib <- function(n) {
  CALL_COUNTER <<- CALL_COUNTER + 1
  if (n == 1 | n == 2) {
    return(1)
  } else {
    answer <- fib(n-1) + fib(n-2)
    return(answer)
  }
}

info_rows <- rstack()
for(i in seq(1, 15)) {
  CALL_COUNTER <<- 0
  answer <- fib(i)
  row <- list(n = i, fibn = answer, calls = CALL_COUNTER)
  info_rows <- insert_top(info_rows, row)
}

infodf <- as.data.frame(info_rows)
p <- ggplot(infodf) +
  geom_line(aes(x = n, y = fibn), color = "orange") +
  geom_line(aes(x = n, y = calls), color = "purple")
plot(p)
```

Figure 4.12: Computing and displaying the number of calls required to compute fib(n) using the recursive method.

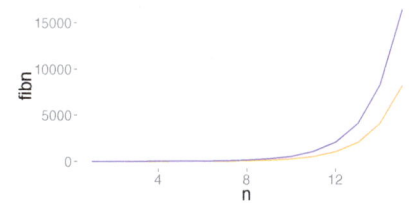

Figure 4.13: Output for code listing in Figure 4.12: for each n, the orange line shows fib(n), and the purple line shows the number of recursive calls needed to compute fib(n).

	n	fibn	calls
1	15	8192	16383
2	14	4096	8191
3	13	2048	4095
4	12	1024	2047
5	11	512	1023
6	10	256	511

Figure 4.14: The first few rows of infodf produced in Figure 4.12.

4.3 The Call Stack

One may wonder–how does the R interpreter manage the magic of local variables, the things that enable the remarkable process we call recursion? Different languages manage the process differently in the details, but they nearly all utilize a stack for the process. Each function call (represented by the set of local variables defined by the function call) becomes an element of this *call stack*, pushed when the call happens, and popped when the function returns.

Consider a function A() that has two parameters (which, we'll recall, are also local variables) a1 and a2. Suppose this function calls B(), which itself calls C() and then D(); each of these has local variables too. The "call tree" can be illustrated as in Figure 4.15. When function A() is called, its information (parameters and other local variables) are pushed onto the top of the call stack. When B() is called, its information is then placed onto the call stack, and similarly for the call to C(). When C() returns however, the information related to that call will be removed from the top of the call stack. Since B() later calls D(), the D() information will then be added. When D() returns, its information is removed, and so on

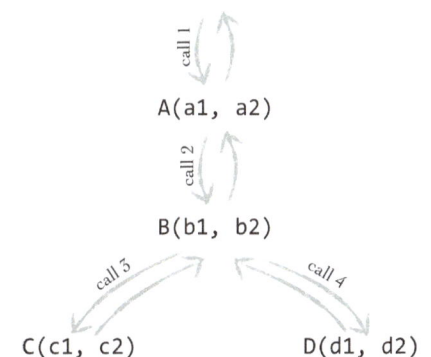

Figure 4.15: A simple call tree.

(Figure 4.16).

This same process happens when we call a recursive function, like fib() (see Figures 4.18 and 4.17).

Each of the individual elements on the stack (all of the local variables associated with a function call, as well as some other book-keeping information used to determine where return values should be assigned and so on) is called a *stack frame*.

Because function calls simply require pushing and popping from the call stack, they are very fast (since those operations are $O(1)$ for stacks). In most languages, the total number of elements the call stack can hold is limited; when the call stack runs out of room a *stack overflow* error occurs and the program crashes.[4]

Normally, we can't see the contents of the call stack, and usually we wouldn't want to. If we did want to, we could use our own stack in a global variable named CALL_STACK, to keep track of some of the same information. Every time the function is called, we'll push some information (a "stack frame") onto this stack, and before any return we'll remove the information, just as is done under the hood for the true call stack.

In the code (Figure 4.19), the global variable CALL_STACK is initialized before the fib() function is first called, and CALL_STACK is modified immediately after each call (at the top of the function) and immediately before each return, just as the the real call stack.

This is all well and good, but to get a sense of the process we should also print the contents of CALL_STACK after each modification, perhaps by writing an auxiliary function print_string_stack() dedicated to nicely printing the contents of a stack of strings. This function will first convert the stack to a list with the as.list() function, which will then be converted to a character vector with as.character() before being printed.

This would be almost correct, except that it would cause the stack contents to be printed in top-to-bottom order (and since R output is left-aligned, the visualization wouldn't match the growth of the stack). To rectify this, we'll print it in bottom-to-top order by adding a rev() to reverse the vector before printing.

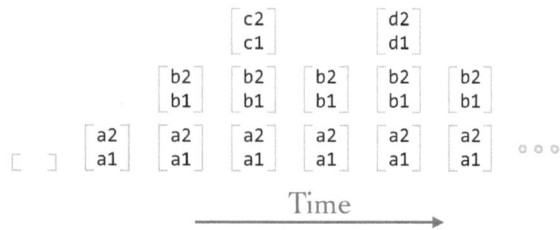

Figure 4.16: Call stack over time for the call tree illustrated in Figure 4.15. Local variables for each call are illustrated in brackets.

[4] R somewhat erroneously calls stack overflow errors "infinite recursion" errors, since recursion that never reaches a base case is the most common reason this happens.

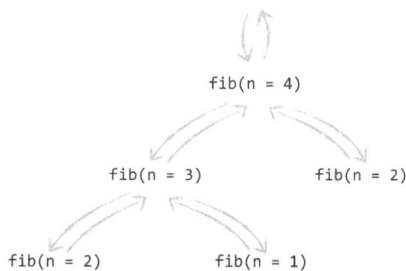

Figure 4.17: Call tree for fib(4).

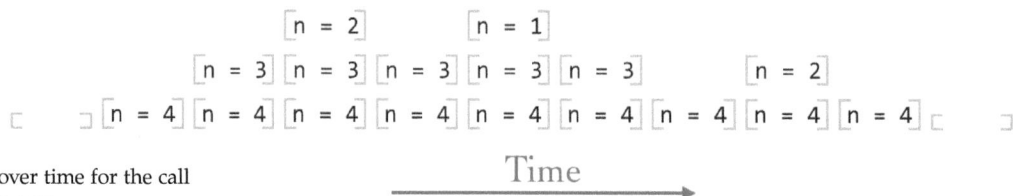

Figure 4.18: Call stack over time for the call tree illustrated in Figure 4.17.

```
print_string_stack <- function(s) {
  char_vec <- as.character(as.list(s))
  print(rev(char_vec))
}

fib <- function(n) {
  this_frame <- str_c("fib: n = ", n)
  CALL_STACK <<- insert_top(CALL_STACK, this_frame)
  print_string_stack(CALL_STACK)
  if(n == 1) {
    CALL_STACK <<- without_top(CALL_STACK)
    print_string_stack(CALL_STACK)
    return(1)
  } else if(n == 2) {
    CALL_STACK <<- without_top(CALL_STACK)
    print_string_stack(CALL_STACK)
    return(1)
  } else {
    answer <- fib(n-1) + fib(n-2)
    CALL_STACK <<- without_top(CALL_STACK)
    print_string_stack(CALL_STACK)
    return(answer)
  }
}

CALL_STACK <<- rstack()   # initialize global stack before calling
print(fib(8))             # prints 21
```

Figure 4.19: Modified `fib()` function that keeps a "shadow" call stack indicating the local parameter `n` for each call.

With these modifications in place, the output shows the contents of the call stack over time for the Fibonacci function (Figure 4.20). There are a few things to note about this result. First, the call stack is only ever as deep as the initial `n` (and thus we needn't worry about stack overflows, unless *n* is very large). Second, although functions call and returns are fast operations, there are quite a few calls made even for `fib(8)`, indicating that the computation is taking a long time. (For a more dramatic experiment, try viewing the output for a call like `fib(14)`.)

```
[1] "n = 8"
[1] "n = 8" "n = 7"
[1] "n = 8" "n = 7" "n = 6"
[1] "n = 8" "n = 7" "n = 6" "n = 5"
[1] "n = 8" "n = 7" "n = 6" "n = 5" "n = 4"
[1] "n = 8" "n = 7" "n = 6" "n = 5" "n = 4" "n = 3"
[1] "n = 8" "n = 7" "n = 6" "n = 5" "n = 4" "n = 3" "n = 2"
[1] "n = 8" "n = 7" "n = 6" "n = 5" "n = 4" "n = 3"
[1] "n = 8" "n = 7" "n = 6" "n = 5" "n = 4" "n = 3" "n = 1"
[1] "n = 8" "n = 7" "n = 6" "n = 5" "n = 4" "n = 3"
[1] "n = 8" "n = 7" "n = 6" "n = 5" "n = 4"
[1] "n = 8" "n = 7" "n = 6" "n = 5" "n = 4" "n = 2"
[1] "n = 8" "n = 7" "n = 6" "n = 5" "n = 4"
[1] "n = 8" "n = 7" "n = 6" "n = 5"
[1] "n = 8" "n = 7" "n = 6" "n = 5" "n = 3"
[1] "n = 8" "n = 7" "n = 6" "n = 5" "n = 3" "n = 2"
[1] "n = 8" "n = 7" "n = 6" "n = 5" "n = 3"
[1] "n = 8" "n = 7" "n = 6" "n = 5" "n = 3" "n = 1"
[1] "n = 8" "n = 7" "n = 6" "n = 5" "n = 3"
[1] "n = 8" "n = 7" "n = 6" "n = 5"
[1] "n = 8" "n = 7" "n = 6"
[1] "n = 8" "n = 7" "n = 6" "n = 4"
[1] "n = 8" "n = 7" "n = 6" "n = 4" "n = 3"
[1] "n = 8" "n = 7" "n = 6" "n = 4" "n = 3" "n = 2"
[1] "n = 8" "n = 7" "n = 6" "n = 4" "n = 3"
[1] "n = 8" "n = 7" "n = 6" "n = 4" "n = 3" "n = 1"
[1] "n = 8" "n = 7" "n = 6" "n = 4" "n = 3"
[1] "n = 8" "n = 7" "n = 6" "n = 4"
[1] "n = 8" "n = 7" "n = 6" "n = 4" "n = 2"
[1] "n = 8" "n = 7" "n = 6" "n = 4"
[1] "n = 8" "n = 7" "n = 6"
[1] "n = 8" "n = 7"
[1] "n = 8" "n = 7" "n = 5"
[1] "n = 8" "n = 7" "n = 5" "n = 4"
[1] "n = 8" "n = 7" "n = 5" "n = 4" "n = 3"
[1] "n = 8" "n = 7" "n = 5" "n = 4" "n = 3" "n = 2"
[1] "n = 8" "n = 7" "n = 5" "n = 4" "n = 3"
[1] "n = 8" "n = 7" "n = 5" "n = 4" "n = 3" "n = 1"
[1] "n = 8" "n = 7" "n = 5" "n = 4" "n = 3"
[1] "n = 8" "n = 7" "n = 5" "n = 4"
[1] "n = 8" "n = 7" "n = 5" "n = 4" "n = 2"
[1] "n = 8" "n = 7" "n = 5" "n = 4"
[1] "n = 8" "n = 7" "n = 5"
[1] "n = 8" "n = 7" "n = 5" "n = 3"
[1] "n = 8" "n = 7" "n = 5" "n = 3" "n = 2"
[1] "n = 8" "n = 7" "n = 5" "n = 3"
[1] "n = 8" "n = 7" "n = 5" "n = 3" "n = 1"
[1] "n = 8" "n = 7" "n = 5" "n = 3"
[1] "n = 8" "n = 7" "n = 5"
[1] "n = 8" "n = 7"
[1] "n = 8"
[1] "n = 8" "n = 6"
[1] "n = 8" "n = 6" "n = 5"
[1] "n = 8" "n = 6" "n = 5" "n = 4"
[1] "n = 8" "n = 6" "n = 5" "n = 4" "n = 3"
[1] "n = 8" "n = 6" "n = 5" "n = 4" "n = 3" "n = 2"
[1] "n = 8" "n = 6" "n = 5" "n = 4" "n = 3"
[1] "n = 8" "n = 6" "n = 5" "n = 4" "n = 3" "n = 1"
[1] "n = 8" "n = 6" "n = 5" "n = 4" "n = 3"
[1] "n = 8" "n = 6" "n = 5" "n = 4"
[1] "n = 8" "n = 6" "n = 5" "n = 4" "n = 2"
[1] "n = 8" "n = 6" "n = 5" "n = 4"
[1] "n = 8" "n = 6" "n = 5"
[1] "n = 8" "n = 6" "n = 5" "n = 3"
[1] "n = 8" "n = 6" "n = 5" "n = 3" "n = 2"
[1] "n = 8" "n = 6" "n = 5" "n = 3"
[1] "n = 8" "n = 6" "n = 5" "n = 3" "n = 1"
[1] "n = 8" "n = 6" "n = 5" "n = 3"
[1] "n = 8" "n = 6" "n = 5"
[1] "n = 8" "n = 6"
[1] "n = 8" "n = 6" "n = 4"
[1] "n = 8" "n = 6" "n = 4" "n = 3"
[1] "n = 8" "n = 6" "n = 4" "n = 3" "n = 2"
[1] "n = 8" "n = 6" "n = 4" "n = 3"
[1] "n = 8" "n = 6" "n = 4" "n = 3" "n = 1"
[1] "n = 8" "n = 6" "n = 4" "n = 3"
[1] "n = 8" "n = 6" "n = 4"
[1] "n = 8" "n = 6" "n = 4" "n = 2"
[1] "n = 8" "n = 6" "n = 4"
[1] "n = 8" "n = 6"
[1] "n = 8"
```

Figure 4.20: Printed call stack for `fib(8)` over time.

Exercises

1. Use the `CALL_COUNTER` technique along with a simple recursive function to determine how deep the call stack can go on your own instance of R.

2. Stacks are easily implemented as a nested linked list, where elements are only appended to or removed from the front. Implement non-recursive `append_front()`, `without_front()` and `peek_front()` functions for such lists.

4.4   Depth-First Search

In some languages (including R), the total number of stack frames the call stack can hold is relatively limited. This prevents us from relying on recursion when there is a potential that the recursion will be very deep: doing so may result in a stack overflow error (or "infinite recursion" error in R). For some problems this may not be an issue. A balanced binary tree of n nodes for example has depth $O(\log_2(n))$, and since searching the tree requires a recursion depth equal to the tree depth, trees of billions of nodes are easy to work with. But for other problems–functions operating on the nested lists of Chapter 2 come to mind–this can be a serious problem.

Fortunately, many procedures that are most easily described recursively can be implemented with loops and supporting structures like lists and stacks (we assume that stacks other than the call stack are not limited in size).[5] Consider the toy problem of collecting all of the elements of a tree that are consonants, i.e., not in the set c("A", "E", "I", "O", "U") (such as in Figure 2.22 on page 34, reproduced in Figure 4.21).

```r
consonants_list <- function(data) {
  if(is.null(data)) {
    return(list())  # if tree is empty, there are no consonants
  }

  left <- data[[1]]
  el <- data[[2]]
  right <- data[[3]]

  answer <- list()
  if(!el %in% c("A", "E", "I", "O", "U")) {
    answer <- c(answer, el)
  }

  left_answer <- consonants_list(left)
  right_answer <- consonants_list(right)

  answer <- c(answer, left_answer, right_answer)
  return(answer)
}

print(consonants_list(chars3)) # prints "C", "B", "F", "D"
```

The function in Figure 4.22 operates recursively. First, if the central element is a consonant, it is added to the answer. Next, sub-answers are computed for the left and right and added to the answer list as well.

Consider the call stack for this recursive function: it begins with just the "C" tree, then adds "A", and then adds "B" (following the

[5] In fact, any recursive function be implemented without recursive calls. In some languages, this can be accomplished by using goto statements along with stacks to emulate the jumping-around of execution performed by function calls. In languages without a goto statement the process is more sophisticated, requiring refactoring functions to use only a single function call at the end of any function (so called *continuation-passing style*) and then converting these "tail calls" to loops using the technique of *tail-call elimination*.

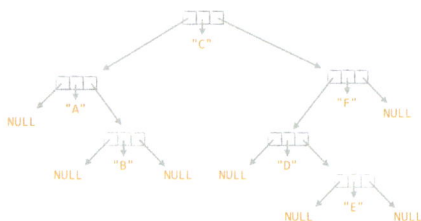

Figure 4.21: The chars3 binary tree from Figure 2.22.

Figure 4.22: Collecting the consonants of a tree into an R list via recursion.

recursive calls made); this returns, and the "A" call returns, then "F" is added, then "D", and so on (Figure 4.23). Each time a call is made, the central element is considered for consonant-ness and added to the answer list if necessary.

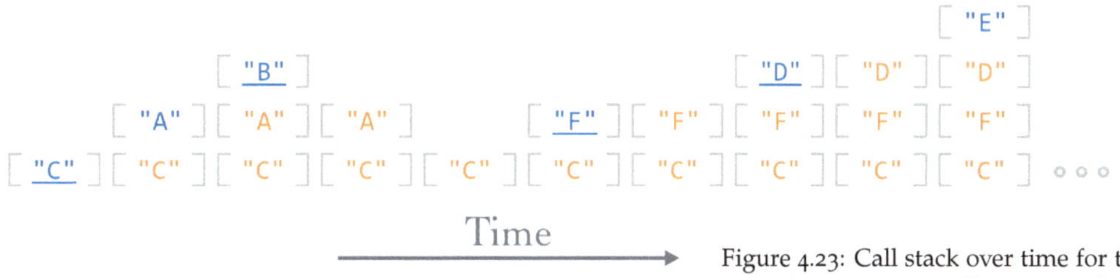

Figure 4.23: Call stack over time for the recursive consonant-collecting method of Figure 4.22. Elements are colored in blue to indicate the first time they are considered during the search, consonants actually added are underlined.

In fact, we can emulate this process using a simple loop and a stack of our own that keeps track of which nodes still need to be searched. To start with, we'll add the "C" tree to the stack. Then, in a loop running so long as any nodes still need to be considered (i.e., the stack is not empty), we'll: 1) Pull the top node off of the stack, considering its element for inclusion in the answer, and 2) If the top node's right and left are not NULL, then they can be added to the stack to be searched later (Figure 4.24).

Figure 4.24: Using a stack and a loop to collect consonants from the tree.

```
search_stack <- rstack()
search_stack <- insert_top(search_stack, chars3)
answer <- list()

while(!empty(search_stack)) {
  data <- peek_top(search_stack)
  search_stack <- without_top(search_stack)

  left <- data[[1]]
  el <- data[[2]]
  right <- data[[3]]

  if(!el %in% c("A", "E", "I", "O", "U")) {
    answer <- c(answer, el)
  }

  if(!is.null(right)) {
    search_stack <- insert_top(search_stack, right)
  }

  if(!is.null(left)) {
    search_stack <- insert_top(search_stack, left)
  }
}
```

For the case of "C", this means that the "F" tree will be added and then the "A" tree will be added *on top of it*. Thus, "F" and all of it's sub-tree will not be considered until "A" and all of its sub-tree

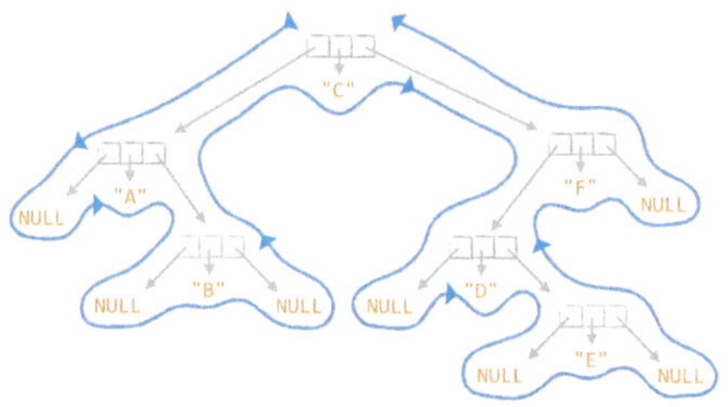

Figure 4.25: The search path in the tree for the depth-first search. This search path mirrors the call tree of the recursive method.

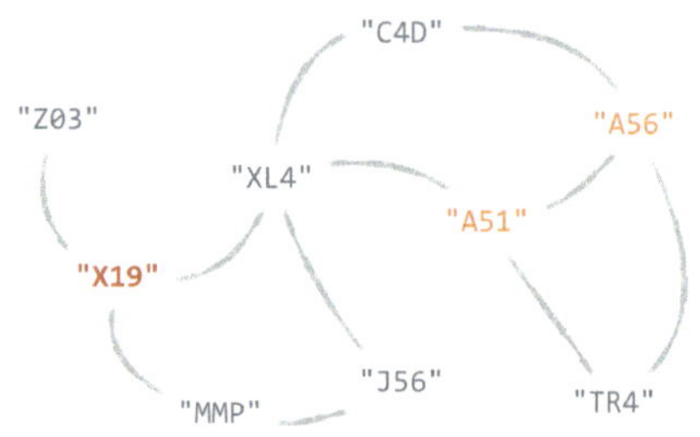

Figure 4.26: An example protein-protein interaction network. We are interested in discovering (computationally) which nodes in the network may be reached from "X19" whose identifiers begin with "A".

Figure 4.27: R code for an edge-matrix representation of a graph.

```
    Z03 XL4 X19
Z03   0   0   1
XL4   0   0   1
X19   1   1   0
```

Figure 4.28: Output for code in Figure 4.27.

are finished. This exactly matches the search done by the recursive method above, printing "C", "B", "F", and "D".

This pattern of searching deeply along one branch before considering other branches is known as *depth-first search*. For an example of why depth-first search could be useful, consider the problem of finding the smallest element of a tree with a certain property. Using depth-first search, as soon as a node satisfies the condition, we can return it, or short-circuit the search loop, thus preventing us from having to search the whole tree.

4.5   Graphs, Depth- vs. Breadth-First Search

Depth-first search is useful for finding nodes in structures more general than trees, called *graphs*. A graph consists of a set of nodes, some of which are connected by a set of edges. For a biologically inspired example, many researchers construct "protein-protein interaction networks" by assaying which proteins in a cell interact physically with other proteins. These collections of interactions can lead to novel insights, for example by revealing which genes regulate others in cascading effects. Figure 4.26 shows an example; the protein of interest "X19" interacts with "Z03", "XL4", and "MMP", and these in turn interact with others. We are interested in identifying which proteins are part of the interaction network whose identifiers begin with "A" (supposing this indicates some biologically important feature).

The first challenge we must solve is how to represent this graph in code. Generally graphs are represented in one of two ways: with an *edge matrix*, or with an *adjacency list*. An edge matrix represents each node as a column and row of a matrix, and connection information is stored in the cells. Figures 4.27 and 4.28 illustrate such a matrix in R for a sub-graph of three nodes.

```
g <- matrix(0, nrow = 3, ncol = 3,
            dimnames = list(c("Z03", "XL4", "X19"),
                            c("Z03", "XL4", "X19")))
g["Z03", "X19"] <- 1
g["X19", "Z03"] <- 1
g["XL4", "X19"] <- 1
g["X19", "XL4"] <- 1

print(g)
```

For our purposes, we'll use an adjacency-list representation. Here, each element of a list is a mapping from a node to a list of other nodes it connects to. We could use the binary search trees or nested lists discussed in Chapter 2 for this, but a named R list of vectors will work fine (Figure 4.29).

```
g <- list()
g[["X19"]] <- c("MMP", "XL4", "Z03")
g[["Z03"]] <- c("X19")
g[["XL4"]] <- c("X19", "J56", "A51", "C4D")
g[["MMP"]] <- c("X19", "J56")
g[["J56"]] <- c("MMP", "XL4")
g[["C4D"]] <- c("XL4", "A56")
g[["A51"]] <- c("XL4", "TR4", "A56")
g[["A56"]] <- c("C4D", "A51", "TR4")
g[["TR4"]] <- c("A56", "A51")
```

Figure 4.29: R code for an adjacency-list representation of a graph.

For the search, we're going to use the same loop-and-stack based depth-first search technique as the last section. However, because our structure is not a tree, we'll run into a problem: when we remove a node from the stack to consider, we'll want to add it's neighbors to the stack for later consideration. But, this could allow each node to be placed on the search stack more than one time. (In fact, "X19" will add "Z03", and then at some point "Z03" will add "X19", resulting in an infinite loop.) To avoid this problem, we will "mark" nodes using a separate structure to indicate if they've been added already, and only add unmarked ones to the search stack (Figure 4.30).

```
marking_list <- list()
marking_list[["Z03"]] <- "unmarked"
marking_list[["X19"]] <- "unmarked"
marking_list[["XL4"]] <- "unmarked"
marking_list[["MMP"]] <- "unmarked"
marking_list[["J56"]] <- "unmarked"
marking_list[["C4D"]] <- "unmarked"
marking_list[["A51"]] <- "unmarked"
marking_list[["A56"]] <- "unmarked"
marking_list[["TR4"]] <- "unmarked"
```

Figure 4.30: A named R list to indicate which nodes have/haven't been added to the search stack already.

The depth-first-search code in Figure 4.31 is quite similar to that of Figure 4.24, with the main adjustments being the need to consider all (unmarked) neighbors of a node in the graph rather than the two children of a node in a tree.[6] And, of course, that we've changed the feature of interest we are searching for.

[6] This depth-first search would work just as well on a tree, if we were to put the tree into adjacency-list representation rather than as a nesting structure.

WHAT IS THE ADVANTAGE OF THIS over simply looking at all the nodes in the graph in arbitrary order? First, consider that there may be other nodes which are not reachable from "X19"; in this case we say the graph is composed on multiple *connected components*, where each component represents a set of nodes reachable from one another. Searching in this way means we will only consider the connected component the target node is in, which might be much smaller than the overall dataset.

Figure 4.31: Depth-first-search of a graph. Notice the similarity between this code and Figure 4.24.

```
to_search <- rstack()
to_search <- insert_top(to_search, "X19")
marking_list[["X19"]] <- "marked"
answer <- list()

while(!empty(to_search)) {
  node <- peek_top(to_search)
  to_search <- without_top(to_search)

  neighbors <- g[[node]] # a vector of neighbors of the node
  if(str_detect(node, "A")) {
    answer <- c(answer, node)
  }

  for(neighbor in neighbors) {
    if(marking_list[[neighbor]] == "unmarked") {
      marking_list[[neighbor]] <- "marked"
      to_search <- insert_top(to_search, neighbor)
    }
  }
}

print(answer)           # prints "A56" and "A51"
```

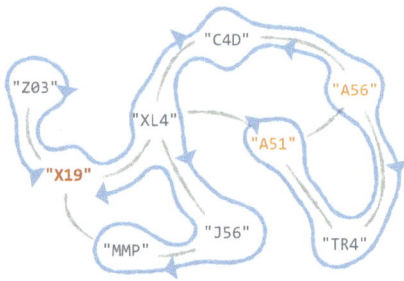

Figure 4.32: Depth-first search path in the protein-protein interaction network.

Figure 4.33: Inspecting the contents of the search stack over time.

Further, note that depth-first search, just like when operating in a tree and as its name implies, tends to go "deep" into the graph before backtracking to try other paths. Figure 4.32 shows the search path taken in this case. To see why this is, our friend print_string_stack() (from Figure 4.19, page 63) can help us inspect the search stack over time, by adding calls to print_string_stack(to_search) before and after grabbing the next element out of to_search (Figure 4.33).

```
# ...
while(!empty(to_search)) {
  node <- peek_top(to_search)
  print_string_stack(to_search)        # a)
  to_search <- without_top(to_search)
  print_string_stack(to_search)        # b)

# ...
```

Figure 4.34 shows the result, though we've added some annotation to help clarify the output. Each line is labeled with *a)* or *b)* to indicate which of the print() calls produced it. Additionally, for *a)* lines, we've colored blue the nodes that were added in the previous iteration of the loop, and we've underlined the nodes which are being removed and inspected during the current iteration.

When using a depth-first search on a graph, the order in which nodes are considered is largely determined by which "deep path" the search decides to check first, and this is determined by the order of the neighbor listing in the adjacency-list representation. In this example, "A56" was identified as a potential downstream target of "X19" before "A51" was. What if we wanted to identify these targets in order of their distance from "X19"? We could try to modify the adjacency-list representation so that close nodes will be searched first, but we don't know this information *a-priori*. Instead, we need to change our search strategy, specifically the way in which nodes are added and removed from to_search. The modification is as simple as replacing the stack with another similar structure called a *queue*.

```
a) [1] "X19"
b) character(0)
a) [1] "MMP" "XL4" "Z03"
b) [1] "MMP" "XL4"
a) [1] "MMP" "XL4"
b) [1] "MMP"
a) [1] "MMP" "J56" "A51" "C4D"
b) [1] "MMP" "J56" "A51"
a) [1] "MMP" "J56" "A51" "A56"
b) [1] "MMP" "J56" "A51"
a) [1] "MMP" "J56" "A51" "TR4"
b) [1] "MMP" "J56" "A51"
a) [1] "MMP" "J56" "A51"
b) [1] "MMP" "J56"
a) [1] "MMP" "J56"
b) [1] "MMP"
a) [1] "MMP"
b) character(0)
```

Figure 4.34: Depth-first search stack contents over time. Labels *a*) and *b*) correspond to print() calls in Figure 4.33, blue elements are newly added, and underlined elements ready for removal and inspection. character(0) indicates that the stack is empty.

THE QUEUE DATA STRUCTURE is in many ways similar to a stack, which we'll recall is a "Last In, First Out" (LIFO) structure. A queue on the other hand is "First In, First Out" (FIFO). Queues support a different kind of constant-time push, pop, and peek: pushes occur at the "back" of a queue, pops remove from the "front" of the queue, and peeks inspect the element at the front without removing. Whereas the rstack structures from the rstackdeque package support insert_top(), without_top(), and peek_top(), rpqueue structures support insert_back(), without_front(), and peek_front() (they both support empty()).

To modify the search procedure, we simply need to replace in Figure 4.31 stack operations with queue operations. Instead of to_search <- rstack(), we'd use to_search <- rpqueue(); similarly to_search <- insert_top(to_search, "X19") becomes to_search <- insert_back(to_search, "X19"), node <- peek_top(to_search) becomes node <- peek_front(to_search), to_search <- without_top(to_search) becomes to_search <- without_front(to_search), and finally to_search <- insert_top(to_search, neighbor) is replaced with to_search <- insert_back(to_search, neighbor). (These queues also support empty(), as.list(), and other helper functions just like stacks.)

Now, with these modifications, what will happen? Let's take it step-by-step. When the initial "X19" is removed, its neighbors "MMP", "XL4", and "Z03" are added to the queue, leaving "MMP" at the front. This is then removed and inspected, and its (unmarked) neighbor "J56" is added to the back of the queue. The next node ready for removal and inspection is again at the current front of the queue– "XL4". This node's unmarked neighbor ("C4D") is added, and then the front of the queue is "Z03". And so on.

In this process, nodes are removed and considered in a "wave" emanating from the target node, level-by-level. In fact, it is relatively easy to stop the search process after some number of levels have

push   peek   pop

Figure 4.35: A queue.

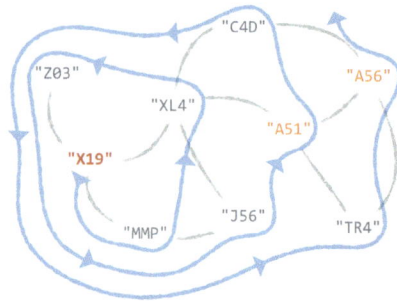

Figure 4.36: Breadth-first search path in the protein-protein interaction network.

```
a) [1] "X19"
b) character(0)
a) [1] "Z03" "XL4" "MMP"
b) [1] "Z03" "XL4"
a) [1] "J56" "Z03" "XL4"
b) [1] "J56" "Z03"
a) [1] "C4D" "A51" "J56" "Z03"
b) [1] "C4D" "A51" "J56"
a) [1] "C4D" "A51" "J56"
b) [1] "C4D" "A51"
a) [1] "C4D" "A51"
b) [1] "C4D"
a) [1] "A56" "TR4" "C4D"
b) [1] "A56" "TR4"
a) [1] "A56" "TR4"
b) [1] "A56"
a) [1] "A56"
b) character(0)
```

Figure 4.37: Breadth-first search stack contents over time. Labels *a)* and *b)* correspond to print() calls in Figure 4.33 (but queue operations are used), blue elements are newly added, and underlined elements ready for removal and inspection. The back of the queue is toward the left, the front toward the right.

been searched, so that only nodes within a certain distance of the target node are considered. Figure 4.36 shows the search path, and this method is known as *breadth-first search*. Figure 4.37 illustrates the contents of the queue over time; here the back of the queue (where new elements are inserted) is toward the left, and the front (where elements are removed) is toward the right.

Although breadth-first search is very useful, recursive methods are naturally depth-first, owing to the use of the call stack. Computing fib(8) requires computing both fib(7) and fib(6); using the recursive method of this chapter, the entirety of fib(7) is computed before work begins on fib(6). In the next chapters we'll see another method for solving problems defined recursively without using explicit recursion, called dynamic programming.

Exercises

1. Suppose a graph has *n* nodes and *m* edges between them. What is the runtime of depth-first search in order-notation, in terms of *n* and *m*? What about for breadth-first search?

2. Assuming there is never more than one edge connecting any two nodes, how many possible edges can there be amongst *n* nodes?

3. Graphs can be used to represent mazes (with nodes being rooms and edges corridors between them). Depth-first search can be used to find a path from the start to the finish. Write a depth-first search which searches for an "end" node from a "start" node, and see if you can have it print the nodes on the solution path found.

4. Breadth-first search can also be used to solve mazes, though the implementation is trickier. What special property would a breadth-first search have for maze solving?

5 Hash Tables, Memoization, and Dynamic Programming

One of the curious features of the Fibonacci sequence is that ratios of successive Fibonacci numbers quickly converge to approximately 1.618, also known as ϕ or the "golden ratio."

$$\lim_{n \to \infty} \frac{fib(n+1)}{fib(n)} = \phi \approx 1.61803 \,.$$

This golden ratio, an irrational number (indeed, the "most" irrational number in that it is particularly difficult to approximate in fractional form), occurs frequently in nature and mathematics. We may explore that later; for now, it suffices to note that this means that each Fibonacci number is an approximate 1.618 multiple of the last. Thus, the Fibonacci numbers are an exponentially growing series, as previously illustrated in Figure 4.13. Also illustrated in Figure 4.13 is that the number of function calls required to compute fib(n) is approximately twice fib(n) itself. Thus, even though calling a function and returning from it is quick, the work required to compute fib(n) in this way grows exponentially with n as well: on my computer, running fib(20) takes about 1.6 seconds, fib(24) 10.5 seconds, and fib(28) 70 seconds.

However, if we look closely at the call stack for fib() (Figure 4.20), or even better the call tree (Figure 5.1), we can see a lot of redundant work being done. The third call computes the result for n = 4; later this same result is computed again utilizing the same recursive process. Similarly, the answer for n = 3 is recomputed three times.

Instead of recomputing these results, we should save them in a lookup table for future use: before any result is to be returned, the answer is saved in the lookup table, and before any computation is

Figure 5.1: Call tree for fib(6) illustrating redundant computation.

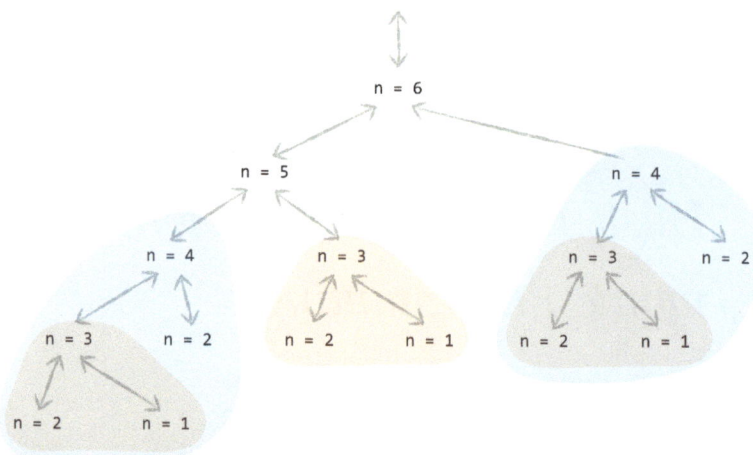

computed the table is consulted (based on the input parameters to the function) to see if the answer has previously been produced and saved. If so, the answer may simply be referred to from the table, also known as the *cache*. This technique, when applied to recursive methods where the sub-problems "overlap" in this way, is known as *memoization*.

It is important to note that we can apply a strategy like memoization only if the function in question is *pure*, which is to say that the returned value will always be the same for the same input parameters. If the function's output depended on any global variables that might change over time, or random choices, then caching answers based only on the input parameters might not produce correct results.

Now, how might we implement a lookup-table cache? Often, a *hash table* (stored as a global variable) is used for this purpose. A hash table is a data structure providing fast lookup of "values" by "keys." (The keys are often character strings, and the values may be numbers, lists, or other structures.) How fast? In practice, in a constant amount of time ($O(1)$) no matter how many keys are present, the same as pushing or popping from a stack. Many languages have explicit data structures for hash tables (such as Python's dict() and Java's HashMap()). By contrast, R does not, but R's environment() type has many of the properties of hash tables and can be used in that capacity. The hash package serves as a wrapper around environments providing the usual features of hash tables: insert values for specific keys, extract values for specific keys, and determine if a given key exists.

Hash tables are one-way structures; given a key, the value can be assigned or extracted, but given a value it is not possible (without much effort) to determine the associated key. Figure 5.2 contains some example code illustrating the basic usage of a hash table to store values (ages) associated with keys (names) with functions provided by the hash library.

```
cache <- hash()
cache[["Bob"]] <- 24
cache[["Mary"]] <- 34

print(cache[["Bob"]])              # prints 24

print(has.key("Mary", cache))      # prints TRUE
print(has.key("Maureen", cache))   # prints FALSE

name <- "Mary"
if(has.key(name, cache)) {
  age <- cache[[name]]
  print(age)
}

print(keys(cache))        # prints character vector "Bob" "Mary"
```

Figure 5.2: Example usage of a hash data structure.

Although this code makes it appear as though the keys are stored in the same order they are added to the hash, this is not the case. Hash tables have no intrinsic order for the key/value pairs, and the character vector returned by keys() shouldn't be assumed to have any particular order.

AN ASIDE: why do we say that key/value lookup for a hash table is constant time "in practice," why is it that the key/value pairs don't have any particular order, and why are hash tables "one way" mappings from keys to values? This relates to how hash tables are implemented. The binary search trees described on page 34 implement some of this functionality: we can store values to keys and later search for those keys to extract the values. As discussed earlier, if the binary search tree is balanced, this can be done fairly quickly in $O(\log_2(n))$ time.

Let's instead consider using the nested lists (linked-lists) described in Chapter 2 instead, as these are more often found as the basis for hash tables. Recall that we can use the append_end() function to create a nested list and append elements to the end, in series (Figure 5.3).

```
nlist <- NULL
nlist <- append_end(nlist, "C")
nlist <- append_end(nlist, "D")
nlist <- append_end(nlist, "A")

print_list(nlist)      # prints "C" "D" and "A"
```

Figure 5.3: Revisiting nested lists.

We can store key/value pairs in such a list as well; after all, the function is agnostic as to what the elements are (Figure 5.4).[1] However, in order to extract a value given a particular key, we need

[1] For this application we should modify the append_end() function so that duplicate keys can not be stored. Instead, if the user attempts to re-enter a value for a key the original value should be replaced. This is a fairly easy fix—see if you can modify append_end() to do so.

to write a new recursive function, get_val(). If the input list is NULL, the function can return NA, the default for non-existent data. Otherwise, the function can extract the list into el and rest, where el is the first key/value pair stored, and rest is all the others. If the key stored in el, el[[1]], is equal to the key being searched for, we can return the value stored in el[[2]]. Otherwise, we must keep searching, recursively (Figure 5.5).

Figure 5.4: Storing key/value pairs in nested lists.

```
nlist <- NULL
nlist <- append_end(nlist, list("Bob", 24))
nlist <- append_end(nlist, list("Mary", 34))
nlist <- append_end(nlist, list("Joe", 19))
```

Figure 5.5: Retrieving a value for a key in a nested key/value list.

```
get_val <- function(data, key) {
  if(is.null(data)) {
    return(NA)
  }

  el <- data[[1]]
  rest <- data[[2]]

  if(el[[1]] == key) {
    return(el[[2]])
  } else {
    answer <- get_val(rest, key)
    return(answer)
  }
}

print(get_val(nlist, "Mary"))    # 34
print(get_val(nlist, "Ken"))     # NA
```

How fast is this operation? It may be that the key being searched for is all the way at the end of the list, which means that if there are n elements, this is an $O(n)$ operation. Hash tables extend this concept by using a large collection of small lists, or "buckets", rather than a single large list. If each bucket has only a few elements, n will never be large–provided we can figure out which bucket to search in. Let's create a miniature list of buckets (Figure 5.6).

Figure 5.6: A list of buckets, all initially empty.

```
hash_buckets <- list(NULL, NULL, NULL, NULL, NULL, NULL, NULL)
```

This is the primary trick of hash tables: we need a large collection of buckets, we need to be able to quickly determine which bucket a given key will should be found or stored in, and we want the key/value pairs distributed fairly evenly across the buckets. Enter the *hash function*, a function that takes some data (usually a string) and returns a pseudo-random, but repeatable, output (usually an integer). Figure 5.7 shows an example hash function–it begins with an initial val of 2, and then inspects every character of the input string. If the lower-case version of the character is before "m" in the alphabet, val is multiplied by three, otherwise we add ten to it.[2]

```
compute_hash <- function(s) {
  val <- 2
  for(i in seq(1, nchar(s))) {
    chari = tolower(str_sub(s, i, i))
    if(chari < "m") {
      val <- val * 3
    } else {
      val <- val + 10
    }
  }
  return(val)
}

print(compute_hash("Bob"))    # 48
print(compute_hash("Mary"))   # 56
print(compute_hash("Bob"))    # 48
```

Figure 5.7: A very simple hash function.

[2] This is a very poor hash function. Real hash functions strive for a number of additional properties: 1) there should by a very large number of potential hash values, 2) a small change in the input should produce a large change in the hash value, and 3) it should be extremely difficult to start with a hash value and determine which keys can produce it, or find two keys that produce the same hash value. Good hash function are very useful for cryptographic applications.

These more-or-less random values are then used to determine the bucket number, by taking the value modulo the number of buckets (the remainder after integer division). In our example we have 7 buckets, and Mary's hash value of 56 results in bucket number 56 %% 7, or bucket 0. (56 divided 7 is 8, remainder 0). Because R starts indices from 1 rather than 0, we'll need to add one to this answer to get to the true bucket number. While Mary goes in bucket 1, Bob goes in bucket 48 %% 7 + 1, which is bucket 7.[3] Now we can write a function that inserts a key/value pair into our hash_buckets (Figure 5.8).

[3] Another strategy uses a number of buckets which is a power of 2, say 2^b. Then, determining which bucket an element belongs to is a matter of selecting the lowest b bits from the hash output, and using that number (as a binary number) to determine the bucket number.

```
insert_hash <- function(buckets, el) {
  key <- el[[1]]
  bucket_num <- compute_hash(key) %% length(buckets) + 1
  buckets[[bucket_num]] <- append_end(buckets[[bucket_num]], el)
  return(buckets)
}

hash_buckets <- insert_hash(hash_buckets, list("Bob", 24))
hash_buckets <- insert_hash(hash_buckets, list("Mary", 34))
hash_buckets <- insert_hash(hash_buckets, list("Joe", 19))
```

Figure 5.8: A function to insert key/value pairs into a hash-bucket list.

To determine the value for a given key, we just need to determine the bucket number in the same way, and use get_val() to extract the appropriate value for that bucket (Figure 5.9).

For a hash table to work properly, we want the number of buckets to be larger than the number of elements stored, so that each bucket has only a few items to search through providing the performance we want ($O(1)$, or constant time, in practice). We don't want it to

Figure 5.9: A function to retrieve the value for a given key from a hash-bucket list.

```
get_val_hash <- function(buckets, key) {
  bucket_num <- compute_hash(key) %% length(buckets) + 1
  answer <- get_val(buckets[[bucket_num]], key)
  return(answer)
}

print(get_val_hash(hash_buckets, "Mary"))     # 34
print(get_val_hash(hash_buckets, "Bob"))      # 24
print(get_val_hash(hash_buckets, "Joe"))      # 19
```

be too large, though, otherwise we're wasting memory by storing many empty buckets. Real hash tables generally start with a modest number of buckets, and once enough elements have been added perform a slow "rehash" step, where a larger bucket list is created and every key/value pair is migrated to it. We additionally want the items to be distributed equally across the buckets: if they stack up in a single bucket we've lost the benefit altogether. A good hash function helps with this. It's also no coincidence that we used a prime number (7) as the number of buckets; if there are any patterns in the hash function (for example, if it were more likely to produce even numbers) then taking the modulo of a prime will help mitigate them.

LET'S RETURN TO THE TASK AT HAND, memoizing our fib() function. We'll define a global FIB_CACHE hash table, and as soon as the function is called we'll first check to see if the answer is already present in the cache. If so, we can simply return the cached value rather than continuing with the rest of the function. Before each other return, we'll be sure to save the computed value in the cache for future lookups.

We'll leave our simulation of the call stack intact. In fact, we can use the same strings recording the parameters passed to each call for both the call-stack simulation and memoization hash-table keys (Figure 5.11). With this accomplished, the time to complete fib(28) is much shorter at only 0.4 seconds. The printed call stack for fib(8) is also a much shorter listing (Figure 5.12), reflecting the removal of redundant computations.

It is enlightening to visualize the call tree for this version as well, which we show in Figure 5.10, where a + indicates a result that is added to the cache (followed by the order in which it is added in parentheses) and a check-mark indicates a result found in the cache. Of particular interest is the *order* in which answers are added to the memoization

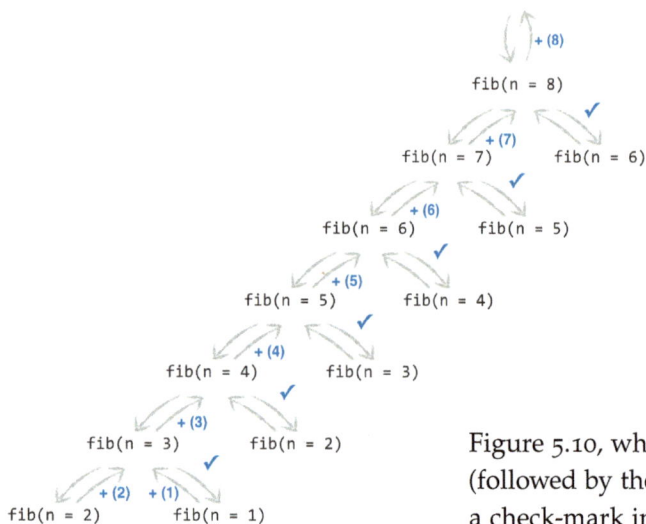

Figure 5.10: Call tree for memoized fib(8).

cache: from smallest (n = 1 and n = 2) to largest (n = 8).

Finally, recursive functions are only worth memoizing (and developing dynamic programs for, as discussed next) if the subproblems indeed overlap. Some recursive methods utilize subproblems, but the inputs to them are always different throughout the process. The recursive functions of Chapters 2 and 3 were all of this type. In these cases, caching solutions that will never be reused would simply be a waste of resources. Additionally, a function can only be memoized if the output is deterministic and depends entirely on the given parameters (i.e., is pure).

```
FIB_CACHE <<- hash()

fib <- function(n) {
  this_frame <- str_c("n = ", as.character(n))
  CALL_STACK <<- insert_top(CALL_STACK, this_frame)
  print_string_stack(CALL_STACK)

  if(has.key(this_frame, FIB_CACHE)) {
      CALL_STACK <<- without_top(CALL_STACK)
      print_string_stack(CALL_STACK)
      return(FIB_CACHE[[this_frame]])
  }

  if(n == 1) {
    CALL_STACK <<- without_top(CALL_STACK)
    print_string_stack(CALL_STACK)
    FIB_CACHE[[this_frame]] <<- 1
    return(1)
  } else if(n == 2) {
    CALL_STACK <<- without_top(CALL_STACK)
    print_string_stack(CALL_STACK)
    FIB_CACHE[[this_frame]] <<- 1
    return(1)
  } else {
    a <- fib(n - 1)
    b <- fib(n - 2)
    answer <- a + b
    FIB_CACHE[[this_frame]] <<- answer
    CALL_STACK <<- without_top(CALL_STACK)
    print_string_stack(CALL_STACK)
    return(answer)
  }
}
```

Figure 5.11: Memoization modification for the recursive Fibonacci function.

```
[1] "n = 8"
[1] "n = 8" "n = 7"
[1] "n = 8" "n = 7" "n = 6"
[1] "n = 8" "n = 7" "n = 6" "n = 5"
[1] "n = 8" "n = 7" "n = 6" "n = 5" "n = 4"
[1] "n = 8" "n = 7" "n = 6" "n = 5" "n = 4" "n = 3"
[1] "n = 8" "n = 7" "n = 6" "n = 5" "n = 4" "n = 3" "n = 2"
[1] "n = 8" "n = 7" "n = 6" "n = 5" "n = 4" "n = 3"
[1] "n = 8" "n = 7" "n = 6" "n = 5" "n = 4" "n = 3" "n = 1"
[1] "n = 8" "n = 7" "n = 6" "n = 5" "n = 4" "n = 3"
[1] "n = 8" "n = 7" "n = 6" "n = 5" "n = 4"
[1] "n = 8" "n = 7" "n = 6" "n = 5" "n = 4" "n = 2"
[1] "n = 8" "n = 7" "n = 6" "n = 5" "n = 4"
[1] "n = 8" "n = 7" "n = 6" "n = 5"
[1] "n = 8" "n = 7" "n = 6" "n = 5" "n = 3"
[1] "n = 8" "n = 7" "n = 6" "n = 5"
[1] "n = 8" "n = 7" "n = 6"
[1] "n = 8" "n = 7" "n = 6" "n = 4"
[1] "n = 8" "n = 7" "n = 6"
[1] "n = 8" "n = 7"
[1] "n = 8" "n = 7" "n = 5"
[1] "n = 8" "n = 7"
[1] "n = 8"
[1] "n = 8" "n = 6"
[1] "n = 8"
```

Figure 5.12: Visualization for the call stack over time for the memoized Fibonacci function.

5.1 Dynamic Programming

We've done quite a lot of work for the simple computation of the nth Fibonacci number! Surely the simplest way to compute the

n^{th} Fibonacci number is simply to compute the first two, and then compute them in sequence until we reach the nth, using a loop, as in Figure 5.13.

Figure 5.13: Dynamic programming (loop-based) solution for computing the nth Fibonacci number.

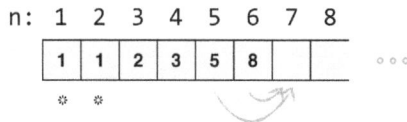

```r
fib <- function(n) {
  # initialize a vector of length n
  fibs <- seq(1, n)

  # set the first two
  fibs[1] <- 1
  fibs[2] <- 1

  # set the rest
  for(i in seq(3, n)) {
    fibs[i] <- fibs[i-1] + fibs[i-2]
  }

  return(fibs[n])
}
```

Figure 5.14: Illustration of the dynamic program for computing the nth Fibonacci number.

This strategy, precomputing subproblem answers in the order in which they will be needed, is known as *Dynamic Programming*. This is a very simple case; some might not even consider it worthy of the term, but it does capture the essence of the technique. The origin of the term is amusing, and helps to explain its esoteric nature. In the 1950's, a mathematician named Richard Bellman was working with the Department of Defense on mathematical computation. To quote Bellman's autobiography, *Eye of the Hurricane*:

> An interesting question is, 'Where did the name, dynamic programming, come from?' The 1950s were not good years for mathematical research. We had a very interesting gentleman in Washington named Wilson. He was Secretary of Defense, and he actually had a pathological fear and hatred of the word, research. I'm not using the term lightly; I'm using it precisely. His face would suffuse, he would turn red, and he would get violent if people used the term, research, in his presence. You can imagine how he felt, then, about the term, mathematical. The RAND Corporation was employed by the Air Force, and the Air Force had Wilson as its boss, essentially. Hence, I felt I had to do something to shield Wilson and the Air Force from the fact that I was really doing mathematics inside the RAND Corporation. What title, what name, could I choose? In the first place I was interested in planning, in decision making, in thinking. But planning, is not a good word for various reasons. I decided therefore to use the word, 'programming.' I wanted to get across the idea that this was dynamic, this was multistage, this was time-varying–I thought, let's kill two birds with one stone. Let's take a word that has an absolutely precise meaning, namely dynamic, in the classical physical sense. It also has a very interesting property as an adjective, and that is it's impossible to use the word, dynamic, in a pejorative sense. Try thinking of some combination that will possibly give it a pejorative meaning. It's impossible. Thus, I thought dynamic programming was a good name. It

was something not even a Congressman could object to. So I used it as an umbrella for my activities.

This technique–given a name not even a member of Congress could object to–is not only related to very powerful and beautiful concepts in computer science and mathematics, but also serves as the foundation for a number of important techniques in modern bioinformatics.

Here we'd like to point out the relationships between our recursive definition, proof-by-induction, recursion, memoization, and dynamic programming, as these concepts are are all quite closely related. Having started with the mathematical observation regarding bee generations (page 55), we continued with an inductive proof for its correctness in describing ancestor counts for honeybee family history. This proof had base cases and an inductive case, just as did the recursive function for computing the nth Fibonacci number (page 57). The "order of operations" for these was reversed: the inductive proof started with the base cases, whereas the recursive function started with the largest cases and recursed until a base case was reached.

Later we memoized the recursive solution, and upon inspecting the call tree discovered that solutions were cached starting with the base cases (Figure 5.10), which is exactly what the loop-based dynamic program accomplished in a loop-based, pre-organized manner (Figure 5.14). And this is, of course, the same bottom-up logic followed by the inductive proof! (One might even directly compare Figures 4.3 and 5.14.)

Why might dynamic programming be preferred over a memoized recursive solution, even if the latter might be more directly related to the problem one wishes to solve? There are several reasons:

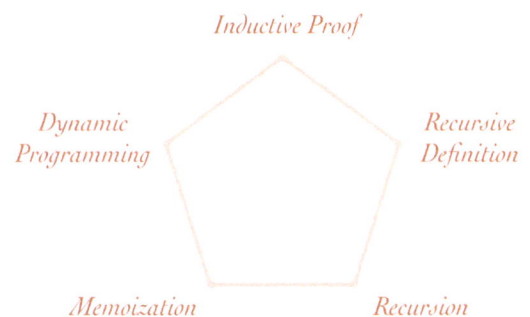

Figure 5.15: A concept map.

- Although calling functions is very efficient, looping over tables is even more efficient. In particular, there's no need for the computer to keep track of local variables, the call stack, and so on.

- Many programmers find dynamic programming solutions more "natural," as they can be seen as a direct fallout of an inductive proof. On the other hand, some problems are more naturally understood in terms of (memoized) recursion, with the dynamic program being an optimization.

- Most importantly, memoized recursive calls are limited by the size of the call stack. Although a computation like fib(1000) might run fast because of memoization, this requires the insertion of 1,000 elements onto the call stack, which is likely to produce a stack overflow error. By contrast, the dynamic programming solution for fib(1000) has no such limitation. (Although in this case, the fact that fib(1000) is a ridiculously large number is a limitation in itself.)

Exercises

1. An earlier exercise (page 58) asked you to program a pair of recursive functions for a predator/prey model. Your task now is to memoize these functions with a pair of global hash tables. Your "key" should be a string that identifies all of the parameters, as in this skeleton code:

```
predators <- function(n, r, b, c, d) {
  this_call <- str_c(n, ";", r, ";", b, ";", c, ";", d)
  # ...
```

2. Next, create a dynamic programming solution for the predator/prey model. This will require two tables of the right design (or, alternatively, a matrix with two rows). You may need to draw a diagram of the subproblems and their dependencies: what does predators(n) depend on? What about prey(n)?

3. Complete the hash table example, by first adjusting append_end() so that duplicate keys cannot be stored within the same nested list, and if a user attempts to do so the value for that key is overwritten. Further, implement a has_key() method which takes a list of buckets, and returns TRUE if a given key is present, and FALSE otherwise. Try using your custom hash table to memoize fib().

5.2   *Notes on Software Engineering*

Many programmers dislike the use of global variables that are updated across function calls, and for good reason: they add complexity and "state" within the program for the programmer to keep track of. A function that reads and writes global data can no longer be thought of as a black box that only turns given parameters into required outputs. Even our relatively benign memoization caches will be cumbersome, since we need to remember to initialize them before using them.

Functional languages like R provide some unique tricks to help manage this complexity. As you've perhaps surmised, functions in R are types of data like any other, and their names are the variables holding the data. Consider the syntax for our fib() function: fib <- function(n) .... Here, fib is a variable name that we've assigned data (the function) to using <-. This allows us to do interesting things like pass function as parameters to other functions–we saw an example of this when we wrote nested_lapply() in Chapter 2.

Additionally, we know that variables assigned to within a function with <- are *local*, meaning they are unique to that function call and disappear when the call ends. This important feature not only enables recursion, but also keeps code clean and manageable.

Combining these two facts, we find that we can define *local functions* within other functions. Figure 5.16 show an outer function definition, and within it an inner function definition.

```
fib <- function(n) {

  fib_inner <- function(n_inner) {
    if(n_inner == 1 | n_inner == 2) {
      answer_inner <- 1
      return(answer_inner)
    } else {
      answer_inner <- fib_inner(n_inner - 1) +
                      fib_inner(n_inner - 2)
      return(answer_inner)
    }
  }

  answer <- fib_inner(n)
  return(answer)
}

print(fib(20))      # 6765
```

Figure 5.16: A function defined locally within another.

Here, fib() defines a local variable fib_inner (which happens to be a function), and then later calls fib_inner() to produce answer. If we call fib(), the inner function fib_inner() will be created, but it will only exist as long as the outer fib() is executing.

Perhaps you can see where we're headed: we're going to memoize fib_inner(), and the cache will be a local variable of the outer fib() (Figure 5.17).

Now when we call fib(), it 1) defines a local fib_inner() function, 2) defines a local fib_cache hash table, and 3) calls fib_inner(), which makes use of the cache as a "global" variable. How does this work, given that earlier in the book we said that <<- assigns to a global variable, but now we are assigning to a local variable of the outer function? Actually, we fibbed a bit earlier. What <<- really does is assign "up" the hierarchy of calls (up the variables in the call stack!) Even if we are deep within a nest of calls, <<- will assign to the first outer variable of that name that it can find.

Thus, from the perspective of outside the main fib() call, there are no global variables and no extra state to keep track of; fib() itself handles initializing the cache, using it, destroying it when

Figure 5.17: Memoizing an inner function.

```r
fib <- function(n) {

  fib_inner <- function(n_inner) {
    key <- str_c("n_inner: ", n_inner)
    if(has.key(key, fib_cache)) {
      return(fib_cache[[key]])
    }

    if(n_inner == 1 | n_inner == 2) {
      answer_inner <- 1
      fib_cache[[key]] <<- answer_inner
      return(answer_inner)
    } else {
      answer_inner <- fib_inner(n_inner - 1) +
                      fib_inner(n_inner - 2)
      fib_cache[[key]] <<- answer_inner
      return(answer_inner)
    }
  }

  fib_cache <- hash()
  answer <- fib_inner(n)
  return(answer)
}

print(fib(20))      # 6765
```

done. In fact, if we are comfortable enough with local variables shadowing external variables, we don't even need the awkward names of fib_inner, n_inner, and answer_inner (which we used purely for clarity). We could replace these with fib, n, and answer and the code would work identically.

In future chapters we won't be encapsulating our memoized functions along with their caches in outer functions. We'll instead opt to keep the code simpler–but potentially more difficult to manage–by using global variables and focusing on the theoretical topics at hand.

6 Alignment

The topics covered in the previous chapters–recursion, induction, memoization, dynamic programming–are important and powerful, but using them to compute Fibonacci numbers isn't that useful. In this chapter we'll bring these ideas together to solve one of the most important problems in bioinformatics: sequence alignment. The problem is defined as follows: given two DNA strings α and β of length n and m, produce a "good" alignment of these by inserting "-" ("gap") characters so that they are the same length. As an example, consider Figure 6.1; the output produces modified versions of α and β by inserting gaps.

Input:

α : ACTAGC

β : ATACC

Output:

ACTAGC
| | | |
A-TACC

Total Score: +1

Figure 6.1: An example sequence alignment.

What makes a "good" alignment? Intuitively, a good alignment produces a large number of matches (four in this example). But this is not the only possible criteria, and the details of defining goodness depend on what the goal is. We are often interested in aligning DNA sequences because we want to compare their sequences after evolutionary divergence. Consider the hemoglobin protein, which carries oxygen in red blood cells. This protein is defined by an A/C/G/T DNA sequence in animal genomes, from fish to humans to mice. All of these animals share a common ancestor, and this ancient ancestor also had an "original" hemoglobin sequence. As time passed and species diverged, the hemoglobin sequence changed via mutation in different ways for different species, and some of these changes were kept or lost by evolutionary pressures (Figure 6.2).

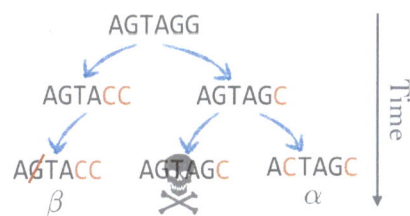

Figure 6.2: Sequence divergence over evolutionary time. Modern species shared common ancestors in the past, and thus also common DNA sequences. Over time the species diverged (and some went extinct), and so did the sequence, leaving us to find only α and β.

[1] Determining scoring rules that match evolutionary history is a large area of study in itself. For example, we also know that A/T and C/G switches are more common than others, so we might score those mismatches slightly higher. In protein sequences we have strings of 20 letters (e.g. "LPEAF...") with varying probabilities of switching. Large sets of genes are analyzed to determine these probabilities empirically, and the scoring points are determined from them.

[2] Computer scientists and mathematicians use the term "optimal" precisely: it is almost exclusively used to describe the best possible solution, or an algorithm that provably delivers one.

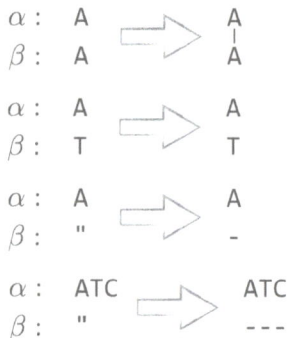

α :   A $\Longrightarrow$ A
β :   A   A

α :   A $\Longrightarrow$ A
β :   T   T

α :   A $\Longrightarrow$ A
β :   "   -

α :   ATC $\Longrightarrow$ ATC
β :   "   - - -

Figure 6.3: Easy cases of the sequence alignment problem: when both are only a single character, or one sequence is empty.

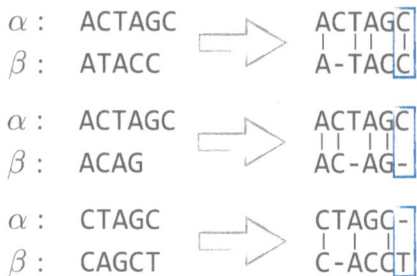

α :   ACTAGC $\Longrightarrow$ ACTAGC
β :   ATACC   A-TACC

α :   ACTAGC $\Longrightarrow$ ACTAGC
β :   ACAG   AC-AG-

α :   CTAGC $\Longrightarrow$ CTAGC-
β :   CAGCT   C-ACCT

Figure 6.4: Any alignment can only end in one of three possible ways.

So, we would expect the hemoglobin sequence to be very similar, but not identical, between humans and mice. Further, we now know certain things about how DNA sequences mutate over time. For example, the loss of a DNA base (which would require inserting a gap in the alignment) is rarer than a DNA-base switch. As such, we should prefer alignments with fewer gaps even if in some cases it means accepting more mismatches. In practice this means alignments are evaluated based on a scoring scheme: for example, +2 points for a match, −3 for a mismatch, and −4 for a gap.[1] With these rules in place, the goal is to produce an alignment that maximizes the score. We call such an alignment *optimal* with respect to the scoring scheme. (There may be a number of different optimal alignments with the same score; we're interested in finding any one.[2])

It should be noted that a scoring scheme like this makes sense only if matching bases are worth more than mismatches and gaps: gap score < mismatch score < 0 < match score. (Imagine what would happen if the gap score was +2 and the others were −2: the score could be maximized by adding millions of gap characters!)

In very simple cases, finding an optimal alignment is easy. Because gaps are scored lower than mismatches (scored lower than matches), if α and β are only one character each, then the optimal alignment is simply the two inputs. Although odd to consider, if one of the sequences is "empty" (i.e. ""), then the optimal alignment simply pads out the empty sequence with gaps to make it the same length as the other (Figure 6.3).

What about more complex cases? Consider some optimal alignments as shown in Figure 6.4 (which we've perhaps computed by hand). In all three cases, the end of the alignments have either a gap (-) or the last base of one or both of the input sequences. And after all, how could they be anything else?

In fact, if we go so far as to say that all sequences begin with an identical common character like @, then even some of the simple cases become complex cases. For example, aligning just "A" with just "T" can be recast as aligning "@A" with "@T", a complex case. We consider this now as it will make the code later much simpler, as we have only two types of cases to deal with: simple cases (where one or both of the sequences are just "@") and complex ones (all others, Figure 6.5). For scoring purposes, we'll assume that "@" aligned with "@" has a score of 0.

For convenience, let's create some definitions. Given two strings α and β, let p_α be the "prefix" of α (containing all but the last character), and e_α be the "end" of α (the last character). Define p_β and e_β similarly for β (Figure 6.6). We'll also define a function $S()$ that represents the score of an alignment or a pair of characters as defined by whatever scoring scheme we're using.

Based on the observation above about how alignments can end, there are three possibilities for the alignment of α and β and their scores, based on sub-alignments that we'll call *left*, *center*, and *right* for reasons that will become clearer in a bit:

$$
\underbrace{\left(\begin{array}{c} p_\alpha \text{ aligned w/} \\ p_\beta e_\beta \end{array} \right)}_{left} \begin{array}{c} e_\alpha \\ - \end{array}, \quad score = S(left) + S(e_\alpha, -)
$$

$$
\underbrace{\left(\begin{array}{c} p_\alpha \text{ aligned w/} \\ p_\beta \end{array} \right)}_{center} \begin{array}{c} e_\alpha \\ e_\beta \end{array}, \quad score = S(center) + S(e_\alpha, e_\beta) \qquad (6.1)
$$

$$
\underbrace{\left(\begin{array}{c} p_\alpha e_\alpha \text{ aligned w/} \\ p_\beta \end{array} \right)}_{right} \begin{array}{c} - \\ e_\beta \end{array}, \quad score = S(right) + S(-, e_\beta)
$$

The optimal alignment (the answer) is thus the best scoring of these three options, if the *left*, *center*, and *right* sub-alignments are themselves optimal. This relationship is often written in a more obtuse (but precise) mathematical notation:

$$
S(\alpha_{1,i}, \beta_{1,j}) = \max \begin{cases} S(\alpha_{1,i-1}, \beta_{1,j}) + S(\alpha_i, \text{-}), \\ S(\alpha_{1,i-1}, \beta_{1,j-1}) + S(\alpha_i, \beta_j), \\ S(\alpha_{1,i}, \beta_{1,j-1}) + S(\text{-}, \beta_j), \end{cases}
$$

where $S()$ is the scoring function, $X_{a,b}$ represents the subsequence of X from position a to position b, and X_i is just the ith base of sequence X.

THERE IS A SIMILARITY HERE between solving the alignment problem and the "bees" problem of previous chapters. We've identified the patterns that we think we can use, in terms of very simple cases and more complex ones that depend on solving subcases (*left*, *center*, and *right*). In fact, what we have is a recursive definition! The argument we've put together for the solution of the problem is pretty strong. But does it constitute a proof? Could there be some outside possibility that using a recursive method in this way won't generate *optimal* alignments in the sense of maximizing the score? To be thorough, we can provide a proof-by-induction for this methodology.

Complex Examples:

$\alpha:$ @A $\Longrightarrow$ @A
$\beta:$ @T $\qquad$ @T

$\alpha:$ @ACTAGC $\Longrightarrow$ @ACTAGC
$\beta:$ @ATACC $\qquad$ @A-TACC

Simple Examples:

$\alpha:$ @A $\Longrightarrow$ @A
$\beta:$ @ $\qquad$ @-

$\alpha:$ @ $\Longrightarrow$ @---
$\beta:$ @ATC $\qquad$ @ATC

$\alpha:$ @ $\Longrightarrow$ @
$\beta:$ @ $\qquad$ @

Figure 6.5: With the appropriate representation, "simple" cases of the alignment problem are those where at least one sequence is just "@"; all others can be considered as a complex case.

$$
\begin{array}{ccc} & p_\alpha & e_\alpha \\ \alpha: & \text{@ACTAG} & \text{C} \end{array}
$$
$$
\begin{array}{ccc} \beta: & \text{@ATA} & \text{CC} \\ & p_\beta & e_\beta \end{array}
$$

Figure 6.6: Definitions for p_α, p_β, e_α and e_β for sequences α and β.

6.1   Proofs-by-Contradiction

BEFORE WE CONTINUE, we need to cover another topic in the area of proofs. It's one thing for a statement to be true, or that a method will work, but it's another to argue rigorously for it. There are of course various levels of rigor: the most stringent would be a set of sentences starting from axioms and employing only basic rules of logic to build to the conclusion. Less stringent is an informal argument where we can assume the reader knows of (and believes) previously shown results, and can make jumps in logic. On the other hand, generating a pattern for a specific subset of cases does not usually constitute a proof–just because my neighbor has only black cats does not make all cats black.

We've seen one proof technique already, proof-by-induction, wherein we argue for the truth of a statement (or correctness of an algorithm) by starting with base cases, and showing that the truth of smaller cases implies the truth of larger ones. This is often the strategy needed for self-defined procedures like recursion.

Another beautiful proof technique, arguably the most powerful and commonly used, is proof-by-contradiction. Here we *assume the opposite* of what it is we are trying to prove. If we can argue that this leads to a contradiction or impossibility, then it must mean that the assumption is wrong, and the statement we want to show must be true. Here's a simple example:

Theorem 1. *There is no smallest integer.*

Proof of Theorem 1. For a proof by contradiction, assume the opposite: that there *is* a smallest integer. Let this integer be i. By the rules of integer arithmetic, $i - 1$ is also an integer, and is smaller than i, a contradiction with i being the smallest. So the assumption is false and it is true that there is no smallest integer.[3]   □

This technique is a bit trickier when there are multiple assumptions involved, or an if/then relationship. Here's a more involved example:

Theorem 2. *If a car's battery is dead and the key is turned, it won't start.*

Proof of Theorem 2. For a proof by contradiction, we assume the opposite: 1) it starts, even though 2) the key is turned and 3) the battery is dead.

Since it starts, it must use the starter, which is an electrical device. This needs energy. The only source of energy (before the car is running) is the battery. Thus, the battery must have supplied energy to the starter. But the battery is dead, and so we have a contradiction.   □

In this proof we are trying to prove a statement with a form of $(a$ and $b) \rightarrow c$; the opposite is $(a$ and $b)$ and $(\text{not } c)$. We assumed the opposite and argued to a contradiction. From this contradiction, one of three things must be the case. Either:

1. the car can't start, or

2. the battery must not actually be dead, or

3. the key wasn't actually turned.

Pedantically, any of these three statements could be true. But we want to prove option 1. We can get there so long as we *continue to assume* that the battery is dead and the key is turned, which is no more or less than the form of the theorem, $(a$ and $b) \rightarrow c$. We've proven the implication itself true, rather than any part of it.

The beauty and power of proof-by-contradiction lies in the freedom to explore. There are many facts we can bring to bear to search for a contradiction, and many lines of argument we could use as well. Any contradiction will suffice, even if it has seemingly little to do with what we wanted to prove. All that is needed is to show that the assumed "hypothetical world" is absurd in some way. (The Latin term for proof-by-contradiction is *reductio ad absurdum*, which translates to *reduction to absurdity*.)

NOW WE CAN PROVIDE A PROOF for the correctness of recursively computing an optimal alignment. The proof a mix of both proof-by-induction and proof-by-contradiction.

Proof of correctness for recursive sequence alignment. Let the base cases be defined as above: where one or both of α or β are of length one (just "@"). If both are just "@", the optimal alignment is "@" and "@" itself with a score of 0. If only one sequence is just "@", the optimal alignment must pad this length-one sequence out with gaps to equal the length of the other.

Any other pair of sequences α and β must each have length at least 2, and so can be handled by the inductive case.

Inductive case: assume that the 3 sub-alignments *left*, *center*, and *right* have been computed and are optimal (i.e., $S(center)$ is the maximum score aligning p_α and p_β, etc.) We wish to show that one of the three overall options, from Equation 6.1, is optimal.

For a sub-proof by contradiction, assume further than the optimal alignment of α and β, which we'll call Z, has a higher score than the three options shown in Equation 6.1; Z is neither $(left)\,{}^{e_\alpha}_{-}$, nor $(center)\,{}^{e_\alpha}_{e_\beta}$, nor $(right)\,{}^{-}_{e_\beta}$. (This is the opposing assumption–we wish to show that one of these three options are optimal, thus we assume that none are.)

We do know, though, that Z must end in either $\frac{e_\alpha}{-}$, or $\frac{e_\alpha}{e_\beta}$, or $\frac{-}{e_\beta}$ (any other possibility would mean that Z is not actually an alignment for the input sequences). Without loss of generality (which means that that argumentation will be the same for other cases), suppose that Z ends in $\frac{e_\alpha}{e_\beta}$, and it can thus be represented as:

$$\underbrace{\left(\begin{array}{c} p_\alpha \text{ aligned w/} \\ p_\beta \end{array} \right)}_{Z'} \begin{array}{c} e_\alpha \\ e_\beta \end{array} \quad score = S(Z') + S(e_\alpha, e_\beta) ,$$

where Z' is the sub-alignment of p_α and p_β used by Z. The assumption is that the score of Z is greater than all other options, including $(center)\frac{e_\alpha}{e_\beta}$. Thus,

$$S(Z) > S(center) + S(e_\alpha, e_\beta)$$
$$S(Z') + S(e_\alpha, e_\beta) > S(center) + S(e_\alpha, e_\beta)$$
$$S(Z') > S(center) .$$

This implies that Z', Zs alignment of p_α and p_β, is better than *center*, our own alignment of p_α and p_β. But this contradicts the inductive assumption above that *left*, *center* and *right* are optimal alignments.

$\square$

6.2   Directionality

Our recursive definition in Equation 6.1 breaks sequences up into two parts, the prefix p_α and the end e_α. But, at least in terms of alignment, our sequences have no "direction." We could just as easily have split α into a "beginning" character b_α and the suffix (all but the beginning character) s_α. Our recursive relationship would then be

$$\begin{array}{c} b_\alpha \\ - \end{array} \underbrace{\left(\begin{array}{c} s_\alpha \text{ aligned w/} \\ b_\beta s_\beta \end{array} \right)}_{left} , \quad score = S(left) + S(b_\alpha, -)$$

$$\begin{array}{c} b_\alpha \\ b_\beta \end{array} \underbrace{\left(\begin{array}{c} s_\alpha \text{ aligned w/} \\ b_\beta \end{array} \right)}_{center} , \quad score = S(center) + S(b_\alpha, b_\beta) \qquad (6.2)$$

$$\begin{array}{c} - \\ b_\beta \end{array} \underbrace{\left(\begin{array}{c} b_\alpha s_\alpha \text{ aligned w/} \\ s_\beta \end{array} \right)}_{right} , \quad score = S(right) + S(-, b_\beta) .$$

Everything else, including the inductive proof and the code of the next sections, could then be modified in a straightforward way to also produce correct alignments. We mention this because in the next chapter we'll be referring back to it.

6.3 Recursive Sequence Alignment

As much fun as all of this theory is, we should start coding! The pattern will be similar to our earlier solution for computing elements of the Fibonacci sequence–after all, we have base cases and recursive cases–but more detail will be required. Partly this is because the method is simply more sophisticated, but also we'll have to encode these concepts in R, a language not known for working with character sequences.

To start with, the default R datatype for string data is the character vector, where each element is a multi-character string, as in seq <- c("@ACGTA", "@AC", "@TTAC"). Here, seq[3] returns the length-one vector identical to c("@TTAC"). Ideally, we'll want to easily extract and compare single characters, so instead of storing a sequence as c("@TTAC"), we'll encode them as c("@", "T", "T", "A", "C"). This will allow us to more easily work with these; for example seq[1:length(seq) - 1] returns the prefix of seq, while seq[length(seq)] returns the last character.

To make this easier, we'll write some helper functions to convert between these two formats (Figure 6.7). (And lest we forget, we assume we've loaded the packages stringr, rstackdeque, and others as described at the end of Chapter 1.)

```r
# eg "@ACT" -> c("@", "A", "C", "T")
char_vec <- function(input) {
  c_vec <- str_split(input, "")[[1]]
  return(c_vec)
}

# e.g. c("@", "A", "T") -> "@AT"
unvec_char <- function(input) {
  ret <- str_c(input, collapse = "")
  return(ret)
}
```

Figure 6.7: Helper functions for working with character vectors.

Next, unlike for the Fibonacci problem, an "answer" to the alignment problem contains three pieces of information: the gapped version of α, the gapped version of β, and the score. We'll encode an answer as a named list of this information, using "a_in" instead of α and "b_in" instead of β. We'll store in an answer not only the aligned sequences ("a_out" and "b_out") and the score, but also the original inputs as well. Figure 6.8 shows an example answer list.

Of course, we'll be writing functions that generate such answers programmatically. A good place to start will be to write a function that, given two single-element, single-character vectors, returns a score according to some scoring scheme (Figure 6.9). Similarly, we can make use of this function to score any equal-length pair of sequences that might represent an alignment (Figure 6.10).

Figure 6.8: Encoding for a sequence alignment answer.

```
answer <- list(a_in = c("@", "A", "C", "T", "A", "G", "C"),
               b_in = c("@", "A", "T", "A", "C", "C"),
               a_out = c("@", "A", "C", "T", "A", "G", "C"),
               b_out = c("@", "A", "-", "T", "A", "C", "C"),
               score = 1)
```

Figure 6.9: A simple function that scores a pair of bases according to scoring rules. If both are just "@" the score is 0.

```
score_pair <- function(a_base, b_base) {
  if(a_base == "@" & b_base == "@") {
    return(0)                           # @ vs @: 0
  }

  if(a_base == b_base) {
    return(2)                           # match
  } else if(a_base == "-" | b_base == "-") {
    return(-4)                          # gap
  } else {
    return(-3)                          # mismatch
  }
}

print(score_pair("C", "T"))            # -3
print(score_pair("A", "A"))            # 2
print(score_pair("-", "G"))            # -4
```

Now we can write a function that produces an answer list for the base cases of our recursion. Based on the discussion on page 84, these are the cases where either a_in or b_in is just "@"; in our encoding, this happens when length(a_in) == 1 or length(b_in) == 1. In the case where they are both of length 1, the score is 0 and we can set a_out and b_out to also be "@" (Figure 6.11). This function uses R's rep() function to produce a sequence of gap characters of the same length as answer$b_out, but of course the first character should be "@" rather than a gap to fit our encoding convention. Example output for this function can be seen in Figure 6.12.

Figure 6.10: A simple function that scores a pair of sequences representing an alignment.

```
score_aln <- function(a_in, b_in) {
  score <- 0
  for(i in seq(1,length(a_in))) {
    score <- score + score_pair(a_in[i], b_in[i])
  }
  return(score)
}

print(score_aln(char_vec("@CAT"), char_vec("@C-G")))  # -5
```

```
base_case <- function(a_in, b_in) {
  answer <- list(a_in = a_in, b_in = b_in,
                 a_out = "", b_out = "", score = 0)

  if(length(a_in) == 1 & length(b_in) == 1) {    # empty/empty
    answer$a_out <- "@"
    answer$b_out <- "@"
  } else if(length(a_in) == 1) {                 # a_in is just @
    answer$a_out <- rep("-", length(answer$b_out))
    answer$b_out <- b_in
    answer$a_out[1] <- "@"
  } else {                                       # b_in is just @
    answer$a_out <- a_in
    answer$b_out <- rep("-", length(answer$a_out))
    answer$b_out[1] <- "@"
  }

  answer$score <- score_aln(answer$a_out, answer$b_out)
  return(answer)
}

str(base_case(char_vec("@"), char_vec("@")))
str(base_case(char_vec("@"), char_vec("@A")))
str(base_case(char_vec("@TAC"), char_vec("@")))
```

Figure 6.11: A function that computes an answer for simple base-cases: those where either one or both input sequences are empty.

```
List of 5
 $ a_in : chr "@"
 $ b_in : chr "@"
 $ a_out: chr "@"
 $ b_out: chr "@"
 $ score: num 0
List of 5
 $ a_in : chr "@"
 $ b_in : chr [1:2] "@" "A"
 $ a_out: chr [1:2] "@" "-"
 $ b_out: chr [1:2] "@" "A"
 $ score: num -4
List of 5
 $ a_in : chr [1:4] "@" "T" "A" "C"
 $ b_in : chr "@"
 $ a_out: chr [1:4] "@" "T" "A" "C"
 $ b_out: chr [1:4] "@" "-" "-" "-"
 $ score: num -12
```

Figure 6.12: Output for Figure 6.11, showing base-case answers encoded as named R lists.

WITH THE NECESSARY TOOLS IN PLACE, now we can work on the fun part: the main recursive function. Like base_case(), it will take in two character vectors a_in and b_in, and return an answer list containing the alignment and its score. We'll call our recursive function global_aln(). The first thing it can do is check to see if the inputs represent a base case: if so, then the answer can simply be returned from the base case() function (Figure 6.13.1).

```
global_aln <- function(a_in, b_in) {
  if(length(a_in) == 1 | length(b_in) == 1) {
    return(base_case(a_in, b_in))
  }
  # to be continued...
```

Figure 6.13.1: The start of the recursive alignment function. If the inputs represent a simple base case, then the answer from base_case() can be returned.

If the inputs aren't a base case, we need to follow the recursive pattern by extracting p_α, e_α, p_β, and e_β, which we'll call p_a_in, e_a_in, p_b_in, and e_b_in (Figure 6.13.2). (The syntax x[1:m] returns the sub-vector of x from index 1 to index m, inclusive.)

```
p_a_in <- a_in[1:(length(a_in) - 1)]
e_a_in <- a_in[length(a_in)]
p_b_in <- b_in[1:(length(b_in) - 1)]
e_b_in <- b_in[length(b_in)]
# to be continued...
```

Figure 6.13.2: Extracting p_α, e_α, p_β, and e_β from α and β.

Let's revisit our recursive definition from Equation 6.1:

$$\underbrace{\left(\begin{array}{c} p_\alpha \text{ aligned w/} \\ p_\beta e_\beta \end{array}\right)}_{left} \begin{array}{c} e_\alpha \\ - \end{array}, \quad score = S(left) + S(e_\alpha, -)$$

$$\underbrace{\left(\begin{array}{c} p_\alpha \text{ aligned w/} \\ p_\beta \end{array}\right)}_{center} \begin{array}{c} e_\alpha \\ e_\beta \end{array}, \quad score = S(center) + S(e_\alpha, e_\beta)$$

$$\underbrace{\left(\begin{array}{c} p_\alpha e_\alpha \text{ aligned w/} \\ p_\beta \end{array}\right)}_{right} \begin{array}{c} - \\ e_\beta \end{array}, \quad score = S(right) + S(-, e_\beta)$$

We need to produce the sub-alignments `left`, `center`, and `right` recursively. For `left`, for example, we do this by aligning p_α against $p_\beta e_\beta$, which is also the entirety of β. We could do this by simply using `b_in`, or we could concatenate the pieces we've already produced with `c(p_b_in, e_b_in)`. To stick with our notation, we'll choose the latter, even though re-concatenating the vectors is less efficient (Figure 6.13.3).

Figure 6.13.3: Recursive calls for computing *left*, *center*, and *right* sub-alignments.

```
left   <- global_aln(p_a_in, c(p_b_in, e_b_in))
center <- global_aln(p_a_in, p_b_in)
right  <- global_aln(c(p_a_in, e_a_in), p_b_in)
# to be continued...
```

Just as in the `fib()` function, notice the similarity between our code and the conceptual definition! Now, we can use the answers for these sub-alignments to produce three potential overall answers for the problem, accessing parts of the answers to sub-problems as needed using $-notation (Figure 6.13.4).

Figure 6.13.4: Computing three potential answers to aligning α and β according to the recursive definition.

```
answer_left <- list(a_in = a_in, b_in = b_in,
                    a_out = c(left$a_out, e_a_in),
                    b_out = c(left$b_out, "-"),
                    score = left$score +
                            score_pair(e_a_in, "-"))
answer_center <- list(a_in = a_in, b_in = b_in,
                      a_out = c(center$a_out, e_a_in),
                      b_out = c(center$b_out, e_b_in),
                      score = center$score +
                              score_pair(e_a_in, e_b_in))
answer_right <- list(a_in = a_in, b_in = b_in,
                     a_out = c(right$a_out, "-"),
                     b_out = c(right$b_out, e_b_in),
                     score = right$score +
                             score_pair("-", e_b_in))
# to be continued...
```

All that is left is to determine which of these three (`answer_right`, `answer_center`, or `answer_left`) is the best, defined as having the largest score, and return it. We can do this in a straightforward manner, and of course we need to include the final brace that closes our function (Figure 6.13.5).

```
best <- answer_left
best_score <- answer_left$score
if(answer_center$score > best_score) {
  best <- answer_center
  best_score <- answer_center$score
}
if(answer_right$score > best_score) {
  best <- answer_right
  best_score <- answer_right$score
}

return(best)
}
```

Figure 6.13.5: Determining and returning the best answer by selecting the one with the largest score.

And that's it! We've turned our recursive definition (which we also proved correct via induction) into a recursive algorithm. (The full function is simply the concatenation of Figures 6.13.1, 6.13.2, 6.13.3, 6.13.4, and 6.13.5.) Figure 6.14 shows a usage attempt, and Figure 6.15 reveals the printed output.

```
a <- char_vec("@TATCGG")
b <- char_vec("@TTCG")
answer <- global_aln(a, b)
str(answer)                       # See margin
print(unvec_char(answer$a_out))   # @TATCGG
print(unvec_char(answer$b_out))   # @T-TCG-
```

Figure 6.14: Using the recursive alignment function.

```
List of 5
 $ a_in : chr [1:7] "@" "T" "A" "T" ...
 $ b_in : chr [1:5] "@" "T" "T" "C" ...
 $ a_out: chr [1:7] "@" "T" "A" "T" ...
 $ b_out: chr [1:7] "@" "T" "-" "T" ...
 $ score: num 0
[1] "@TATCGG"
[1] "@T-TCG-"
```

Figure 6.15: Output for Figure 6.14.

Exercises

1. Implement the code in this chapter, but modify the scoring rules such that A/T and C/G mismatches are scored at -2 rather than -3.

2. What is the maximum depth of the call stack in relation to `length(a_in)` and `length(b_in)` for `global_aln()`? Prove that your answer is correct.

3. Prove the correctness of the recursive definition in equation 6.2, and implement the recursive method it describes. You may need to create an alternate representation as well, since in this case a sequence like "TAGC" should be represented the vector `c("T", "A", "G", "C", "@")`.

7 *Fast Alignment, Local Alignment*

> Scientists often have a naïve faith that if only they could discover enough facts about a problem, these facts would somehow arrange themselves in a compelling and true solution.
>
> ———————————————
> Theodosius Dobzhansky, 1962

In the previous chapter we developed and proved correct a recursive method for computing what are known as *global* sequence alignments. A global alignment of two sequences requires that all portions of both sequences are used in the alignment–later in this chapter we'll explore other types of alignments that are particularly good for finding matching *subsequences* of two sequences, known as local alignments.

Before we can do that, however, we should evaluate the speed of our algorithm. If we try to use this method to align two longish sequences (as in Figure 7.1), we'll find that we must wait for a surprisingly long time.

```
a <- char_vec("@TATCGGCGATCGATTAGCCC")
b <- char_vec("@TTGGCGATCGACCATCC")
answer <- global_aln(a, b)       # waiting...
```

Figure 7.1: Attempting to use the recursive method from the last chapter on long sequences takes a very long time.

The recursive global_aln() function operates not too dissimilarly from the fib() function of Chapter 4, except instead of making two recursive calls it makes *three*! And, just like the fib() function, the recursive calls only get closer to a base case one step at a time: if α has n characters and β has m, computing just the *center* subalignment requires aligning $n - 1$ and $m - 1$ characters. Contrast this to many of the methods in Chapter 3, where recursive calls were made to subproblems of *half* the original size. Indeed, just as we wrote a recurrence relation for quicksort() (page 51), we can write a recurrence relation for global_aln(). Let $T(n, m)$ be the time needed to align two sequences of length n and m. Then:

$$T(n,m) = \begin{cases} T(n-1,m) + T(n-1,m-1) + T(n,m-1) + O(n+m), & \text{if } n > 1 \text{ and } m > 1, \\ O(m), \text{ if } n = 1, \\ O(n), \text{ if } m = 1. \end{cases}$$

[1] The $O(n+m)$ comes from lines like a_out = c(center$a_out, e_a_in), which requires copying the data from center$a_out into a new vector. Even without an $O(n+m)$ term in the recurrence (which can be avoided with the creative use of stacks), the method would still be exponentially slow.

We won't solve this recurrence exactly, other than to say that just like the basic fib() function, the runtime is *exponential* in m and n.[1] But, also like the fib() function, many of the recursive calls solve overlapping subproblems. Consider the call tree for an alignment where $\alpha = $ @TATC and $\beta = $ @TTGT (Figure 7.2; hopefully it's clear now why we named the subproblems *left*, *center*, and *right*!)

In Figure 7.2 we've highlighted the largest overlapping and redundant subproblems, but there are many in the full tree even for short input sequences. Obviously, memoizing our global alignment function using the techniques of Chapter 4 will speed things up considerably. We'll use as keys into the memoization cache the result of concatenating the unvec_char()'d versions of a_in and b_in (Figure 7.3).

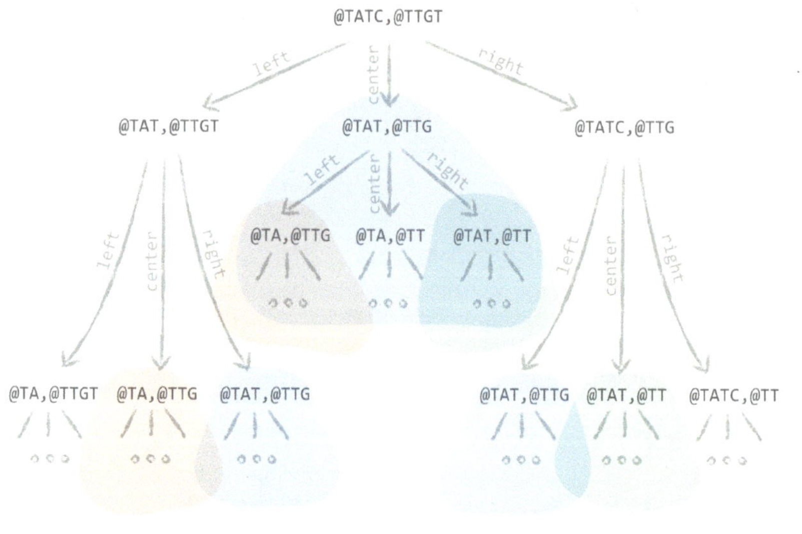

With memoization our recursive function runs much faster, even for long input sequences. Just *how* fast remains to be seen.

Figure 7.2: Call tree for global_aln() on sequences @TATC and @TTGT, with several redundant computations highlighted.

7.1   Inspecting the Cache

In an effort to determine how much time and effort the memoized alignment algorithm takes, we can take a detailed look at the cache. After all, each entry in the cache represents a chunk of work performed by some function call. We're going to visualize the contents of the cache using the ggplot2 R package.

But in order to plot anything with ggplot2, the data to plot must exist in a dataframe–a table of columns and rows. As shown in Figure 4.10 on page 60, the contents of an rstack can easily be converted to a data frame. Unfortunately, our data exists as entries of a hash table, for which no such convenient conversion exists. Our strategy will be to use an rstack as an intermediary (Figure 7.4, ignoring the highlighted lines).

As we do this, we'll also (using an internal loop) run unvec_char() on any elements of answer that are character vectors, effectively converting entries like a_out so they are represented as c("@CATG") instead of c("@", "C", "A", "T", "G") (highlighted lines in Figure

```
GLOBAL_ALN_CACHE <<- hash()

global_aln <- function(a_in, b_in) {
  key <- str_c(unvec_char(a_in), unvec_char(b_in), sep = ",")
  if(has.key(key, GLOBAL_ALN_CACHE)) {
    return(GLOBAL_ALN_CACHE[[key]])
  }

  if(length(a_in) == 1 | length(b_in) == 1) {
    answer <- base_case(a_in, b_in)
    GLOBAL_ALN_CACHE[[key]] <- answer
    return(answer)
  }

  # rest of function...

  GLOBAL_ALN_CACHE[[key]] <<- best
  return(best)
}
```

Figure 7.3: Modifications to memoize the global_aln() function.

7.4).

```
hash_values_as_dataframe <- function(thehash) {
  tempstack <- rstack()

  for(key in keys(thehash)) {
    answer <- thehash[[key]]

    for(index in seq(1, length(answer))) {
      if(is.character(answer[[index]])) {
        answer[[index]] <- unvec_char(answer[[index]])
      }
    }

    tempstack <- insert_top(tempstack, answer)
  }

  return(as.data.frame(tempstack, stringsAsFactors = FALSE))
}
```

Figure 7.4: Modifying hash_values_as_dataframe() so that any character vectors are run through unvec_char() for the resulting data frame.

Of course, if we are interested in inspecting the cache for a given run of global_aln(), we should be sure to clear it out before we call global_aln() (Figure 7.5).

```
a <- char_vec("@TATCTGCAACGA")
b <- char_vec("@TTGTGC")
GLOBAL_ALN_CACHE <<- hash()
answer <- global_aln(a, b)

cache_df <- hash_values_as_dataframe(GLOBAL_ALN_CACHE)
print(head(cache_df))
```

Figure 7.5: Using hash_values_to_dataframe() to summarize the memoization cache. Notice that we reset GLOBAL_ALN_CACHE before each call to global_aln().

```
            a_in     b_in          a_out          b_out  score
1 TATCTGCAACGA TTGTGC TATCTGCAACGA @-TGTGC-----    -22
2 TATCTGCAACGA  TTGTG TATCTGCAACGA @-TGTG------    -28
3 TATCTGCAACGA   TTGT TATCTGCAACGA @-TGT-------    -34
4 TATCTGCAACGA    TTG TATCTGCAACGA @-T--G------    -35
5 TATCTGCAACGA     TT TATCTGCAACGA @-T---------    -41
6 TATCTGCAACGA      T TATCTGCAACGA @----------    -47
```

Figure 7.6: Output for Figure 7.5; each row of the dataframe contains information for a subproblem solved and cached by the recursive method.

Based on the output (Figure 7.6), each row of the dataframe clearly holds the information for a subproblem solved during the recursion, including the inputs (a_in and b_in) and the outputs (a_out, b_out, and score).

Let's use ggplot2 to plot the subproblems in terms of their *inputs* and the score output. We'll do so by plotting the cache's a_in and b_in values in a grid, organized by lengths of a_in and b_in along with the optimal alignment score for that subproblem (Figure 7.7).

```
p <- ggplot(cache_df) +
    geom_tile(aes(x = reorder(a_in, nchar(a_in)),
                  y = reorder(b_in, -1*nchar(b_in)),
                  fill = score)) +
    geom_text(aes(x = reorder(a_in, nchar(a_in)),
                  y = reorder(b_in, -1*nchar(b_in)),
                  label = score)) +
    coord_equal() +
    scale_x_discrete(name = "a_in") +
    scale_y_discrete(name = "b_in") +
    theme_bw(16) +
    theme(axis.text.x = element_text(angle = 25, hjust = 1))

plot(p)
```

Figure 7.7: Using ggplot2 to visualize the subproblems stored in the memoization cache; here a_in sequences are arranged by length on the x axis and b_in sequences are arranged by length (in reverse order, as is standard for this particular type of visualization) along the y axis.

For those unfamiliar with the particulars of ggplot2, the geom_tile() "layer" is specifying that values for the x-axis should be drawn from the b_in column of the dataframe, ordered by nchar(a_in) (number of characters) in those entries and colored by the score column. We use -1*nchar(b_in) for the y-axis to place larger entries toward the bottom. The geom_text() layer adds the numeric scores; coord_equal() ensures that the plotted cells are squares, and the theme() lines set the font size and rotation for the x-axis labels.

Figure 7.8: Graphical output from Figure 7.7.

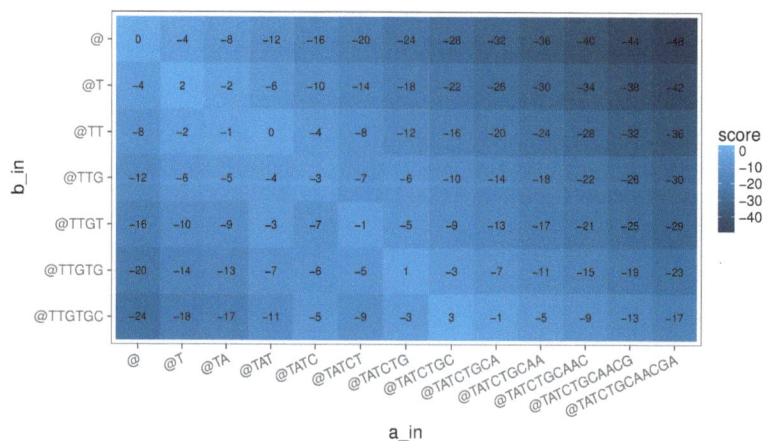

The plot in Figure 7.8 shows each subproblem in a grid along with the optimal score for solving it. If a_in is of length n and b_in is of length m, then there are clearly $n \times m$ cells in this table, meaning $n \times m$ subproblems were solved. Each cell here represents a single call to global_aln() that took more than $O(1)$ time (which is to say, those subproblems whose answers weren't already computed and in the cache). How much time was used for each cell? Well, the function includes lines like a_out = c(center$a_out, e_a_in), which runs in $O(n)$ time (since it copies all the data in center$a_out), and b_out = c(center$b_out, e_b_in), which runs in $O(m)$ time. Thus, each cell takes $O(m + n)$, and so the entire process runs in $O(nm(n + m))$; not great, but much better than the non-memoized, purely recursive, exponential-time solution of the last chapter.[2]

7.2 Subproblems are Organized

Let's take a detailed look at the upper-left corner of this grid of scores (Figure 7.9). First, note that the cells along the top and left-hand side correspond to base cases, where either a_in was just "@" (on the left) or b_in was just "@" (on the top). In the far upper-left, "@" aligned with "@" has a score of 0. What is far more interesting is the cell representing the problem @TAT,@TT (green arrow, also corresponding to the green subproblem in Figure 7.2), and the spatial relationship to its subproblems. The *left* subproblem occurs immediately to its left, *center* along the diagonal, and *right* above. (If we tilt our heads 45° to the left, the subproblems are still *left*, *center*, and *right*!) The overall solution for @TAT,@TT relied upon the answers to these three neighboring cells.

Additionally, exactly *one* of these neighboring cells contributed to the best answer; in this case it was subproblem *center* which had a score of 2 and led to an optimal overall score of 0 (−2 plus 2 for the T versus T match). (The other alternatives were *left* at −1 plus a gap cost of −3, or *right* at −6 plus a gap cost of −3.) In a sense, we can say that the optimal solution for @TAT,@TT came "from" the subproblem @TA,@TT.

In code, we might even want to record this information in an answer list, as in answer$from_a_in = "@TA", answer$from_b_in = "@TT". Of course, this "from" information should be added programmatically. We'll need to add it for the base-cases as well for consistency, but in this case we'll say that from_a_in is equal to a_in itself to make the eventual plot cleaner (Figure 7.10).

In the recursive function, we need to determine the "from" information for each potential answer before we figure out which is best (Figure 7.11).

Because our hash_values_to_dataframe() function is general enough that it keeps all information in the answer lists and con-

[2] It is possible to implement this solution without using the slow c() function at all. Rather than storing answer$a_out as a vector, we could store it as an rstack, which supports fast additions to one end. Then, rather than a_out = c(center$a_out, e_a_in), we could use a line like a_out = insert_top(center$a_out, e_a_in). This approach would make the method truly $O(nm)$, but would require more code to visualize and interpret the answers since the stacks holding the alignment would need to be deconstructed. Such a solution would be best served by storing a_in and b_in as stacks as well, allowing e_a_in <- peek_top(a_in) and p_a_in <- without_top(a_in).

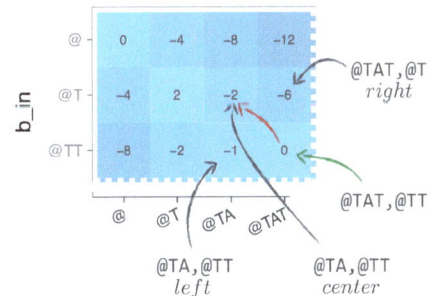

Figure 7.9: Detailed view of Figure 7.8. The subproblem aligning a_in = "@TAT", b_in = "@TT" is indicated by a green arrow, and the corresponding *left*, *center*, and *right* subproblems are indicated by gray arrows. The red arrow indicates that the *center* subproblem was the one that produced the best overall answer (−2 plus a match score of 2 equals 0).

Figure 7.10: Adjustment to the base_case() function to keep track of "from" information.

```r
base_case <- function(a_in, b_in) {
  answer <- list(a = a_in, b = b_in,
                 aaln = "", baln = "", score = 0,
                 from_a_in = a_in, from_b_in = b_in)

  # continue with rest of function ...
```

Figure 7.11: Adjustments to the global_aln() function to keep track of "from" information for each subproblem.

```r
  # ...
  answer_left <- list(a_in = a_in, b_in = b_in,
                      a_out = c(left$a_out, e_a_in),
                      b_out = c(left$b_out, "-"),
                      score = left$score +
                              score_pair(e_a_in, "-"),
                      from_a_in = left$a_in,
                      from_b_in = left$b_in)
  answer_center <- list(a_in = a_in, b_in = b_in,
                        a_out = c(center$a_out, e_a_in),
                        b_out = c(center$b_out, e_b_in),
                        score = center$score +
                                score_pair(e_a_in, e_b_in),
                        from_a_in = center$a_in,
                        from_b_in = center$b_in)
  answer_right <- list(a_in = a_in, b_in = b_in,
                       a_out = c(right$a_out, "-"),
                       b_out = c(right$b_out, e_b_in),
                       score = right$score +
                               score_pair("-", e_b_in),
                       from_a_in = right$a_in,
                       from_b_in = right$b_in)
  # ...
```

	a_in	b_in	a_out	b_out	score	from_a_in	from_b_in
1	@TATC	@TTG	@TATC	@T-TG	-3	@TAT	@TT
2	@TATC	@TT	@TATC	@T-T-	-4	@TAT	@TT
3	@TATC	@T	@TATC	@T---	-10	@TAT	@T
4	@TATC	@	@TATC	@----	-16	@TATC	@
5	@TAT	@TTG	@TAT	@TTG	-4	@TA	@TT
6	@TAT	@TT	@TAT	@T-T	0	@TA	@T

Figure 7.12: Example cache dataframe with "from" information included.

verts all characters vectors with unvec_char(), this from_a_in and from_b_in information will be represented in the cache_df dataframe holding all the information of the memoziation cache. An example for the shorter inputs $\alpha = $ @TATC and $\beta = $ @TTG is shown in Figure 7.12.

With this information in the dataframe, we can add a layer to our ggplot2 code to represent these "from" arrows for all subproblems. We'll also add a slight bit of jitter to the arrow endpoints for readability (Figure 7.13).

The output in Figure 7.14 is again enlightening; the optimal alignment for these two sequences is @TATCTGCAACGA and @T-TGTGC-----; notice the trend in "from" arrows corresponding to the nature of the alignment!

```
p <- ggplot(cache_df) +
      geom_tile(aes(x = reorder(a_in, nchar(a_in)),
                    y = reorder(b_in, -1*nchar(b_in)),
                    fill = score)) +
      geom_text(aes(x = reorder(a_in, nchar(a_in)),
                    y = reorder(b_in, -1*nchar(b_in)),
                    label = score)) +
      geom_segment(aes(x = a_in, y = b_in,
                       xend = from_a_in, yend = from_b_in),
                   arrow = arrow(length = unit(0.4,"cm")),
                   position = position_jitter(width = 0.1,
                                              height = 0.1),
                   color = "red") +
      # ...
```

Figure 7.13: Adjustments to the ggplot code to plot "from" arrows, indicating which subproblems contributed to the best answer for each cell.

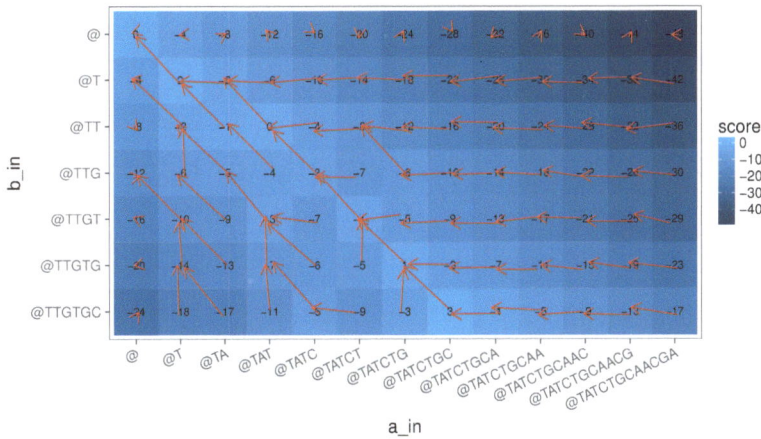

Figure 7.14: Using ggplot2 to visualize the subproblems stored in the memoization cache, including the "from" information indicating which subproblems contributed to the best answer for each cell.

7.3   The Dynamic Program

Something to notice about our cache-inspection plots (Figures 7.8 and 7.14) is that they don't display in any way the alignments for any of the subproblems. All we see are subproblem inputs (on the x and y axes), the optimal scores, and the "from" information. Is it perhaps possible to reconstruct the optimal alignment for any subproblem given just this information?

Let's consider this information as shown in Figure 7.15. The lower-right of this zoomed view represents the subproblem of aligning $\alpha = $ "@TAT" with $\beta =$ "@TT". The optimal alignment would be @TAT and @T-T, with a score of 0. The arrow in this cell points along the diagonal, indicating that the optimal solution was built upon the optimal solution for its *center* subproblem, aligning "@TA" against "@T". This means that the ending T from α and the ending T

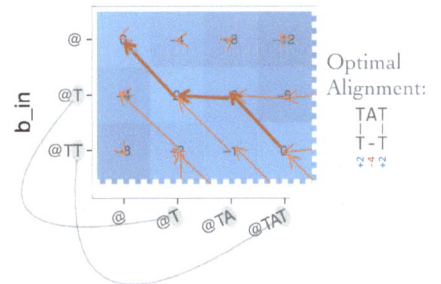

Figure 7.15: Detailed view of "from" information for the upper-left section of the score table. Gray lines between bases indicate letters matched in the optimal output (these also have diagonal arrows), and bold red arrows indicate the path "traced back" from the lower-right to the upper-left.

in

Recursion:

$$n: 1 \quad 2 \quad 3 \quad 4 \quad 5 \quad 6 \quad 7 \quad 8 \quad 9 \quad 10$$

Dynamic Programming:

$$n: 1 \quad 2 \quad 3 \quad 4 \quad 5 \quad 6 \quad 7 \quad 8 \quad 9 \quad 10$$

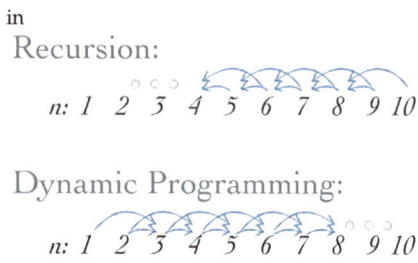

Figure 7.16: When using recursion, we start at the solution for the large problem, and compute the answers to subproblems recursively "as needed." Dynamic programming, by contrast, pre-computes answers to subproblems in a guided, bottom-up manner.

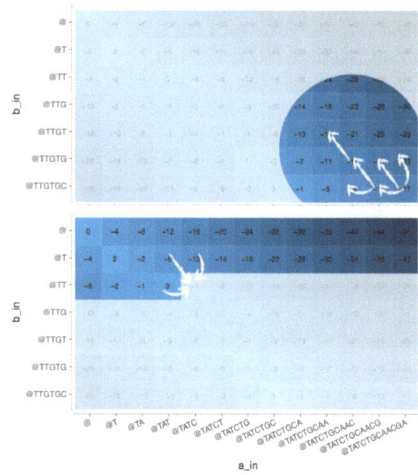

Figure 7.17: For the sequence alignment problem, the recursive method attempts to compute answers starting from the lower right to the upper left, on an as-needed basis (top). Given that we know the cell dependencies, we'll fill the table in from the upper-left (bottom).

from β were aligned against each other:

$$\underbrace{\begin{pmatrix} \text{@TA aligned w/} \\ \text{@T} \end{pmatrix}}_{center} \begin{matrix} \text{T} \\ \text{T,} \end{matrix} \quad score = S(center) + S(\text{T}, \text{T})$$

The arrow from *this* cell (α = "@TA" versus β = "@T") points leftward, indicating that the best solution is built upon the solution to the left subproblem, "@T" vs "@T", where the A from α has been aligned with a gap character -. (If the arrow had pointed up, we'd have analygous case with a character from β being aligned with a gap.)

$$\left(\underbrace{\begin{pmatrix} \text{@T aligned w/} \\ \text{@T} \end{pmatrix}}_{left} \begin{matrix} \text{A} \\ \text{-} \end{matrix} \right) \begin{matrix} \text{T} \\ \text{T,} \end{matrix} \quad score = \left(S(left) + S(\text{A}, \text{-}) \right) + S(\text{T}, \text{T})$$

Another diagonal arrow indicates that the *center* subproblem from that point was used, and the ending T characters were aligned together:

$$\left(\left(\underbrace{\begin{pmatrix} \text{@ aligned w/} \\ \text{@} \end{pmatrix}}_{center} \begin{matrix} \text{T} \\ \text{T} \end{matrix} \right) \begin{matrix} \text{A} \\ \text{-} \end{matrix} \right) \begin{matrix} \text{T} \\ \text{T,} \end{matrix} \quad score = \left(\left(S(center) + S(\text{T}, \text{T}) \right) + S(\text{A}, \text{-}) \right) + S(\text{T}, \text{T}$$

Finally we've reached a base case: "@" aligned with "@" is just "@" and "@" with a score or 0.

In general we can use these *traceback* rules to reconstruct the same result the recursive solution found given only the "from" information. In fact, if we were to modify the arrows along the top row to always point left, and the arrows along the left column to always point up, then the traceback rules would fill out the gaps even for base-cases like "@TAGA" versus just "@".

To summarize: for a given subproblem, if the arrow points diagonally, we can align the last bases of the subproblems together. If it points left, the last base in the α subproblem is aligned with a gap, and if it points up, the last base in the β subproblem is aligned with a gap. In all cases, we "move" to the next subproblem indicated by the arrow to continue on.

Further, I'm sure it hasn't escaped your attention that the last bases in these subproblems organized in this way are the characters of the original α and β inputs themselves! Thus, we if we had the matrix of arrows, we wouldn't even need to store the full axis labels (the subproblem inputs)–the bases to be aligned together could simply be read as indices into the original sequences. To put this in more concrete terms, if a_in = c("@", "T", "A", "T") and b_in = c("@", "T", "T"), the diagonal arrow in column 4, row 3 of Figure 7.9 indicates that a_in[4] ("T") should be aligned with b_in[3] (also "T").

BEFORE WE GO MUCH FUTHER, let's recall from our Fibonacci example of Chapter 4 how dynamic programming relates to memoized recursion. In recursion, we are solving subproblems on an as-needed basis (memoizing, a.k.a. cacheing, for speed if necessary). With dynamic programming, we smartly deduce which subproblems will need to be computed and their relationships, and pre-compute them from the "bottom up" (Figure 7.16).

For the sequence alignment problem, the subproblems can be organized in a table, and the recursive algorithm is solving them (and filling the memoization cache with those solutions) in an as-needed fashion from the lower-right corner. But we know that any given cell depends on the solutions for the *left*, *center*, and *right* cells (which we'll soon be denoting "left," "diag," and "up"), so for the dynamic program we'll fill in the table starting from the upper-left corner. Specifically, we'll complete the top row left-to-right, then the second row left-to-right, and so on (Figure 7.17).

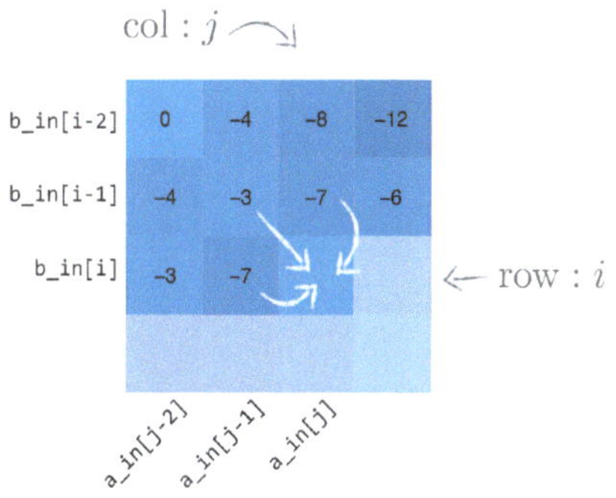

NOW, AS DISCUSSED ABOVE, to compute an optimal alignment all we really need is the matrix of "from" information–from this the path of optimal solutions can be traced back. During this process the bases to be aligned can be indexed from the original input sequences. However, in order to actually compute the "from" arrow for a given cell, we need the *scores* of those neighboring cells. Our strategy will be to store two matrices: one called score (a numeric matrix of scores) and one called from (a character matrix with entries like "left", "diag", and "up").

These two matrices will be filled in much the same way the information is stored in the memoization cache. Consider as an example Figure 7.18, wherein we are attempting to determine the optimal score for the cell at row i column j (score[i,j]) partway through the process. This is dependent on the maximum score contributions from the left, diagonal, and upper cells: if the score to the left (score[i-1,j]) plus the cost of aligning a gap to a_in[j] is the best option, then score[i,j] is set to score[i-1,j] + score_pair(a_in[j], "-") and from[i,j] can be set to "left".[3] On the other hand, if score[i-1,j-1] + score_pair(a_in[j], b_in[i]) is larger then score[i,j] can be set to that and from[i,j] can be set to "diag". Figure 7.19 summarizes for all three cases.

Figure 7.18: Computing the score for the cell scores[i,j].

[3] Indices in a_in are along columns, and so are associated with the j index, since we're going to stick with a *row, column* notation for indexing into matrices.

Figure 7.19: Letting scores be a matrix of score values and from be a matrix of direction strings, the maximum of the three possible scores defines the score for the cell and the "from" direction.

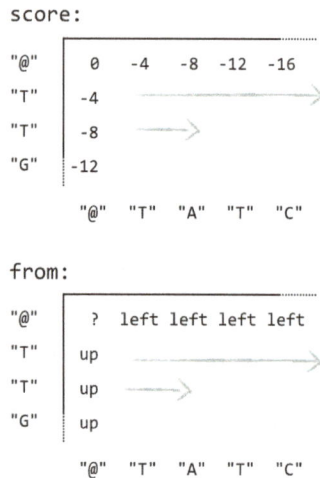

$$\text{score}[i,j] = \max \begin{cases} \text{score}[i,j-1] + \text{score\_pair}("-", a[j]); & \text{from}[i,j] = "left" \\ \text{score}[i-1,j-1] + \text{score\_pair}(b[i], a[j]); & \text{from}[i,j] = "diag" \\ \text{score}[i-1,j] + \text{score\_pair}(b[i], "-"); & \text{from}[i,j] = "up" \end{cases}$$

The number of columns of the matrix will be length(a_in), and the number of rows will be length(b_in). In order to fill in the rows from top to bottom and left to right, we'll first need to fill out the top row and the left-hand side–note that these correspond to base cases in the recursion and can be simply filled in with increasing gap costs. For the arrows, we'll see that cells along the left-hand column always point "up" and those along the top always point "left"–this way during the traceback once we hit these walls the traceback will continue through to the upper-left hand corner. We'll use for-loops for this, and then we can use loops to fill out the interior of the table (Figure 7.20).

Now would be a good time to write some code. Starting with the inputs a_in and b_in, we'll create a score and from matrix of the appropriate size; initially all entries in score will be 0 and all entries in from will be "?" (Figure 7.21.1).

Next we can fill in the base-cases along the first row and column (Figure 7.21.2). (The upper-left hand corner is already set with a score of 0, and the from entry there won't matter during the trace-back.) Notice that along row 1, the score in score[row,col] is equal to the score of score[row,col-1] plus the gap cost; if we were to compute it properly via the score_pair() function it would be score[row,col - 1] + score_pair("-", a_in[j]), even though in this implementation score_pair() always returns −4 if one of the inputs is "-".

score:

```
"@"  │   0    -4    -8   -12   -16
"T"  │  -4    ─────────────────────>
"T"  │  -8    ─────────>
"G"  │ -12

        "@"   "T"   "A"   "T"   "C"
```

from:

```
"@"  │   ?   left  left  left  left
"T"  │  up    ─────────────────────>
"T"  │  up    ─────────>
"G"  │  up

        "@"   "T"   "A"   "T"   "C"
```

Figure 7.20: A two-table solution for computing the scores and "from" information. After the base cases have been taken care of, the table can be filled out row-by-row, column-by-column (gray arrows).

Figure 7.21.1: The start of the dynamic programming solution for sequence alignment.

```
global_aln_dp <- function(a_in, b_in) {
  score <- matrix(0, ncol = length(a_in), nrow = length(b_in))
  from <- matrix("?", ncol = length(a_in), nrow = length(b_in))
  # to be continued...
```

```
  row <- 1
  for(col in seq(2, length(a_in))) {
    score[row,col] <- score[row,col-1] + score_pair("-", a_in[col])
    from[row,col] <- "left"
  }

  col <- 1
  for(row in seq(2, length(b_in))) {
    score[row,col] <- score[row-1,col] + score_pair(b_in[row], "-")
    from[row,col] <- "up"
  }
  # to be continued...
```

Figure 7.21.2: Filling in the base cases of the dynamic programming tables.

Now we need to fill up the rest of these two tables in a top-to-bottom, left-to-right order so that we can ensure the appropriate neighboring cells have been completed when we attempt to fill the next. First, in a nested for-loop accessing each cell, we compute the potential possibilities for the three scores (Figure 7.21.3).[4]

[4] This sort of matrix programming can be very confusing, especially for those with dyslexic tendencies. Be careful, and try to use rules like "always *row, column* order."

```
for(row in seq(2, length(b_in))) {
  for(col in seq(2, length(a_in))) {
    leftscore <- score[row,col-1] +
                     score_pair(b_in[row], "-")
    diagscore <- score[row-1,col-1] +
                     score_pair(b_in[row], a_in[col])
    upscore   <- score[row-1,col] +
                     score_pair("-", a_in[col])
    # to be continued...
```

Figure 7.21.3: Computing the three potential scores for score[row,col].

Now we need to decide which of the three scores is the largest, and set the score[row,col] entry and from[row,col] entries accordingly (Figure 7.21.4).

```
    bestscore <- leftscore
    bestfrom <- "left"
    if(diagscore > bestscore) {
      bestscore <- diagscore
      bestfrom <- "diag"
    }
    if(upscore > bestscore) {
      bestscore <- upscore
      bestfrom <- "up"
    }

    score[row,col] <- bestscore
    from[row,col] <- bestfrom
  }
}
# to be continued...
```

Figure 7.21.4: Computing the best of the three potential scores and setting score[row,col] and from[row,col].

This ends the nested for-loop. At this point we have the entire table of "from" information that is needed to recreate the optimal alignment, and the optimal score is sitting in the lower-right hand corner of score. To process the traceback, we'll start by setting currentrow <- length(b_in) and currentcol <- length(a_in) as an index into the lower-right cell. We'll build the aligned sequences in rstacks, since these make it efficient to add characters one-at-a-time during the traceback (Figure 7.21.5).

Finally we can use a while-loop to perform the traceback–we'll follow "from" arrows until currentrow == 1 and currentcol == 1. At each iteration we'll look at from[currentrow, currentcol]; if it's "left" we need to align the appropriate base in a_in with a gap and move left one column. Other "from" rules are processed as described earlier (Figure 7.21.6)

Figure 7.21.5: Initiating the traceback in the lower-right hand corner of the dynamic program tables.

```
currentrow <- length(b_in)
currentcol <- length(a_in)
a_out <- rstack()
b_out <- rstack()
best_score <- score[currentrow, currentcol]
# to be continued...
```

Figure 7.21.6: Performing the traceback through the "from" information, building aaln and baln one character at a time.

```
while(currentrow != 1 & currentcol != 1) {
  arrow <- from[currentrow, currentcol]
  if(arrow == "left") {
    a_out <- insert_top(a_out, a_in[currentcol])
    b_out <- insert_top(b_out, "-")
    currentcol <- currentcol - 1
  } else if(arrow == "diag") {
    a_out <- insert_top(a_out, a_in[currentcol])
    b_out <- insert_top(b_out, b_in[currentrow])
    currentcol <- currentcol - 1
    currentrow <- currentrow - 1
  } else {
    a_out <- insert_top(a_out, "-")
    b_out <- insert_top(b_out, b_in[currentrow])
    currentrow <- currentrow - 1
  }
}
# to be continued...
```

With this done, the optimal alignment is stored in a_out and b_out (as stacks), and best_score stores the optimal score. Building the aligned sequences in stacks was beneficial for performance reasons, but not very convenient for reading the answer. We can convert a stack of characters to a simple string by first running it through as.list() to convert it to an R list, then through as.character() to convert it to a character vector, and finally through our unvec_char() function to produce a simple string rather than a vector of characters. We'll also finish out the global_aln_dp() function and return the three pieces as an answer (Figure 7.21.7).

Figure 7.21.7: Deconstructing the alignment stacks and returning the answer along with the optimal score.

```
  answer <- list(a_out = unvec_char(as.character(as.list(a_out))),
                 b_out = unvec_char(as.character(as.list(b_out))),
                 score = best_score)
  return(answer)
}
```

Finally, we can run our dynamic programming function (which altogether spans figures 7.21.1 to 7.21.7) in Figure 7.22. The output is shown in Figure 7.23.

```
a <- char_vec("@TAGACGAGACCAGA")
b <- char_vec("@AGACACAGCTG")
answer <- global_aln_dp(a, b)
str(answer)
```

Figure 7.22: Running the dynamic program for global sequence alignment.

THIS DYNAMIC PROGRAM for optimal global sequence alignment is known as the Needleman-Wunsch algorithm, after the authors who developed it in the 1970's for aligning protein sequences. (Actually, the original dynamic program as proposed by Needleman and Wunsch was significantly slower, $O(n^2m)$. Shortly thereafter the method described here was discovered by others.)

The dynamic program may seem quite removed from the recursive formulation described in the last chapter. On the other hand, the same essential ideas are captured, including the relationships between subproblems. The similarity of the memoization cache, dynamic programming tables, and inductive proof also brings us full circle, just as we saw with the Fibonacci function toward the end of Chapter 5.

The runtime for this method is easily described as $O(nm)$, because of the nested for-loops that fill out the tables (and the fact that the tables are of size $n \times m$). This is also the amount of *memory* that is used by this method. If both sequences are millions or billions of characters long, this is quite a lot of time and memory! As such, this method is not usually run on genome-scale DNA sequences, but the Needleman-Wunsch algorithm nevertheless serves as the basis for a variety of other modern techniques in bioinformatics.

While both the dynamic program and the recursive method can be made to run in $O(nm)$ time (via memoization and clever usage of data structures), the dynamic program has an edge in speed, since looping over entries in a matrix is somewhat faster than calling and returning from functions. Additionally, as mentioned in Chapter 5, with the dynamic programming approach we needn't worry about overflowing the call stack with too many recursive calls.

```
List of 3
 $ a_out: chr "AGACGAGACCAGA"
 $ b_out: chr "AGAC-ACAGCTG-"
 $ score: num -5
```

Figure 7.23: Output for Figure 7.22, demonstrating successful alignment via the dynamic programming solution.

7.4   Local Alignment

The dynamic programming tables (representing subproblems organized by their dependencies, pre-solved from simplest to most complex) and their traceback can help us look at the alignment problem in a variety of interesting ways. For example, *any* traceback path starting at any cell represents an alignment according to the traceback rules (Figure 7.15 on page 101). If such a path starts somewhere in the middle of the table and ends in the middle, it effectively ignores the ends of α and β; such an alignment is called a *local alignment*. For example, the trace in Figure 7.24 illustrates a local alignment from TCTG of α to just TG of β.

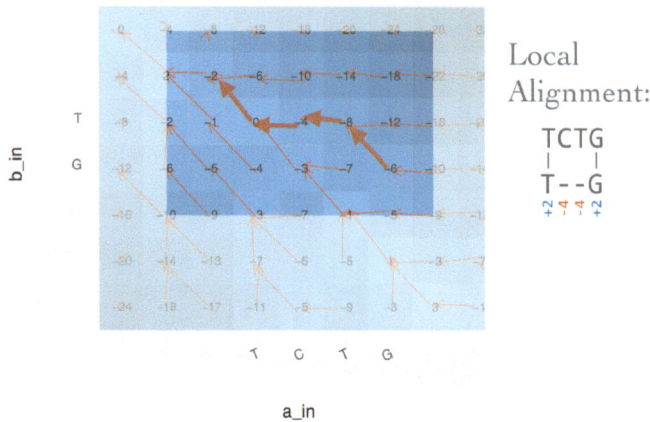

Figure 7.24: A small traceback for a local alignment, aligning the subsequence of α TCTG with the subsequence of β TG.

Local Alignment:

```
TCTG
|  |
T--G
+2 -4 -4 +2
```

In Figure 7.24, the ending score in the path shows a −6, but this would be the score for an optimal alignment all the way back to the start of both sequences. Stopping at the location shown, the path ends at a score of −2; thus the "local score" of the alignment is −6 − −2 = −4; this can also be verified by looking at the local alignment itself (two matches at +2 and two gap costs at −4).

The *local alignment problem* is to find the optimal local alignment, the one with the largest local score. Note that the optimal local alignment should never have a score that is negative. This is because the "empty" alignment, "" versus "", has a score of 0, and by these definitions even the empty alignment is a better local alignment than that shown in Figure 7.24.

We can encode this observation in the building of the score table. Any time we would enter a score that is less than 0, we can simply enter 0 instead, and *during the traceback encountering a 0 indicates a stopping point* (Figure 7.25). By doing this, any score in the table would also be the local score for an alignment ending there, since the last cell in a traceback has score 0 (rather than something like −2 as in the above example). The base cases of the table (cells along the top and left) can also be set to 0, as these are valid stopping points as well.

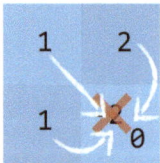

Figure 7.25: When filling the score table for a local alignment, any time a score would be negative we can simply replace it with a 0, indicating that any traceback can stop at this point to maximize the score.

Only a few modifications are necessary for local alignment. First, base-cases should be scored as 0 (Figure 7.26.1). It also doesn't matter what the from entries are for any 0 cells because any traceback will stop when seeing a 0. Second, when computing the best score for a cell, we never let the score be less than 0 (Figure 7.26.2). Third, when computing a traceback, we start not at the lower-right corner of the table, but rather in the largest scoring cell (Figure 7.26.3). Lastly, when computing the traceback, rather than stopping when we reach the upper-left corner of the table, we stop when we reach a score of 0 (Figure 7.26.4).

Everything else is the same, though we might want to rename the function to reflect its change in behavior (example usage in Figure 7.27). This algorithm is known as the Smith-Waterman alignment algorithm (after their 1981 paper describing the method), and forms the foundation for many sequence-matching tools.

```
# ...
row <- 1
for(col in seq(2, length(a_in))) {
  score[row,col] <- 0
}

col <- 1
for(row in seq(2, length(b_in))) {
  score[row,col] <- 0
}
# ...
```

Figure 7.26.1: Modified version of Figure 7.21.2 for local alignment.

```
    # ...
    if(upscore > bestscore) {
      bestscore <- upscore
      bestfrom <- "up"
    }
    score[row,col] <- max(bestscore,0)
    from[row,col] <- bestfrom
    # ...
```

Figure 7.26.2: Modified version of Figure 7.21.4 for local alignment.

```
# ...
best_score <- -1
bestrow <- 1
bestcol <- 1
for(rownum in seq(1, nrow(score))) {      # check every cell
  for(colnum in seq(1, ncol(score))) {    # keep largest location
    if(score[rownum, colnum] > best_score) {
      best_score <- score[rownum, colnum]
      bestrow <- rownum
      bestcol <- colnum
    }
  }
}

currentrow <- bestrow
currentcol <- bestcol

a_out <- rstack()
b_out <- rstack()
# ...
```

Figure 7.26.3: Modified version of Figure 7.21.5 for local alignment.

```
# ...
while(score[currentrow,currentcol] != 0) {
  arrow <- from[currentrow, currentcol]
# ...
```

Figure 7.26.4: Modified version of Figure 7.21.6 for local alignment.

Figure 7.27: Utilizing the dynamic program for determining the optimal *local* alignment. Here the ends of the two sequences purposely include non-matching non-DNA characters for illustration.

```
a <- char_vec("@XXXATGACGATAYYY")
b <- char_vec("@ZZZATGCCATAQQQ")
answer <- local_aln_dp(a, b)
print(unvec_char(answer$a_out))     # ATGACGATA
print(unvec_char(answer$b_out))     # ATGCC-ATA
```

7.5   Heuristification

The dynamic programs in this chapter utilize $O(nm)$ time and memory to fill out and store the score and from tables, where n and m are the lengths of the input sequences. This is quite a lot, especially for local alignment–the time complexity of finding them does not scale with the size of the local match we are looking for, but rather the sizes of the overall input sequences. Finding two matching short sequences (say, 1,000 DNA bases of a gene) amongst two much longer sequences (inside a pair of 100,000,000-character chromosome sequences, for example) becomes nearly impossible.

How might we get around this? Suppose, for the sake of argument, we are busy working on a score table for the local alignment dynamic program (using a pencil and paper rather than a computer). As we are doing so, a wise monk approaches.

"Ah, friends, I see you are working on a dynamic program, seeking a local match between these two very large sequences."

"As it happens, I am well-versed in such matters. I think you will find that there is indeed a good match in this table, and it begins at row 1,456, column 1,672."

This seems a bit odd, but we may as well take the advice and start our search at this cell (ignoring all columns left of 1,672 and all rows above 1,456). In fact, since the monk said that the alignment we would find has a good score, we won't even search all rows and columns to the right and below this position. Rather, we'll fill out the cells rows-by-row, but any scores that are below some threshold we'll simply consider to be $-\infty$ and stop the search along that row. This will restrict the amount of table we need to fill out to be in the area of the optimal alignment. With that done, we can find the highest scoring cell in the searched area, and utilize the traceback rules to construct the local alignment our monk friend hinted at (Figure 7.28).

This strategy may not find the *optimal* local alignment (the maximum scoring one if we had filled out the whole table) for two reasons. First, our friend simply told us where a "good" alignment started, not the optimal. Second, part of the optimal local alignment might lie outside of the searched region; this depends on the cutoff

cell 1456,1672

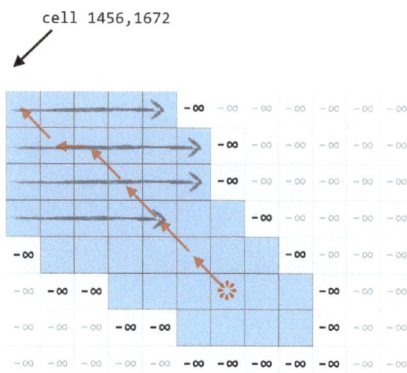

Figure 7.28: Performing a heuristic local alignment, given information that a good local alignment begins in row 1,456 column 1,672.

used to replace low scores with $-\infty$. We are very likely to find a good alignment (perhaps even the optimal one), but we argue for it without giving any guarantees. Such a strategy is known as a *heuristic*.

SADLY, WE HAVE NO ACCESS TO SUCH A WISE MONK. What about a somewhat less-wise monk? We begin another alignment, and he appears:

"Ah, friend. I am but a student of sequence alignment. I cannot tell you the start location for a good local alignment in your table. But, I do know there is a good local alignment present in your table, and I can tell you that the cell at row 256, column 512 is somewhere in the middle of it. I'm sorry, but that's all the help I can provide..."

This second monk provides some valuable information, but can we effectively make use of it? Based on the above we know how to *start* a local alignment at a given cell, but if the cell is in the middle of a good alignment, we'll only recover the latter half of that alignment.

Here is where we refer back to the alternative recursive formulation for sequence alignment in Equation 6.2 (page 88). This formulation prescribes not only an alternative recursive method, but also an alternative dynamic program. In the original dynamic program, scores are computed from the beginning of α and β forwards and the traceback is computed from the ends backwards. In the alternative, scores are computed from the ends backward, and the traceback would occur from the beginnings moving forward (Figure 7.29).

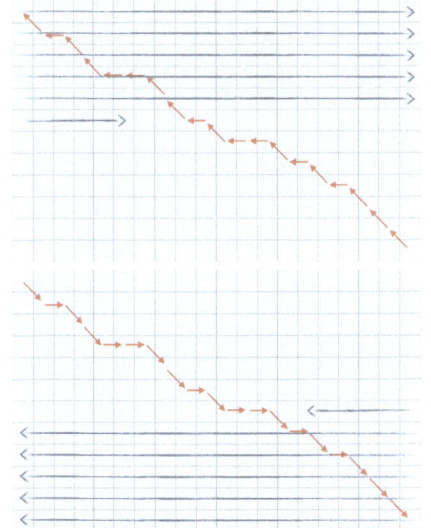

Figure 7.29: In the normal formulation, the scores are computed from the upper-left to the lower right, and the traceback occurs from the lower-right to the upper-left (top). In the alternative formulation these directions are reversed, but both methods produce an optimal alignment, as discussed on page 88.

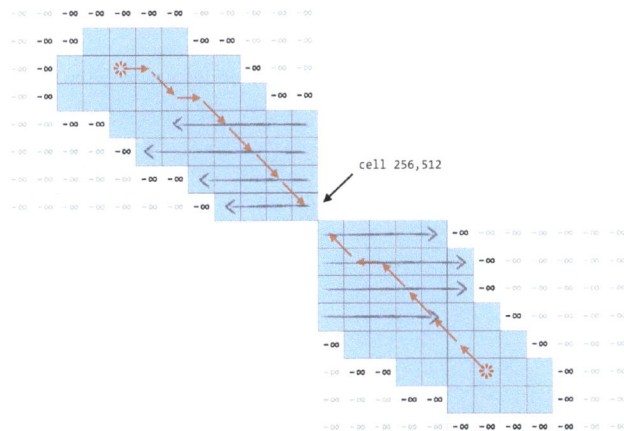

cell 256,512

Figure 7.30: Given the location of a cell in the middle of a good alignment, score-limited normal-formulation and alternative-formulation dynamic programs can be used to compute the left and right halves.

Thus, if we are given information that a cell occurs in the middle of a good local alignment, we can compute its *right* half by using the normal dynamic programming formulation, and its *left* half by using the alternative formulation! This is illustrated in Figure 7.30. Here, we'll refer the reader to a portion of Figure 3 of "Gapped

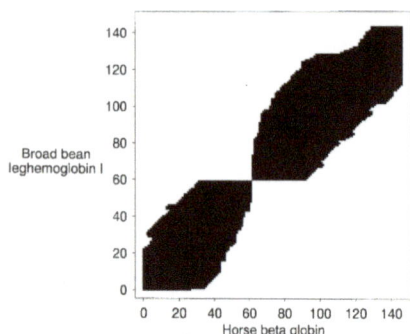

Figure 7.31: A portion of Figure 3 of "Gapped BLAST and PSI-BLAST, a new generation of protein database search programs" by Altschul et al., 1997.

Keys		Values
"ACGACGAGTAC"	->	SeqA@634, SeqB@1328, …
"CGACGAGTACT"	->	SeqA@635, SeqB@1329, …
"GACGAGTACTG"	->	SeqA@636, SeqB@1330, …
…		

Figure 7.32: A hash table storing all 11-base subsequences as keys, with the values indicating which sequences contain those subsequences and at what positions.

[5] Hash tables are sometimes used for this purpose, where *row, column* pairs are used as keys to store the values. Keys not found in the table are assumed to have a default value such as 0 or $-\infty$.

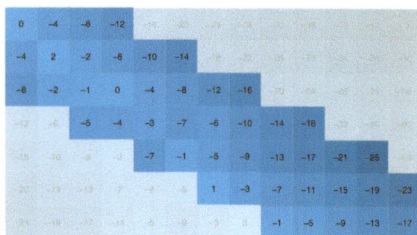

Figure 7.33: In banded alignment, only information for a narrow band around the diagonal is computed. This can be done with a sparse matrix, or by storing the band as a rectangular matrix with each column being associated with an offset.

BLAST and PSI-BLAST, a new generation of protein database search programs" by Stephen Altschul et al., in the Journal Nucleic Acids Research (Vol 25, 1997; Figure 7.31.) The BLAST tool described in this paper uses a refinement of this strategy (along with some sophisticated statistics to consider the fact that local alignments may occur by chance) and is one of the most popular tools in modern computational biology. As of this writing, this paper has over 55,000 citations.

This is all well and good, though we're still making use of a hypothetical "monk" who tells us the locations of cells likely to be contained in good local alignments. One way we could do this for ourselves is to identify small *exact* matches between the two strings, called "seeds." For example, if we knew that ATGACGAGTAC occurred at positions 634–644 of α and positions 1,328–1,338 of β, then the cell at row 1,328 column 634 is likely to be part of a good local alignment since it contains at least 11 exactly matching characters.

In fact, we could pre-compute all the 11-base subsequences of any number of long sequences, and organize them in a hash table! To determine whether a query sequence γ has any matches in this "database," we can simply consider every 11-base subsequence of γ and look up the entries in the table (Figure 7.32). This is essentially the strategy that BLAST uses to search for local matches between a single query and a large set of potentially matching sequences.

THERE ARE A COUPLE OF FINAL OPTIMIZATIONS THAT ARE OFTEN CONSIDERED. The first is that, for local alignment, the area of the score table we are interested in is much smaller than the size of the entire matrix. Considering memory usage, it would be wasteful to only make use of a 100×100 area of a $1,000,000 \times 1,000,000$ score table. (If each entry is one byte, the latter requires 1 Terabyte of memory!) Often, a *sparse matrix* of some kind is used, which acts like a normal matrix but doesn't explicitly store redundant default values.[5]

Are there any alternatives to the large memory requirements for global alignment, where the traceback must follow from the lower-right corner to the upper-left? There are. The first, simplest solution is to use a heuristic known as *banded alignment*. This is similar to the heuristic used by BLAST, where only part of the matrix is considered–in this case a narrow band of cells along the diagonal from lower-right to upper-left (Figure 7.33). It may be that an optimal alignment deviates from this, but if the two sequences are similar this is unlikely. Banded alignment works well for similar sequences, but not so well for alignments requiring many gaps. Some approaches try an initial narrow band, and if the scores indicate it is too narrow, increase the band size and try again.

A beautiful approached for global alignment that uses much less memory ($O(n)$ as opposed to $O(mn)$) is called *Hirschberg's algorithm*. This method fills out the score matrix for the dynamic program and traceback, but does so recursively.[6] The essense of the algorithm lies in identifying–as efficiently (in memory used) as possible–which cells in the middle two rows of the table the traceback path will intersect. This can be done by computing scores (and "from" information) in a row-by-row fashion, but only storing the most recent row in order to compute the next. This proceeds in the forward fashion to the middle row. Next, the same process happens in the reverse starting at the bottom right (using the "alternative formulation" discussed above), and where these two collide provides one small part of the overall traceback path (Figure 7.34, top).

With these neighboring cells identified, the same process can be recursively computed on the upper-left qaudrant of the matrix defined by the cells found, and then again on the lower-right quadrant of the matrix (Figure 7.34, bottom). In this way, at most one or two full rows of information need to stored, even though cell scores will be computed many times. Fortunately, only $1/2$ of the scores will be computed twice, only $1/4$ of the cell scores need to be computed three times, $1/8$ four times, and so on. Because $1 + 1/2 + 1/4 + \cdots \leq 2$, the total runtime of Hirshberg's algorithm is only twice that of normal global alignment (still $O(nm)$) but uses much less memory ($O(n)$, or "linear space").

This is only a sketch of the algorithm; for details we refer the reader to a more comprehensive bioinformatics text such as *An Introduction to Bioinformatics Algorithms* by Neil C. Jones and Pavel A. Pevzner.

[6] Hirschberg's algorithm is particularly fascinating because it recursively solves a dynamic program, itself representing a recursively defined process!

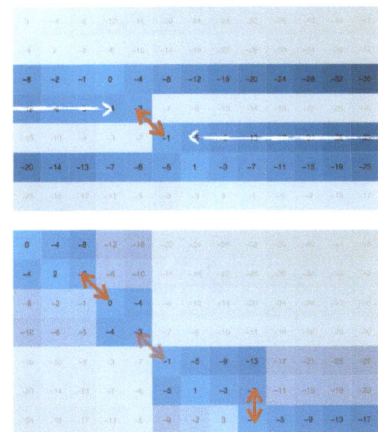

Figure 7.34: Hirschberg's algorithm finds the traceback path in the dynamic programming tables recursively. To start, pairs of rows are scanned from the top and bottom to find a small part of the traceback path near the middle row (top). Then the upper-left quadrant and lower-right quadrants are solved recursively (bottom).

7.6 Alternative Scoring Rules, Multiple Alignment

As we saw, only simple modifications to the scoring and traceback rules were needed to convert global alignment into local alignment. Other adjustments can be used to produce other alignment types.

The first modification is for *end-gap-free alignments*–these allow for overhangs at the start or end of α and/or β to be scored as 0, or "free." These are useful when both sequences are sourced from similar template sequences and potentially overlap (Figure 7.35). This is common in genome assembly applications where short fragments are sequenced from a longer chromosome and need to be pieced back together.

To allow for free end-gaps, the dynamic program is adjusted so that scores along the top row and left-hand column are all 0 (rather than increasingly negative gap costs). This allows the traceback to "stop" anywhere along either sequence (and free gaps are assumed

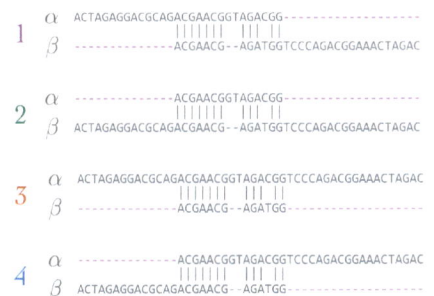

Figure 7.35: In end-gap-free alignment, gaps occurring at the beginning or end of the alignment (shown in purple) do not count against the alignment score, allowing the algorithm to align two sequences drawn from different portions of similar template sequences. The four general types are shown.

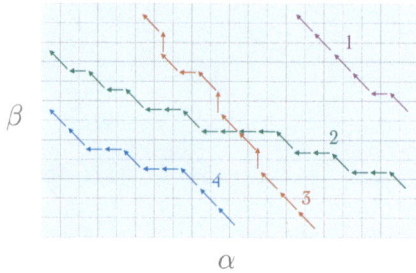

β

α

Figure 7.36: Traceback paths for the four potential types of end-gap-free alignments, which start at the highest-scoring cell along the bottom or right, and end at the first cell encountered along the top or left.

[7] The particulars of this are best left to advanced courses in evolutionary biology. In some cases repeated additions or deletions may not be causal, but an artifact of the non-uniform nature of mutation. In other cases a single modification could increase the likelihood of future mutations. For example, if a removal causes a gene sequence to become non-functional (and this doesn't cause the lineage to go extinct), then future mutations to the same region carry less risk of ill effects.

```
ATACGCTAGCT
| | |     | | |
AAAC- - - -GCT
```

Figure 7.37: Affine-gap alignments score gaps in a series differently that standard alignment; usually the first gap incurs a severe penalty, and subsequent gaps less so to account for evolutionary patterns.

Figure 7.38: The simplest way to implement affine-gap alignment costs is to consider different-length "jumps" for each sub-problem, with each having a different cost associated as desired.

to fill out the rest). The traceback starts not in the lower-right corner, but rather at the largest scoring cell along the bottom row or right-hand column, allowing the free gaps at the other end. Figure 7.36 shows the four possible types of traceback paths corresponding to the four types of alignments in Figure 7.35.

A more sophisticated modification provides for *affine-gap* alignments, which consider a tricky biological reality that not all gaps are created equal. In an evolutionary tree (see Figure 6.2, page 83), once a gap has been introduced by the loss of a DNA base or addition of a new base, it can be more likely that future losses or additions may occur at the same location.[7] To account for this, affine-gap scoring associates a large cost with the first in a series of gaps, but smaller costs with subsequent gaps (Figure 7.37).

There are at least a couple of ways to implement affine-gap penalties. The easiest (and slowest) extends the idea of "from" arrows so that an "up" arrow (or "left" as the case may be) might be longer than a single cell, with the associated cost computed as desired from the length (Figure 7.38). This means, however, that when filling out the score table each cell depends on not just three neighboring subproblems, but many. A more efficient solution makes use of multiple scoring tables with "from" arrows that might move between them. For more information on this topic we again refer to *An Introduction to Bioinformatics Algorithms* by Jones and Pevzner.

FOR THIS CHAPTER AND THE LAST, we've considered aligning only two sequences, α and β. The idea can be extended to three sequences; consider the seven possible ending configurations for sequences α, β, and δ. When computing a multi-way aligment, we consider all combinations for scoring. (An alignment of "T" with "A" with "-", for example, incurs the T/A cost, the A/- cost, and the -/T cost.)

$$\underbrace{\begin{pmatrix} p_\alpha e_\alpha \text{ aligned w/} \\ p_\beta e_\beta \text{ aligned w/} \\ p_\delta \end{pmatrix}\begin{matrix} - \\ - \\ e_\delta \end{matrix}}_{aln_1}, \; score = S(aln_1) + S(-,-) + S(-,e_\delta) + S(e_\delta,-)$$

$$\underbrace{\begin{pmatrix} p_\alpha \text{ aligned w/} \\ p_\beta e_\beta \text{ aligned w/} \\ p_\delta e_\delta \end{pmatrix}\begin{matrix} e_\alpha \\ - \\ - \end{matrix}}_{aln_2}, \; score = S(aln_2) + S(e_\alpha,-) + S(-,-) + S(-,e_\alpha)$$

$$\underbrace{\begin{pmatrix} p_\alpha e_\alpha \text{ aligned w/} \\ p_\beta \text{ aligned w/} \\ p_\delta e_\delta \end{pmatrix}\begin{matrix} - \\ e_\beta \\ - \end{matrix}}_{aln_3}, \; score = S(aln_3) + S(-,e_\beta) + S(e_\beta,-) + S(-,-)$$

$$\underbrace{\begin{pmatrix} p_\alpha e_\alpha \text{ aligned w/} \\ p_\beta \text{ aligned w/} \\ p_\delta \end{pmatrix}}_{aln_4} \begin{matrix} - \\ e_\beta, \\ e_\delta \end{matrix} \ score = S(aln_4) + S(-,e_\beta) + S(e_\beta,e_\delta) + S(e_\delta,-)$$

$$\underbrace{\begin{pmatrix} p_\alpha \text{ aligned w/} \\ p_\beta e_\beta \text{ aligned w/} \\ p_\delta \end{pmatrix}}_{aln_5} \begin{matrix} e_\alpha \\ -, \\ e_\delta \end{matrix} \ score = S(aln_5) + S(e_\alpha,-) + S(-,e_\delta) + S(e_\delta,e_\alpha)$$

$$\underbrace{\begin{pmatrix} p_\alpha \text{ aligned w/} \\ p_\beta \text{ aligned w/} \\ p_\delta e_\beta \end{pmatrix}}_{aln_6} \begin{matrix} e_\alpha \\ e_\beta, \\ - \end{matrix} \ score = S(aln_6) + S(e_\alpha,e_\beta) + S(e_\beta,-) + S(-,e_\alpha)$$

$$\underbrace{\begin{pmatrix} p_\alpha \text{ aligned w/} \\ p_\beta \text{ aligned w/} \\ p_\delta \end{pmatrix}}_{aln_7} \begin{matrix} e_\alpha \\ e_\beta, \\ e_\delta \end{matrix} \ score = S(aln_7) + S(e_\alpha,e_\beta) + S(e_\beta,e_\delta) + S(e_\delta,e_\alpha)$$

Since there are 3 input sequences, there are $2^3 - 1$ ending configurations to consider–2 choices for how we end the α portion (e_α and $-$), times 2 for β, times 2 for δ, minus the obviously unnecessary -/-/- option. A memoized, recursive solution would follow much the same strategy as in the last chapter. Similarly, a dynamic program would follow in the footsteps of this chapter: these seven options can be cast as potential "from" arrows in a 3-dimensional table! (Figure 7.39.) Although more difficult to visualize, aligning four sequences can be accomplished with 4-dimensional matrices, each cell of which depends on $2^4 - 1$ neighboring cells.[8]

While such *multiple alignments* allow biologists to compare many sequences simultaneously, in practice this method is far too slow. If α has n characters, β has m, and δ has l, the time needed to fill out the 3-dimensional table is $O(nml)$. Adding a fourth sequence of length k increases the runtime to $O(nmlk)$. In general, the time necessary grows exponentially with the number of input sequences. Real multiple-alignment programs turn away from this optimal approach and again turn to much faster (but not gauranteed to produce score-maximizing alignment) heuristics.

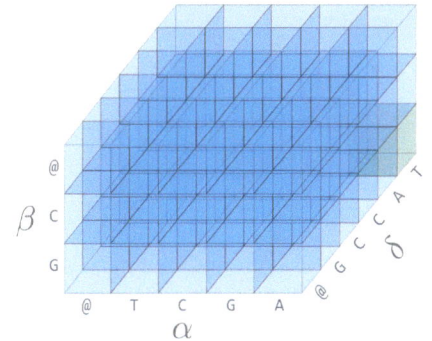

Figure 7.39: The dynamic programming solution for three-sequence multiple alignment would utilize 3-dimensional score and from matrices. The global alignment would start the traceback from the green cell; neighboring solutions are represented by the seven cells touching it.

[8] I find it interesting that "base cases" of higher-dimensional alignments are instances of lower-dimensional alignments. For example, any subproblem along a "wall" of the 3-dimensional table is an instance of 2-dimensional alignment, with the third sequence filled out by gaps. From this, it is possible to design a general n-way dynamic program that relies on itself (recursively) to compute solutions for lower-dimensional walls in dimension $n - 1$.

Exercises

1. Try implementing end-gap-free alignment.

2. Try implementing affine-gap alignment with the naïve algorithm described.

3. Try implementing 3-sequence global alignment, using the algorithm for 2-sequence alignment if one of the three inputs is just "@".

8   Hidden Markov Models

> On two occasions I have been asked, 'Pray, Mr. Babbage, if you put into the machine wrong figures, will the right answers come out?' I am not able rightly to apprehend the kind of confusion of ideas that could provoke such a question.
>
> Charles Babbage, 1864

Many topics in computer science constitute a sort of "algorithmic forensics:" given a set of observations, what happened to produce them? In some cases, we have a good idea of the underlying "model" and our goal is to figure out how our observations fit into the model. Hidden Markov Models (HMMs, after late 19th century Russian mathematician Andrey Markov) are a common example.

Suppose, for the moment, that we are security guards working deep underground for months at a time at the NORAD compound (North American Aerospace Defense Command), inside Cheyenne Mountain in Colorado. As amateur meteorologists, based on historical newspapers we've built a simple weather model: the weather tomorrow will most likely be like the weather today. To quantify this, if any given day is sunny then it will be sunny the next day with 75% probability and rainy with the remaining 25% probability. On the other hand, if it is rainy, then the next day will be rainy 70% of the time and sunny 30% of the time. These two *states*–sunny (s) and rainy (r)–represent our model of the world, and our model satisfies the *Markov property*: that the probability of moving to a state depends only on the immediately previous state. After five rainy days the sixth will be rainy with 70% probability; similarly after ten rainy days the eleventh will also be rainy with 70% probability.

But this is not the entire story. As mere security guards stuck inside, we can't actually observe the weather.[1] Fortunately, our friend the General lives outside the base, and every day he comes to work passing by our security station either carrying an umbrella,

[1] We should probably pick a different hobby. Programming, maybe.

or not. From talking to his friends, we know that he tends to carry an umbrella on rainy days, but he forgets it on about 20% of those rainy days. Similarly, he usually doesn't carry it on sunny days, but brings it just in case 10% of the time. All of this information together represents our Hidden Markov Model, where "umbrella" (u) and "no umbrella" (n) are possible observations influenced by the (hidden from us) states 8.1.

Given a model like this, there are a number of questions we might ask. Supposing we start on a sunny day, what is the probability it will be rainy exactly 10 days later? What is the probability that we'll see an umbrella on day 20? In the long term, what percentage of days will be sunny?

All of these questions can be answered using the many beautiful mathematical theories developed for Hidden Markov Models.[2] For a practical perspective, we'll focus in this chapter on a single question: given a sequence of Umbrella/No Umbrella observations like n, n, n, u, n, u, u, u, u, n, u, n, n, n, what is the *most likely* sequence of underlying states? (More plainly: what was most probably the weather on those days?)

This is a well-formed question. Consider a shorter sequence like n, u. The likelihood that the underlying states were s, s is [probability of n being observed from state s] × [probability that state s transitions to state s] × [probability of u being observed from state s], or $(0.9)(0.75)(0.1) = 0.0675$. A similar calculation shows that the likelihood of s, r is $(0.9)(0.25)(0.8) = 0.18$.[3] Given an observation sequence, we simply want to find a state sequence maximizing this likelihood.

But this is also not an easy question. One possible strategy for finding the most likely state sequence is to consider *all* possible state sequences, compute the likelihood for each as described above, and keep the most likely one. However, the number of possible state sequences is (number of states)$^{\text{(number of observations)}}$ (two possible states for day 1, times two for day 2, and so on). If our sequence was 20 days long, there would be 1,048,576 possible state sequences to check; at 30 days, there are over a billion! Clearly we need a better strategy.

HIDDEN MARKOV MODELS can be used to represent a huge variety of processes. Those involving chance immediately come to mind, such as measurements made with scientific instruments prone to error. Many games like poker and roulette can be modeled probabilistically, though they may or may not have a "hidden" component.

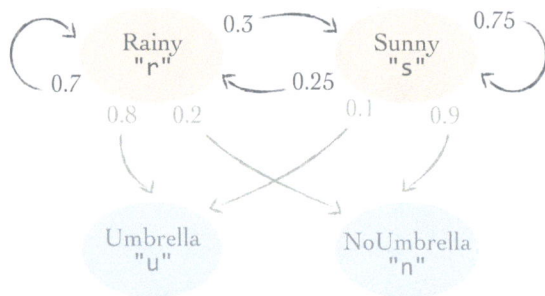

Figure 8.1: Graphical representation for the rainy/sunny Hidden Markov Model, with states shown in pink, and possible observations shown in blue.

[2] The excellent book *Probability and Computing* by Mitzenmacher and Upfal covers a variety of these results.

[3] Although "likelihood" and "probability" are closely related, they are not quite the same thing. Probability measures the chance of an outcome from a random process, while likelihood measures the probability that a hypothesized model produced some outcome (for discrete situations at least, such as our weather model).

HMMs have also been successfully applied to processes that we don't usually think of as random, such as text-to-speech applications where the observations are sound waves, and the hidden states are words or letter combinations. In the realm of bioinformatics, HMMs are commonly used to identify regions of DNA with specific properties.

The "central dogma" of molecular biology holds that "gene" regions of DNA sequences are transcribed into messenger RNA (potentially with some subsections, called introns, removed). These are then translated in three-base chunks into an amino acid sequence that folds in 3 dimensions to become a building block of life: a protein (Figure 8.2).

In many species, the overall makeup of the DNA is biased, for example consisting of 80% As and Ts and only 20% Cs and Gs. Furthermore, there are often patterns and trends that distinguish gene sequences from the surrounding DNA. In real gene finding applications, these patterns and the models that represent them are amazingly complex and are generated by analyzing many sequences in related species.

For this discussion we'll assume an extremely simple model: a genome that is 80% As and Ts in non-gene ("n") regions, and 25% As, Ts, Cs, and Gs in gene ("g") regions. Further, we'll assume that the genome starts in a non-gene region, and that each position can transition from a non-gene position to a gene position with 1% probability, and gene positions can transition to non-gene positions with 5% probability (Figure 8.3).

8.1 Generating Sequences

How might we represent a Hidden Markov Model like the above in code? There are a number of possibilities. We might store the state transition probabilities in a hash table, with a key for each state and the corresponding probabilities as values. Alternatively we could could use a matrix, with each row/column combination representing a particular transition probability. Since R supports matrices natively, we'll use this representation (Figure 8.4).

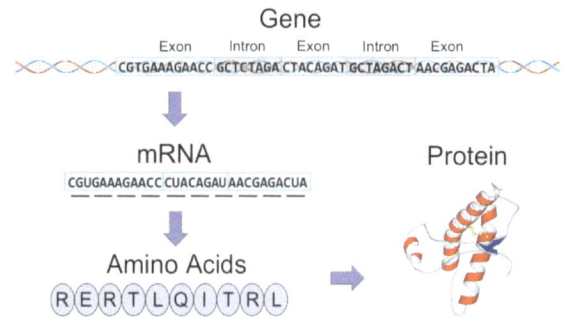

Figure 8.2: The "central dogma" of molecular biology describes the transcription/translation process whereby genic regions in the DNA are turned into functional proteins.

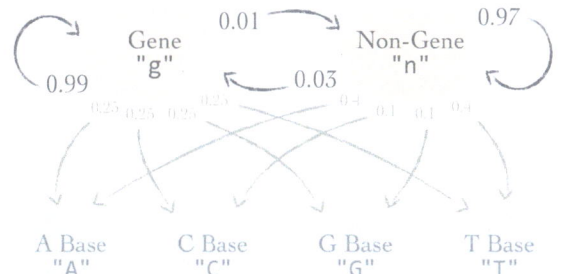

Figure 8.3: Graphical representation for the gene/non-gene Hidden Markov Model.

Figure 8.4: Representing state transition probabilities with an R matrix, including named rows and columns.

```
trans_probs <- matrix(nrow = 2, ncol = 2,
                      dimnames = list(c("g", "n"), c("g", "n")))

trans_probs["g", "g"] <- 0.97
trans_probs["g", "n"] <- 0.03
trans_probs["n", "n"] <- 0.99
trans_probs["n", "g"] <- 0.01

print(trans_probs)
```

```
     g    n
g 0.97 0.03
n 0.01 0.99
```

Figure 8.5: Output for Figure 8.4, representing transition probabilities (from row to column).

The code and printed output (Figure 8.5) reveal that we can name the rows and columns, and access individual entries by name, as in trans_probs["g", "n"], storing the probability of transitioning from a gene to a non-gene state. Similarly, we'll encode the observation probabilities in a two by four matrix (Figure 8.6, output in Figure 8.7).

Figure 8.6: Representing observation probabilities.

```
obs_probs <- matrix(nrow = 2, ncol = 4,
                    dimnames = list(c("g", "n"),
                                    c("A", "C", "G", "T")))
obs_probs["g", "A"] <- 0.25
obs_probs["g", "C"] <- 0.25
obs_probs["g", "G"] <- 0.25
obs_probs["g", "T"] <- 0.25
obs_probs["n", "A"] <- 0.4
obs_probs["n", "C"] <- 0.1
obs_probs["n", "G"] <- 0.1
obs_probs["n", "T"] <- 0.4

print(obs_probs)
```

```
     A    C    G    T
g 0.25 0.25 0.25 0.25
n 0.40 0.10 0.10 0.40
```

Figure 8.7: Output for Figure 8.6, representing observation probabilities.

R provides convenient syntax for working with named matrices. For example, probs <- trans_probs["g",] assigns to probs the "g" row as a named vector; names(probs) thus returns the character vector c("g", "n") while probs itself contains the numeric vector c(0.97, 0.03). The sample() function returns a random sample from a vector; it takes an optional size parameter specifying the sample size, and a prob parameter specifying the sampling distribution vector. Thus, sample(names(probs), size = 1, prob = probs) returns "g" with 97% probability and "n" with 3% probability (representing a random transition from the original "g"). We can use these to write a function random_next_state() that, given the trans_probs matrix and a "current" state, randomly selects a new state and returns it. A very similar function random_obs() generates a random observation from a given state 8.8).

With these functions in hand, we can write another that generates a random sequence of states and corresponding outputs. The function will need both the trans_probs and obs_probs matrices,

```r
random_next_state <- function(trans_probs, current) {
  probs <- trans_probs[current, ]   # named probability vector
  randstate <- sample(names(probs), size = 1, prob = probs)
  return(randstate)
}

random_obs <- function(obs_probs, state) {
  probs <- obs_probs[state, ]
  randobs <- sample(names(probs), size = 1, prob = probs)
  return(randobs)
}

print(random_next_state(trans_probs, "g"))   # e.g. "g"
print(random_obs(obs_probs, "g"))            # e.g. "A"
```

Figure 8.8: Functions for generating a random next states and random observations.

as well as a state to start in and the sequence length to generate (n). But what should this function output? For easy manipulation, we'll return a data frame with three columns: 1) a state column containing each visited state, 2) an observation column obs containing the sequence of observations, and 3) a "position" column pos containing the position of each state in the sequence (1, 2, 3, etc.). We'll initially build this sequence as an rstack of lists for speed, before converting it to a data frame to return (Figure 8.9; we'll also order the table so that state 1 is at the top).

```r
generate_seq <- function(trans_probs, obs_probs, init_state, n) {
  seqstack <- rstack()

  state <- init_state
  for(i in seq(1, n)) {
    # get random observation for the current state:
    obs <- random_obs(obs_probs, state)
    new_row <- list(pos = i, state = state, obs = obs)
    seqstack <- insert_top(seqstack, new_row)
    # update state by random transition:
    state <- random_next_state(trans_probs, state)
  }

  df <- as.data.frame(seqstack, stringsAsFactors = FALSE)
  df <- df[order(df$pos), ]            # order rows by position
  return(df)
}

seq_df <- generate_seq(trans_probs, obs_probs, "n", 500)
print(head(seq_df))
```

Figure 8.9: Generating a random sequence of states and observations as a data frame.

One of the advantages of representing a sequence as a data frame is that we can easily visualize it with ggplot2. We'll color A and T observations red and orange, and C and G observations blue and green, to distinguish the two groups (Figures 8.11 and 8.12).

	pos	state	obs
500	1	n	T
499	2	n	C
498	3	n	T
497	4	n	G
496	5	n	T
495	6	n	A

Figure 8.10: Output for Figure 8.9, a random sequence of states and observations as a data frame.

Figure 8.11: Plotting a state and observation sequence data frame.

```
p <- ggplot(seq_df) +
    geom_tile(aes(x = pos, y = state, fill = obs)) +
    scale_fill_manual(values = c("#CC3300", "#006699",
                                  "#00CC66", "#CC6633"),
                        name = "Observation") +
    scale_x_continuous(name = "Position") +
    scale_y_discrete(name = "State")
plot(p)
```

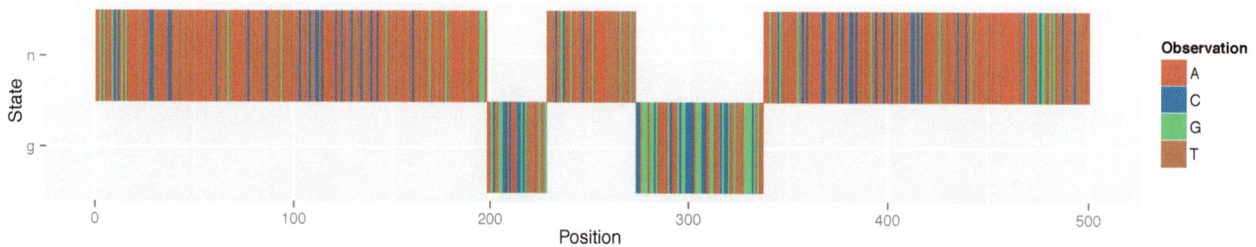

Figure 8.12: Plotted output for Figure 8.11.

Because non-gene regions are biased toward A and T, we see these regions as more strongly red and orange; by contrast genic regions are evenly distributed amongst A, C, T, and G.

8.2 The Viterbi Algorithm

Generating sequences from Markov Models is well and good, but the main problem remains: given only a sequence of observations (as in obs <- seq_df$obs and then ignoring seq_df), what is the most likely sequence of underlying states that generated it? This is sometimes known as "decoding" the observation sequence. The method for decoding is known as the Viterbi algorithm, after the American electrical engineer who invented it in 1967. The Viterbi algorithm is a dynamic programming method, but we'll start with (what else?) a recursive implementation.

Rather than attack the question directly, we break it out into cases. For each possible state s, what is the most likely sequence of states (for the first observation to the last observation) that ends in s? From these choices, we'll just keep the overall most likely. For example, suppose the last observation is A, and the most likely state sequence that ends in n has likelihood 0.000021, while the most likely state sequence that ends in g has likelihood 0.000065. Since g outputs A with 25% probability and n outputs A with 80%, the .....n option has overall likelihood $0.000021 \times 0.80 = 0.0000168$, and the .....g option has overall likelihood $0.000065 \times 0.25 = 0.00001625$. The result? We can conclude that the .....n state sequence is the more likely, with with likelihood 0.0000168.[4]

Of course, for this strategy to work, we need to actually compute

[4] This observation–that an answer must end in one of the valid options–is not too dissimilar from the observation on page 87 than a global sequence alignment must end with $\frac{e_\alpha}{-}$, $\frac{e_\alpha}{e_\beta}$, or $\frac{-}{e_\beta}$!

the most likely state sequence ending in n (or g, as the case may be) and its likelihood. The function we we'll write will operate as decode(trans_probs, obs_probs, obs_vec, end_state), where trans_probs and obs_probs are the transition and observation probability matrices, obs_vec is a vector of observations we are trying to decode, and end_state is the desired ending state (either "n" or "g" here).

```
decode <- function(trans_probs, obs_probs, obs_vec, end_state) {
  # to be continued...
```

Figure 8.13.1: The "signature" for our recursive decoding algorithm. (A function's signature describes its name, the parameters it takes, and sometimes the type of the return value.)

The function should return a list with components representing an answer: an entry for state_vec (a vector holding the most likely state sequence ending in end_state), and lhood (the likelihood). We'll also include the pertinent inputs obs_vec and end_state for later use. The easiest version of the problem (the base case), occurs when length(obs_vec) == 1, or when there is only a single observation. Since the end state is specified, the most likely state sequence is simply that ending state, and its likelihood is just obs_probs[end_state, obs_vec] (Figure 8.13.2).

```
# Base case:
if(length(obs_vec) == 1) {
  answer <- list(state_vec = end_state,
                 lhood = obs_probs[end_state, obs_vec],
                 obs_vec = obs_vec,
                 end_state = end_state)
  return(answer)
}

# to be continued ...
```

Figure 8.13.2: The base case for the decode method.

What if obs_vec is longer? In that case, we are essentially trying to solve a slightly smaller version of the overall problem, by decoding all but the last observation (since our given end_state effectively decodes the last observation). Again, we'll break it into cases: for each possible state s, what is the most likely sequence of states (for the first observation to the *second-to-last* observation) that ends in state s? The overall answer is the one with the largest likelihood, after considering the transition from s to end_state, and the likelihood of the last observation from end_state.

We start by extracting the possible states from the row names of trans_probs, the sub-vector of observations from first to second-to-last, and the last observation. A for-loop calls decode() recursively as needed, and the most likely overall answer is kept and returned (Figure 8.13.3).

To test our function, we can construct a small observation sequence that apparently transitions from non-gene (predominantly As and Ts) to gene (predominantly Cs and Gs; Figure 8.14).

Figure 8.13.3: Calling decode() on sub-problems in a for-loop, one for each possible second-to-last state.

```
# Recursive cases (one for each state):
possible_states <- rownames(trans_probs)
obs_subvec <- obs_vec[1:(length(obs_vec) - 1)]
last_obs <- obs_vec[length(obs_vec)]

best_answer <- list(lhood = -Inf) # a "dummy" answer
for(s in possible_states) {
  subanswer <- decode(trans_probs, obs_probs, obs_subvec, s)

  answer <- list(state_vec = c(subanswer$state_vec, end_state),
                 lhood = subanswer$lhood *
                           trans_probs[s, end_state] *
                           obs_probs[end_state, last_obs],
                 obs_vec = obs_vec,
                 end_state = end_state)

  if(answer$lhood > best_answer$lhood) {
    best_answer <- answer
  }
}

return(best_answer)
}
```

Figure 8.14: A small observation vector for testing.

```
obs <- c("A", "T", "A", "T", "T", "A", "C", "G", "G", "C", "G")
```

Over such a short sequence, however, the probability of a gene to non-gene transition is so unlikely (1%) that the most likely state sequence according to the current model will just be non-gene, or "n", all the way through. To compensate for the short length of this test, we'll adjust the probabilities to make "n" → "g" and "g" → "n" transitions a stronger possibility (Figure 8.15).

Figure 8.15: Alternate probabilities matrix considering state transitions more likely.

```
alt_trans_probs <- matrix(nrow = 2, ncol = 2,
                    dimnames = list(c("g", "n"), c("g", "n")))

alt_trans_probs["g", "g"] <- 0.6
alt_trans_probs["g", "n"] <- 0.4
alt_trans_probs["n", "n"] <- 0.7
alt_trans_probs["n", "g"] <- 0.3
```

Now we can run our algorithm, testing to see whether it is more likely that the most likely state sequence ended in a "g" or an "n" (Figure 8.16). If the number of states was larger than two, we might have decided to use a for-loop to test all of them and keep the largest. (Note that this is exactly what the recursive function does!)

```
answer_g <- decode(alt_trans_probs, obs_probs, obs, "g")
answer_n <- decode(alt_trans_probs, obs_probs, obs, "n")
print("Answer g output:")
print(answer_g)
print("Answer n output:")
print(answer_n)
```

Figure 8.16: Testing the viterbi_recursive() function to determine whether the most likely sequence ending in "g" or "n" is more likely.

The output (Figure 8.17) reveals that the sequencing ending in "gene" ("g") is indeed more likely, and the state_vec correctly identifies a good "n" → "g" transition point.

8.3 Log-Likelihoods

Aside from speed concerns relating to massively redundant computation (try visualizing a call tree for this method), there is one fatal flaw in the function we've implemented. Worse, this flaw wouldn't become apparent until we attempted to analyze a long observation sequence.

To see the issue, let's run decode() on the long sequence of observations from Figure 8.9 and compare the likelihoods for answer_g and answer_n (Figure 8.18 assumes the function has been memoized for speed, which we'll leave as an exercise.) In this test the likelihoods of both answer_g and answer_n are reported as 0, so we can't tell which is more likely. But do either of these answers really have a likelihood of 0? No–the likelihoods are just incredibly small, due to the length of the sequences involved.

```
[1] "Answer g output:"
$state_vec
 [1] "n" "n" "n" "n" "n" "n" "g" "g" "g" "g" "g"

$lhood
[1] 2.613825e-08

$obs_vec
 [1] "A" "T" "A" "T" "T" "A" "C" "G" "G" "C" "G"

$end_state
[1] "g"

[1] "Answer n output:"
$state_vec
 [1] "n" "n" "n" "n" "n" "n" "g" "g" "g" "g" "n"

$lhood
[1] 6.970199e-09

$obs_vec
 [1] "A" "T" "A" "T" "T" "A" "C" "G" "G" "C" "G"

$end_state
[1] "n"
```

Figure 8.17: Output for Figure 8.16.

```
obs <- seq_df$obs
answer_g <- decode(trans_probs, obs_probs, obs, "g")
answer_n <- decode(trans_probs, obs_probs, obs, "n")
print(answer_g$lhood)      # prints 0
print(answer_n$lhood)      # prints 0
```

Figure 8.18: Testing decode() on a length-500 observation sequence. Due to round-off errors, the likelihood for both answer_g and answer_n is reported as 0.

The issue here is that computers are not very good at representing very small numbers accurately. Depending on the encoding scheme used, most "real" numbers are rounded to an accuracy of a couple-dozen decimal places. Even R, which specializes in numerical computation, has a lower limit: print(.Machine) reports a minimum number of 2.2e-308 on many machines. This a large amount of precision, but even so, multiplying hundreds of probabilities will quickly produce numbers smaller than this threshold rending our method useless.

Rather than storing likelihoods (numbers between zero and one), we'll work around this problem by storing quantities that are much larger (or at least, not close to zero) that can be converted to likelihoods when needed. We'll do so by exploiting some properties of the logarithm function, log(). Generally, the logarithm of a product of numbers like a, b, and c is the *sum* of the logarithms of the numbers individually:

$$\log(a \times b \times c) = \log(a) + \log(b) + \log(c) \, .$$

If the numbers are between zero and one, then the logarithm will be negative, with numbers closer to zero resulting in negative numbers further from zero:

$$\begin{aligned}\log(0.1 \times 0.2 \times 0.3) &= \log(0.1) + \log(0.2) + \log(0.3) \\ &= -2.302 + -1.669 + -1.203 \\ &= -5.1159 \, .\end{aligned}$$

Because the logarithm is an invertable function (Figure 8.19), we can always get back to the original product by raising the base of the logarithm used (in this case e) to the power of the end result: $e^{-5.1159} = 0.006 = 0.1 \times 0.2 \times 0.3$. Importantly, none of the terms in the addition are very close to 0, so we have no precision issues when computing in this fashion *until* we attempt to convert a log-likelihood back into a (very small) likelihood.

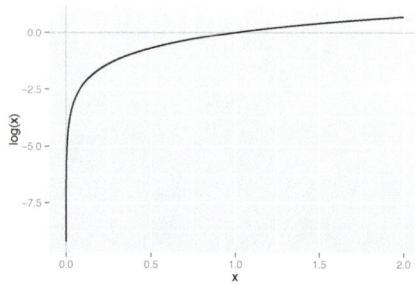

Figure 8.19: The logarithm is an invertable function–given any $log(x)$, we can compute x.

```
# ...
# Base case:
if(length(obs_vec) == 1) {
  answer <- list(state_vec = end_state,
                 lhood = log(obs_probs[end_state, obs_vec]),
                 obs_vec = obs_vec,
                 end_state = end_state)
  return(answer)
}
# ...
```

Figure 8.20.1: Modification for Figure 8.13.2 for computation over log-likelihoods in the base-case.

But, why should we ever need to convert back? Rather than multiply sub-answer likelihoods and transition probabilities, we could simply add sub-answer log-likelihoods to transition log-probabilities. Further, when comparing these values, we simply choose the larger (since if $x > y$, then $\log(x) > \log(y)$). The modification to the function is simple, as shown in Figures 8.20.1 and 8.20.2.

Now, if we redo the test from above, the printed likelihoods are actually log-likelihoods, and we can easily determine which potential answer is most likely (Figure 8.21). In this case the answer ending in "n" is the more likely, matching the true underlying state sequence (Figure 8.12).

```
# ...
for(s in possible_states) {
  subanswer <- decode(trans_probs, obs_probs, obs_subvec, s)

  answer <- list(state_vec = c(subanswer$state_vec, end_state),
                 lhood = subanswer$lhood +
                   log(trans_probs[s, end_state]) +
                   log(obs_probs[end_state, last_obs]),
                 obs_vec = obs_vec,
                 end_state = end_state)
  # ...
```

Figure 8.20.2: Modifications for Figure 8.13.3 for computation over log-likelihoods in the recursive cases.

```
obs <- seq_df$obs
answer_g <- decode(trans_probs, obs_probs, obs, "g")
answer_n <- decode(trans_probs, obs_probs, obs, "n")
print(answer_g$lhood)          # prints -633.288
print(answer_n$lhood)          # prints -628.223
```

Figure 8.21: Long observation sequences can be analyzed using log-likelihoods.

Now we can even visually compare the true state sequence (and the observations) with the computed most likely underlying state sequence. We start by adding a called column to the seq_df data frame that currently contains the true state sequence and observations. The entries of this new column will be either "called_n" or "called_g", generated by concatenating the string "called_" to the most-likely state sequence (Figures 8.22, 8.24).

```
seq_df$called <- str_c("called_", answer_n$state_vec)
print(head(seq_df))

p <- ggplot(seq_df) +
    geom_tile(aes(x = pos, y = state, fill = obs)) +
    geom_tile(aes(x = pos, y = called, fill = obs)) +
    scale_fill_manual(values = c("#CC3300", "#006699",
                                 "#00CC66", "#CC6633"),
                      name = "Observation") +
    scale_x_continuous(name = "Position") +
    scale_y_discrete(name = "State")
plot(p)
```

Figure 8.22: Visualizing the called state sequence in comparison with the true state sequence.

The plotted output (Figure 8.23) shows that even though the Viterbi method computes the *most likely* state sequence, this isn't guaranteed to recapitulate the *true* state sequence. (And after all, if any random process always did the most likely thing, it wouldn't actually be random!)

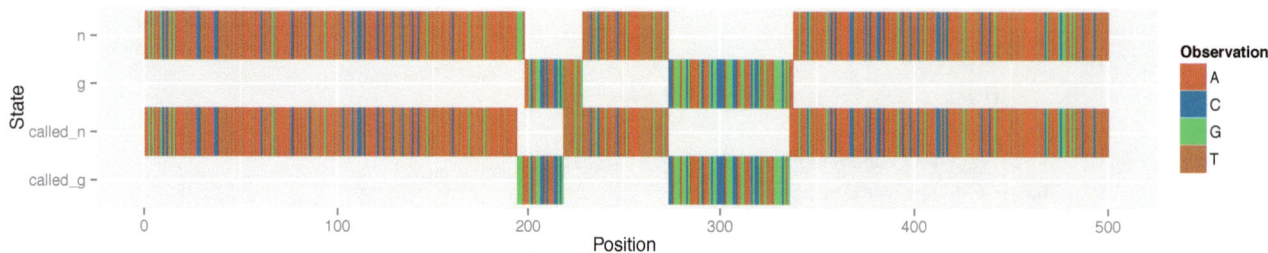

Figure 8.23: Plotted output for Figure 8.22.

	pos	state	obs	called
500	1	n	A	called_n
499	2	n	A	called_n
498	3	n	A	called_n
497	4	n	T	called_n
496	5	n	A	called_n
495	6	n	C	called_n

Figure 8.24: Printed output for Figure 8.22.

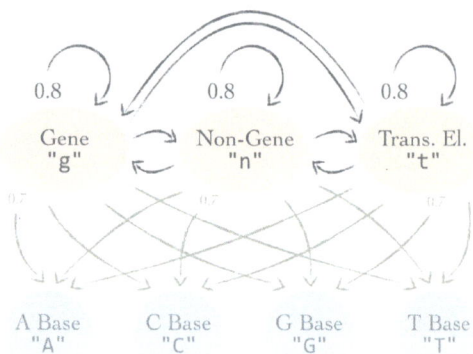

Figure 8.25: Graphical representation for a three-state Hidden Markov Model; all unlabeled edges have weight of 0.1.

Figure 8.26: Generating a moderate-size observation sequence for the three-state model.

8.4   Sub-problems and Dynamic Programming

As with sequence alignment, even though the memoized recursive solution is fast (compared to a non-memoized solution), solving large instances is still impractical due to limitations of the call stack (see page 64). Fortunately, finding most-likely state sequences lends itself well to a dynamic-programming, table-based solution. (As mentioned earlier, the Viterbi algorithm was originally developed as a dynamic program.)

In order to inspect the relationships among sub-problems, we'll plot the sub-problems on a grid as we did for sequence alignment in Figure 7.8 on page 98. To get a better sense of the process, we'll consider a more complex model with another state possibility, "t" for "transposable element." In real genomes, transposable elements are regions of the DNA prone to being replicated in other parts of the genome. For our test we'll represent genic regions as being rich in As, non-gene regions as being rich in Cs, and transposable elements as being rich in Gs. Further, all three states will only transition to another state with 10% probability (Figure 8.25).

After generating transition probability and observation matrices `trans_probs2` and `obs_probs2` (code not shown), we generate a sequence of 50 observations (Figure 8.26).

However, before running `decode()` we need to modify the function so that the answer lists generated store which sub-answer produced the most likely overall answer. This "from" information consists of the sub-answer's input (`obs_vec` and `end_state`). For base cases these will be set to NA. These modifications are found in Figures 8.27.1 and 8.27.2.

```
seq_df2 <- generate_seq(trans_probs2, obs_probs2, "n", 50)
```

Now we can this modified `decode()` function to compute the most likely state sequence for the given observation sequence, `seq_df2$obs`. Rather than consider all three possible answers and

```
# ...
# Base case:
if(length(obs_vec) == 1) {
  answer <- list(state_vec = end_state,
                 lhood = log(obs_probs[end_state, obs_vec]),
                 obs_vec = obs_vec,
                 end_state = end_state,
                 from_obs_vec = NA,
                 from_end_state = NA)
  return(answer)
}
# ...
```

Figure 8.27.1: Modifications to Figure 8.20.1 for keeping track of "from" information in base-case answers.

```
# ...
for(s in possible_states) {
  subanswer <- decode(trans_probs, obs_probs, obs_subvec, s)

  answer <- list(state_vec = c(subanswer$state_vec, end_state),
                 lhood = subanswer$lhood +
                   log(trans_probs[s, end_state]) +
                   log(obs_probs[end_state, last_obs]),
                 obs_vec = obs_vec,
                 end_state = end_state,
                 from_obs_vec = subanswer$obs_vec,
                 from_end_state = subanswer$end_state)
  # ...
```

Figure 8.27.2: Modifications to Figure 8.20.2 for keeping track of "from" information in recursive-case answers.

checking for the most likely, we'll compute just answer_n. Further, we'll assume that VITERBI_CACHE is the name of the memoization cache, and use the hash_values_as_dataframe() function (page 97) to convert the cache into a data frame for plotting (Figure 8.28).

```
DECODE_CACHE <<- hash()    # memoization cache
answer_n <- decode(trans_probs2, obs_probs2, seq_df2$obs, "n")

cache_df <- hash_values_as_dataframe(DECODE_CACHE)
print(tail(cache_df, n = 20))
```

Figure 8.28: Converting the memoization cache for decode() into a data frame.

Using ggplot2, we can then plot a cell for each subproblem solved, colored by the best log-likelihood computed for that subproblem. We organize the cells along the x-axis according to the length of the observation sequence solved for, and we also draw "from" arrows, indicating which state transitions proved most likely (Figure 8.30).

The resulting plot shows each desired ending state on the y-axis and each observation sequence solved for on the x-axis (Figure 8.31). We've also annotated the plot with the true state sequence and the called state sequence contained in answer_n.

```
    state_vec      lhood obs_vec end_state from_obs_vec from_end_state
129 nnnpppn -9.9403791 CCCGGGG       n        CCCGGG              p
130 nnnpppg -9.9403791 CCCGGGG       g        CCCGGG              p
131 nnnpppp -5.3352090 CCCGGGG       p         CCCGG              p
132 nnnnnnn -9.0934979 CCCGGGG       n         CCCGG              n
133 nnnppg  -9.3605607 CCCGGG        g         CCCGG              p
134  nnnp   -4.7553905 CCCGG         p          CCCG              p
135  nnnnn  -6.5677692 CCCGG         n          CCCG              n
136  nnnng  -8.6472108 CCCGG         g          CCCG              n
137   nnnp  -4.1755720 CCCG          p           CCC              p
138   nnnn  -4.0420406 CCCG          n           CCC              n
139   nnng  -6.1214821 CCCG          g           CCC              n
140    nnp  -5.5416636 CCC           p            CC              n
141    nnn  -1.5163119 CCC           n            CC              n
142    nng  -5.5416636 CCC           g            CC              n
143     pp  -4.8283137 CC            p             C              p
144     nn  -0.9364934 CC            n             C              n
145     gg  -4.8283137 CC            g             C              g
146      p  -2.3025851 C             p          <NA>           <NA>
147      n  -0.3566749 C             n          <NA>           <NA>
148      g  -2.3025851 C             g          <NA>           <NA>
```

Figure 8.29: Printed output for Figure 8.28.

Figure 8.30: Using ggplot2 to plot the memoization cache contents, with sub-problems organized by observation sequence length.

```
p <- ggplot(cache_df) +
  geom_tile(aes(x = reorder(obs_vec, nchar(obs_vec)),
                y = end_state, fill = lhood)) +
  geom_segment(aes(x = obs_vec, y = end_state,
                   xend = from_obs_vec, yend = from_end_state),
               arrow = arrow(length = unit(0.2,"cm")),
               position = position_jitter(width = 0.1,
                                          height = 0.1),
               color = "red") +
  scale_y_discrete(name = "State") +
  theme_bw(14) +
  theme(axis.text.x = element_text(angle = 25, hjust = 1))

plot(p)
```

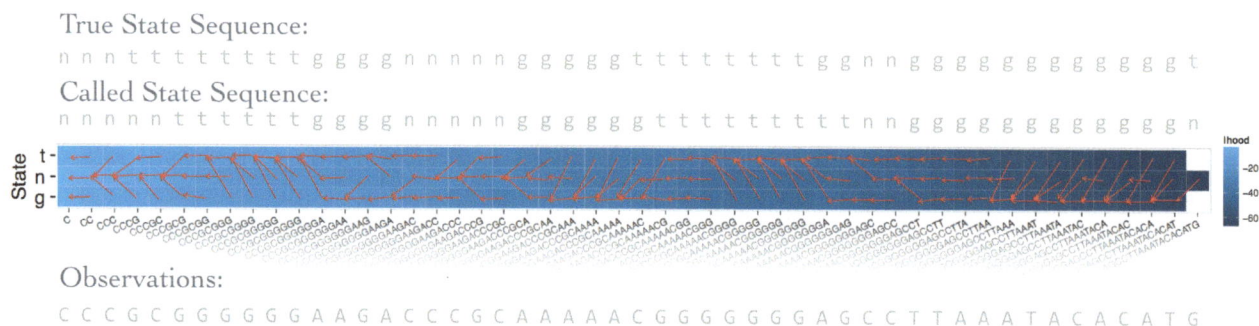

Figure 8.31: Plot inspecting the contents of the memoization cache for decode(). Also shown are the true and called state sequences (top) and the observation sequence (bottom). Values along the x-axis are observation sequences considered in the solution for each sub-problem cell.

Based on this visualization, it is clear that the number of unique sub-problems solved is $O(nk)$, where n is the length of the observation sequence and k is the number of states in the model. However, the total amount of *work* performed by decode() is actually much larger, even for the memoized version. This is because each sub-problem requires considering each possible "from" state in the for-loop, of which there are $O(k)$ (which is to say, for each red arrow visualized in Figure 8.31, k arrows were computed and considered). Thus, the total runtime for the memoized solution is $O(nk^2)$, as will be the runtime for a dynamic programming solution.

Exercises

1. Our gene/non-gene model assumes that "gene" and "non-gene" are equally likely first states, even though the base-case (Figure 8.13.2) considers the relative probability of observations. (To see this clearly, consider what would happen if there was an observation that could be produced by either with equal probability.) In reality, it is extremely unlikely that the first base in a genome is part of a gene.

One easy way to work around this is to introduce an additional "start" state into the model, such that it is only possible to move out of the start state into other states, and the start state only produces a special observation that can be placed at the beginning of an observation sequence (Figure 8.32).

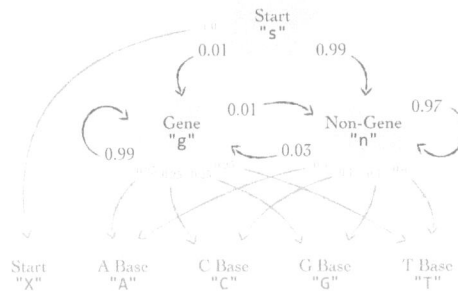

Figure 8.32: A gene/non-gene Hidden Markov Model with an explicit starting state.

Code an HMM with such a start state, and generate a random sequence of states and observations starting from it. Try decoding the observation sequence.

2. Visualize the non-memoized call tree for decode(trans_probs, obs_probs, obs_vec, end_state), with obs_vec <- c("C", "A", "T") and end_state <- "g". (You only need to visualize the contents of obs_vec and end_state at each node, since trans_probs and obs_probs don't change.)

3. Implement a memoized version of the decode() function, using information from obs_vec and end_state for the memoization cache keys. (The trans_probs and obs_probs parameters don't need to be part of the keys, since they don't change.)

4. Implement the dynamic-programming Viterbi algorithm for decoding. As hinted at by Figure 8.31 (and the techniques of Chapter 7), you'll need to produce a table with a column for each observation and a row for each state. A for-loop will be required in computing the log-likelihood for each cell, considering potential log-likelihoods based on all the cells in the column to the left.

Once the log-likelihood and "from" tables are complete, computing the most-likely sequence as a traceback is straightforward.

5. Generate a formal proof of correctness for the recursive decode() function. You will likely need to use an inductive proof similar in structure to that used for global sequence alignment (Chapter 6).

9   Turtle Drawing, L-Systems

The programmer, like the poet, works only slightly removed from pure thought-stuff. He builds his castles in the air, from air, creating by exertion of the imagination. Few media of creation are so flexible, so easy to polish and rework, so readily capable of realizing grand conceptual structures...

Fred Brooks, 1975

Nearly all of the techniques covered in this book have a self-similar beauty to them, and the many figures we've seen show that these ideas can be visualized graphically. The goal of this chapter is to more explicitly explore the idea of *drawing* via recursive and self-similar processes, and as a result will be more whimsical than practical. First though, we will need a way to draw simple lines and shapes programmatically. As it turns out, this functionality will be provided by a turtle–a virtual turtle–provided by the R package TurtleGraphics.

After loading the library (along with others, see page 23), we can run turtle_init(mode = "clip") to initiate and display our turtle in the center of a 100 by 100 "terrarium" (display box). In this box, the lower-left hand corner is at coordinate $(0,0)$. The turtle_getpos() function returns the turtle's current position as a length-2 vector in x, y coordinates. Similarly, turtle_getangle() returns a length-1 vector of his current angle (where 0 is up, -90 is left, 90 is right and 180 is down; Figure 9.2).

```
turtle_init(mode = "clip")
print(turtle_getpos())     # 50 50
print(turtle_getangle())   # 0
```

Our turtle has a pen, which by default is "down" on the paper. We can tell him to move forward 10 units by calling turtle_forward(10), causing him to move and draw a line with his pen. We could then

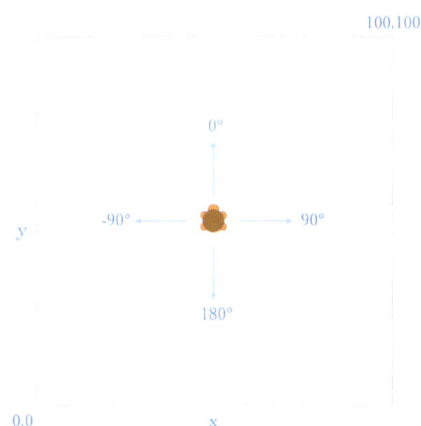

Figure 9.1: The turtle's "terrarium" after calling turtle_init() is 100 units on the x (horizontal) axis and 100 units on the y (vertical), with 0,0 in the lower-left and 100,100 in the upper-right.

Figure 9.2: Initiating a new turtle and printing his initial location and angle.

call turtle_up() and turtle_forward(10) to have him lift his pen and then move forward, followed by turtle_down() and another turtle_forward(10) to have him to put his pen down and move again while drawing.

Figure 9.3: Basic moves for turtle-based drawing.

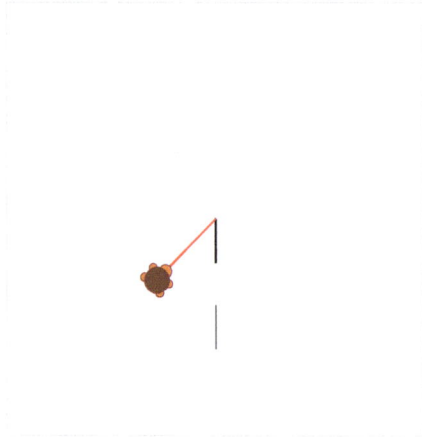

```
turtle_init(mode = "clip")     # initiate turtle at 50,50

turtle_setpos(50, 20)  # set x,y location
turtle_forward(10)     # move forward 10
turtle_up()            # lift drawing pen
turtle_forward(10)     # move forward 10
turtle_down()          # set drawing pen down
turtle_lwd(3)          # set pen size to 3.0
turtle_forward(10)     # move forward 10
turtle_right(45)       # turn 45 degrees right
turtle_col("red")      # set pen color to red
turtle_backward(20)    # move backward 20
```

The mode = "clip" in the turtle_init() function controls what happens if the turtle moves outside the 100×100 window: by default an error occurs, using mode = "clip" lets him simply move outside the box but we won't see any drawing. Figure 9.3 summarizes these basic moves and a few more; the output is shown in Figure 9.4.

Figure 9.4: Displayed output for Figure 9.3.

Unfortunately, after every instruction, the turtle himself needs to be redrawn (at least in the R TurtleGraphics package). Since we will be drawing many lines (in loops and with functions), this dramatically slows down the drawing process. So although the turtle is cute, after running turtle_init(mode = "clip") we'll generally then run turtle_hide() to indicate that we aren't interested in seeing the turtle himself. When we hide the turtle we can efficiently create interesting images, such as a spiral produced by a loop (Figures 9.5 and 9.6).

Figure 9.5: If we are willing to "hide" the turtle himself, we can efficiently produce more complex drawings.

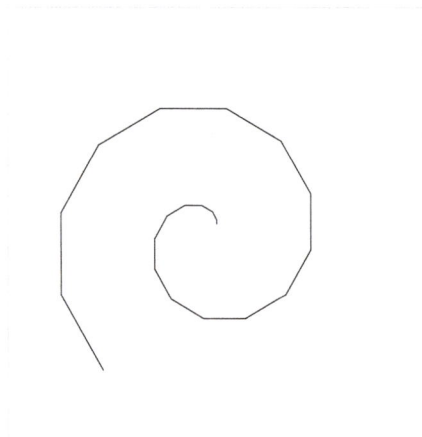

```
turtle_init(mode = "clip")
turtle_hide()

for(dist in seq(1,20)) {
  turtle_forward(dist)
  turtle_left(30)
}
```

Finally, we're also going to write three helper functions. The first, turtle_getstate() will return the turtle's current x and y location as well as his angle as a 3-element vector. Conversely, turtle_setstate() will take such a 3-element vector and set the turtle's current state to that position and angle. The TurtleGraphics package provides no support for having the turtle draw text, so we'll include a custom turtle_text() function that takes a length-1 character vector and plots it at the turtle's current location and

Figure 9.6: Displayed output for Figure 9.5.

angle. This function makes use of the same underlying graphical system used by the `TurtleGraphics` package (Figures 9.7 and 9.8).

```
turtle_getstate <- function() {
  state <- c(turtle_getpos(), turtle_getangle())
  return(state)
}

turtle_setstate <- function(state) {
  turtle_setpos(state[1], state[2])
  turtle_setangle(state[3])
}

turtle_text <- function(label, col = "black", fontsize = 20) {
  grid.text(label,
            turtle_getpos()[1],
            turtle_getpos()[2],
            rot = -1*turtle_getangle(),
            default.units = "native",
            gp = gpar(fontsize = fontsize, col = col))
}

# Example usage:
turtle_init(mode = "clip")
turtle_hide()

start_state <- turtle_getstate()
turtle_forward(20)
turtle_text("After move")
turtle_setstate(start_state)
turtle_text("Back at start")
```

Figure 9.7: Helpful functions for retrieving and setting the turtle's state, as well as drawing text.

After move

Back at start

9.1 *Graphical Recursion*

Turtle graphics are too simple to be used for many applications, like designing user interfaces. On the other hand, they are an excellent tool for visualizing computational processes. Let's start by writing a function that draws a "tree" of a given size (taken as a parameter), where the tree has only two branches, and the turtle is returned to the starting position before the function ends. The overall strategy will be to store the current state, move forward by the size given, turn left, move forward by some fraction of the size given, return to the branching point (without drawing), turn right, move forward again by some fraction of the size given, and finally return to the stored state (Figures 9.9 and 9.10).

We can use this function to draw two simple trees, one in the lower-left with size of 20, and one in the lower-right with size of 0.5 (Figure 9.11).

Figure 9.8: Displayed output for Figure 9.7.

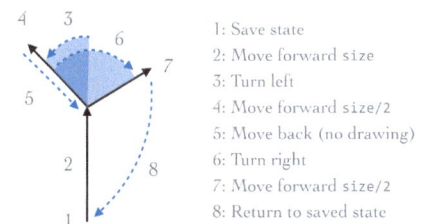

1: Save state
2: Move forward size
3: Turn left
4: Move forward size/2
5: Move back (no drawing)
6: Turn right
7: Move forward size/2
8: Return to saved state

Figure 9.9: Turtle moves for drawing a simple tree with two branches.

Figure 9.10: A function to draw a very simple, two-branch tree of a given size.

```
simple_tree <- function(size) {
  stored_state <- turtle_getstate() # 1
  turtle_forward(size)              # 2
  turtle_left(30)                   # 3
  turtle_forward(size*0.5)          # 4

  turtle_up()
  turtle_backward(size*0.5)         # 5
  turtle_down()

  turtle_right(70)                  # 6
  turtle_forward(size*0.5)          # 7

  turtle_setstate(stored_state)     # 8
}
```

Figure 9.11: Drawing two simple trees of differing sizes.

```
turtle_init(mode = "clip")
turtle_hide()

turtle_setstate(c(30, 20, 0))   # put turtle in lower left
simple_tree(20)                 # draw a tree of size 20
turtle_setstate(c(70, 20, 0))   # put turtle in lower right
simple_tree(0.5)                # draw a tree of size 0.5
```

In the output (Figure 9.12), we see both the large and small trees. The small tree, however, is so small that it's hardly worth the effort for our poor turtle! So, we'll adjust the code such that if the size given is less than 1, then the function can simply do nothing and return (Figure 9.13).

Figure 9.13: Modification for the code in Figure 9.11, simply returning if the given size is too small.

```
simple_tree <- function(size) {
  stored_state <- turtle_getstate() # 1
  if(size < 1) {
      return(invisible())
  }
  # ...
```

What is the advantage of ensuring that our function returns the turtle to his original state after drawing the tree? This allows us to embed "draw a simple tree" within any other drawing process, without compromising it. As an example, Figure 9.14 draws a spiral of trees of varying sizes.

Now, since our simple trees can be drawn inside of any other drawing process, we can actually modify our simple_tree() function so that it draws *smaller* trees at the end of each branch! This would happen between steps 4 and 5, and between steps 6 and 7 (Figure 9.15).

Figure 9.12: Displayed output for Figure 9.11.

```
turtle_init(mode = "clip")
turtle_hide()

for(size in seq(1,20)) {
  turtle_forward(size)
  simple_tree(size)
  turtle_left(30)
}
```

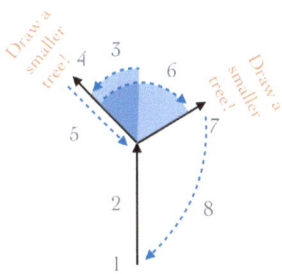

Figure 9.15: A complex tree is a simple tree, with smaller simple trees at the end of each branch.

Figure 9.14: Drawing a spiral of trees.

If the trees get smaller the further we go from the "root," each *recursive* call gets closer to the *base case* of a tree of size less then 1, in which case the function simply returns. This is important–otherwise the function calls would never stop, resulting in an "infinite recursion" error.

The modification for the code is shown in Figure 9.17, consisting of only a couple of additional recursive function calls, one after each branch is drawn. We've made the left sub-trees slightly larger than the right sub-trees. Calling the function (Figure 9.18) results in the striking output shown in Figure 9.19.

```
# ...
turtle_forward(size*0.5)      # 4
simple_tree(size*0.7)
# ...


# ...
turtle_forward(size*0.5)      # 7
simple_tree(size*0.65)
# ...
```

```
turtle_init(mode = "clip")
turtle_hide()

turtle_setstate(c(50, 10, 0))  # set turtle in the bottom-middle
simple_tree(16)                # draw a recursive tree
```

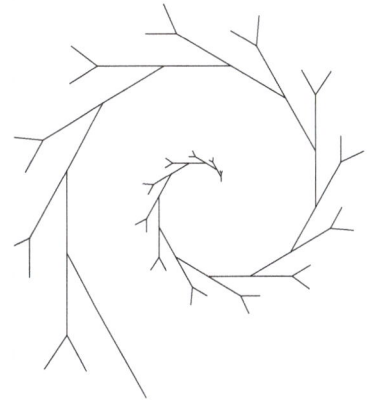

Figure 9.16: Displayed output for Figure 9.14.

Figure 9.17: Further modifications for the code in Figure 9.11, drawing two smaller simple trees at the ends of each branch.

Figure 9.18: Calling the now-recursive tree-drawing function.

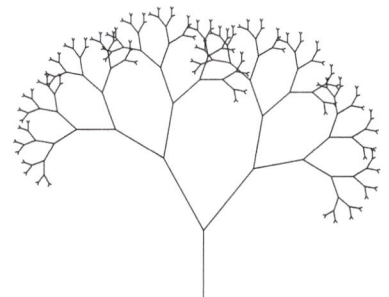

Figure 9.19: Displayed output for Figure 9.18.

THIS RECURSIVELY DRAWN TREE is reminiscent of a call tree, of the sort shown in Figure 4.17 on page 62. Can we write a function that draws its own call tree?

Let's write a `draw_call_tree()` which, like `simple_tree()`, takes a `size` parameter. As part of the process, each call to the function will first use `turtle_text()` to draw this `size` parameter to the window. Since the turtle is doing the drawing, we'll also draw the turtle's location and angle, extracted from `turtle_getstate()` (Figure 9.20.1).

Figure 9.20.1: The start of a function that draws its own call tree. Recall that `str_c()` concatenates character vectors.

```
draw_call_tree <- function(size) {
  state <- turtle_getstate()
  pos <- state[1:2]            # position (x and y)
  angle <- state[3]            # angle

  # draw the current size, position, and angle as text
  turtle_text(str_c("size: ", as.integer(size), "\n",
                    "pos: ", as.integer(pos[1]), ",",
                    as.integer(pos[2]), "\n",
                    "angle: ", as.integer(angle)),
             fontsize = 9, col = "darkblue")

  # to be continued...
```

Parsing the above, recall that `str_c()` pastes multiple character strings together, and `as.integer()` truncates numbers to integers (since we don't need much precision in the drawn information). Each "\n" represents a "newline," breaking the string over multiple lines.

Our base case shall be when `size < 15`, in which case the function will additionally draw "Base Case!" and then just return (Figure 9.20.2).

Figure 9.20.2: Base case for `draw_call_tree()`.

```
  if(size < 15) {
    turtle_up()
    turtle_forward(6) # forward without drawing
    turtle_down()
    turtle_text("Base Case!", fontsize = 9, col = "darkred")
    return(invisible())
  }

  # to be continued...
```

At this point if we called `turtle_init()` and `draw_call_tree(10)`, the output would be "Base Case!; size: 10; pos: 50,50; angle: 0". If `size` is at least 15 though, we'll have the function make two recursive calls with a smaller `size` parameter. Before each, we'll have the turtle turn and move forward while drawing a line. After each, we'll restore the turtle's location and angle with `turtle_getstate()` (Figure 9.20.3).

```
  turtle_left(22)
  turtle_forward(size)
  draw_call_tree(size * 0.64)
  turtle_setstate(state)

  turtle_right(28)
  turtle_forward(size)
  draw_call_tree(size * 0.54)
  turtle_setstate(state)
}
```

Figure 9.20.3: Recursive calls for
draw_call_tree().

Now we can call our graphically-self-descriptive function. Before
we do, we move the turtle to the lower-center of the window and
set his pen color to dark gray (to make the text show more clearly;
Figure 9.21).

```
turtle_init(mode = "clip")   # initiate turtle at 50,50
turtle_hide()

turtle_setpos(50, 15)  # set x,y location
turtle_col("darkgray")
draw_call_tree(36)
```

Figure 9.21: Calling draw_call_tree(), a
function that visualizes its own call tree.

There are only a few nodes in the drawn tree (Figure 9.22), but
they illustrate most of the information stored in local variables for
each call. What this figure is missing is any sense of temporality–
what *order* were the nodes drawn in? To add this information, we'll
keep a global COUNTER variable (initially 0), increment it with each
call, and include it in each displayed node (Figures 9.23 and 9.24,
reference Figure 4.17).

```
COUNTER <<- 0

draw_call_tree <- function(size) {
  COUNTER <<- COUNTER + 1
  state <- turtle_getstate()
  pos <- state[1:2]
  angle <- state[3]

  turtle_text(str_c("size: ", as.integer(size), "\n",
                    "pos: ", as.integer(pos[1]), ",",
                    as.integer(pos[2]), "\n",
                    "angle: ", as.integer(angle), "\n",
                    "counter: ", COUNTER),
              fontsize = 9, col = "darkblue")

  # to be continued...
```

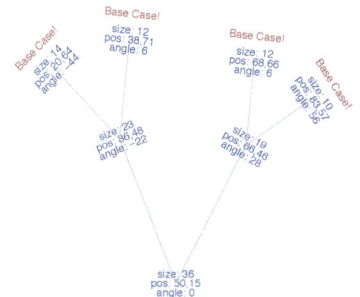

Figure 9.22: Displayed output for Figure 9.21.

Finally, although we could also display the contents of the call
stack programmatically (as we did for Figure 4.20 on page 63),
Figure 9.25 shows a visualization.

Figure 9.23: Modifications to Figure 9.20.1 for
tracking the order of node drawing.

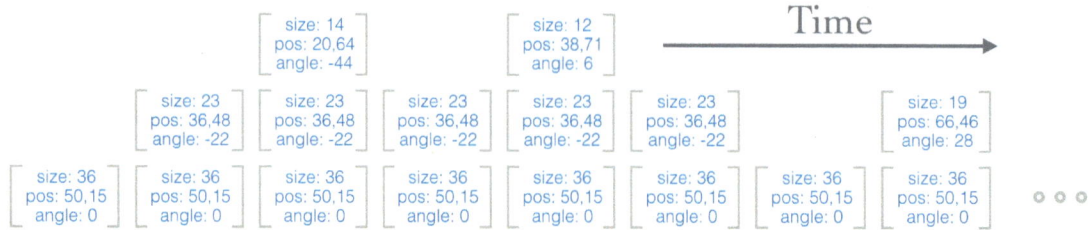

Figure 9.25: Illustrating some of the local variables stored in the call stack during execution of draw_call_tree().

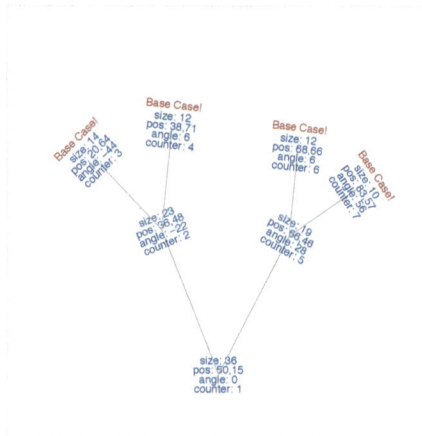

Figure 9.24: Displayed output for draw_call_tree() with modifications from Figure 9.23.

CALL TREES AREN'T THE ONLY RECURSIVE STRUCTURE we've seen that can be visualized with turtle graphics. We can also draw the contents of binary search trees, such as those created with our initial insert_tree() (Figures 2.20 and 2.22 on page 34). We'll start by first creating a nice, full tree (Figure 9.26).

```
t <- NULL
t <- insert_tree(t, "C")
t <- insert_tree(t, "A")
t <- insert_tree(t, "F")
t <- insert_tree(t, "B")
t <- insert_tree(t, "D")
t <- insert_tree(t, "E")
t <- insert_tree(t, "K")
t <- insert_tree(t, "H")
t <- insert_tree(t, "L")
```

Figure 9.26: Creating a binary search tree with nine internal nodes.

Our draw_tree() function will be recursive in nature, and will take the data representing the tree, as well as a size for drawing the branches. Since these trees can be NULL (to represent an empty tree), the base case for drawing will be if data is NULL, in which case we'll just draw a "*" and return (Figure 9.27.1).

Figure 9.27.1: Base case for drawing a binary search tree.

```
draw_tree <- function(data, size) {
  if(is.null(data)) {
    turtle_text("*", fontsize = 14)
    return(invisible())
  }

  # to be continued...
```

On the other hand, if data is not NULL, then it must have exactly three elements: the left subtree, the element itself, and the right subtree. We'll extract these, and then use turtle_text() to draw the element at the turtle's location (Figure 9.27.2).

```
left <- data[[1]]
el <- data[[2]]
right <- data[[3]]

turtle_text(el, fontsize = 14)

# to be continued...
```

Figure 9.27.2: Base case for drawing a binary search tree.

With the central element drawn, we can proceed to draw the left and right subtrees recursively. First we save the turtle's current state (location and angle), so that we can return him to the original point after each recursive call. For the left subtree, we turn left, draw a branch of length size, and make a recursive call to draw the left tree with a smaller size. A similar set of commands draws the right (Figure 9.27.3).

```
 s <- turtle_getstate()

turtle_left(30)
turtle_forward(size)
draw_tree(left, size * 0.8)
turtle_setstate(s)

turtle_right(30)
turtle_forward(size)
draw_tree(right, size * 0.8)
turtle_setstate(s)
}
```

Figure 9.27.3: Recursive cases for drawing a binary search tree.

Code to draw tree t can be found in Figure 9.28, and the drawn output in Figure 9.29. This tree is not drawn top-down as we did for earlier binary search trees, though this could be remedied by initially placing the turtle near the top facing downward. (We'd also need to have the turtle turn right to draw the left subtree. Similar modifications would suffice for a top-down drawing with draw_call_tree().)

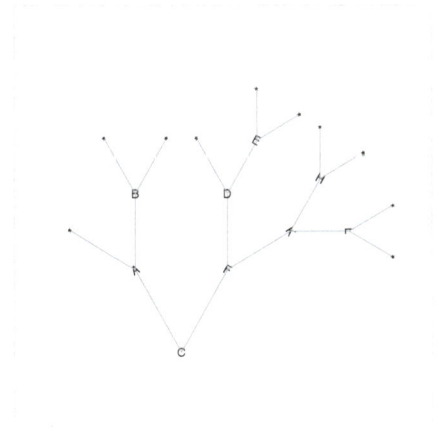

Figure 9.29: Binary search tree constructed in Figure 9.26.

```
turtle_init(mode = "clip")
turtle_hide()

turtle_col("darkgray")
turtle_setpos(40, 20)      # lower center-left
draw_tree(t, 22)
```

Figure 9.28: Calling draw_tree() on the binary search tree t.

NOT ALL RECURSIVELY DRAWN PROCESSES need to return to return to their starting point. A good example of this is the *Koch curve*, named after the Swedish mathematician Helge von Koch who first described it in 1904 (indeed, it was one of the earliest fractals–self-similar geometric patterns–described).

The Koch curve is described directly as a recursive function, taking a size parameter and a limit parameter. The simplest Koch curve is simply a line: if size <= limit, then the turtle simply draws a line of length size. Otherwise, the area to draw in is broken in to three sections: in the first section, a smaller Koch curve is drawn, in the second section, two smaller curves are drawn (but at angles so they fit in the section), and in the final section another smaller curve is drawn. Note that the geometry of the curve is such that each section is of length size/3, so the final product will be of the desired size (Figures 9.30 and 9.31).

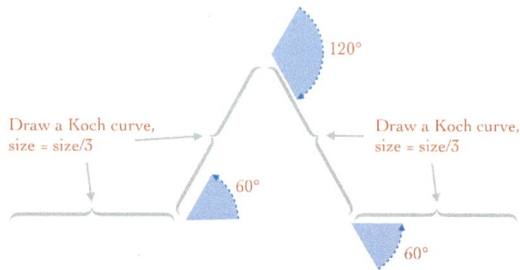

Figure 9.30: Graphical representation of steps required to draw a Koch curve.

Figure 9.31: Recursive function for drawing a Koch curve.

```
koch_curve <- function(size, limit) {
  if(size <= limit) {
    turtle_forward(size)
  } else {
    koch_curve(size/3, limit)
    turtle_left(60)
    koch_curve(size/3, limit)
    turtle_right(120)
    koch_curve(size/3, limit)
    turtle_left(60)
    koch_curve(size/3, limit)
  }
}
```

Setting the turtle at five different locations, we can plot five different curves with decreasing limit parameters (Figure 9.32), illustrating the increasing complexity with deeper recursion (Figure 9.33).

```
turtle_init(mode = "clip")
turtle_hide()

turtle_setstate(c(10, 90, 90))
koch_curve(80, 80)
turtle_setstate(c(10, 65, 90))
koch_curve(80, 40)
turtle_setstate(c(10, 45, 90))
koch_curve(80, 15)
turtle_setstate(c(10, 25, 90))
koch_curve(80, 7)
turtle_setstate(c(10, 5, 90))
koch_curve(80, 1.5)
```

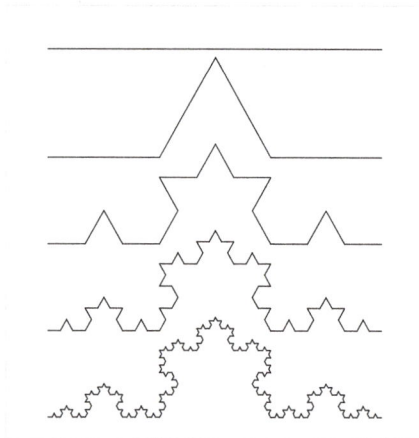

Figure 9.33: Displayed output for Figure 9.32.

Figure 9.32: Using the Koch curve function to draw five curves, with decreasing limit parameters.

FOR ANOTHER LOOK AT PATTERNS found in nature, let's consider *phyllotaxis*: the arrangement of plant parts during growth. Often these arrangements are spirals, such as the seeds of a sunflower or pinecone. As we discovered earlier, we can create spirals with turtle graphics as a repetition of moving and turning. First though, let's create a utility function that instructs our turtle to draw a circle of a given diameter d, centered on himself.

```
turtle_circle <- function(d) {
  s <- turtle_getstate()

  turtle_up()
  turtle_forward(d/2)

  arc_size <- 3.141596 * d / 36
  turtle_right(95)
  turtle_down()

  for(i in seq(1, 36)) {
    turtle_forward(arc_size)
    turtle_right(10)
  }

  turtle_setstate(s)
}
```

Figure 9.34: A function for drawing a circle at the turtle's location.

This function (Figure 9.34) first moves the turtle forward by the radius of the circle without drawing, then turns him rightward by just over 90°. Then, we tell him to draw 36 arcs (lines, really) of length $circumference/36 = \pi * d/36$, turning by 10° each time. Like earlier functions, this one returns the turtle to his original place, so drawing a circle can be embedded in some other drawing process.

Now, let's use this function to create a simple spiral of "leaves." Rather than create a spiral similar to Figure 9.6 however, we're going to use a sharper turning angle of (somewhat arbitrarily) 126° (Figure 9.35, output in Figure 9.36). In this spiral we move forward with `turtle_forward(i/2)` rather than `turtle_forward(i)`, just to fit more leaves in the view.

```
turtle_init(mode = "clip")
turtle_hide()

for(i in seq(1,200)) {
  turtle_forward(i/2)
  turtle_circle(2)
  turtle_right(126)
}
```

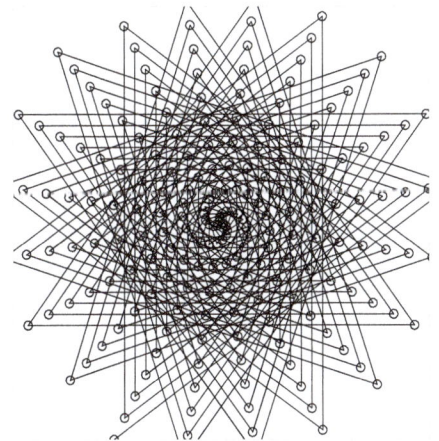

Figure 9.36: Displayed output for Figure 9.35.

Figure 9.35: Drawing a spiral of leaves with a sharp turning angle.

This figure may seem to have little to do with natural growth; certainly plants do not cross their bodies in determining where

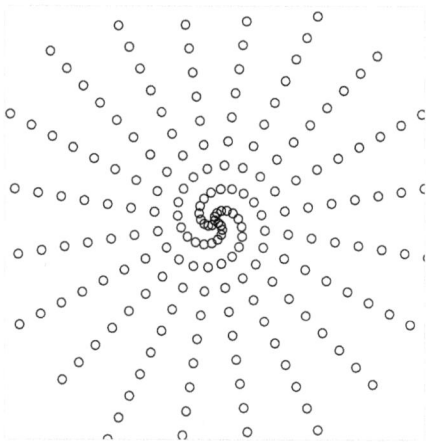

Figure 9.37: Phyllotactic spiral show in Figure 9.36 without lines.

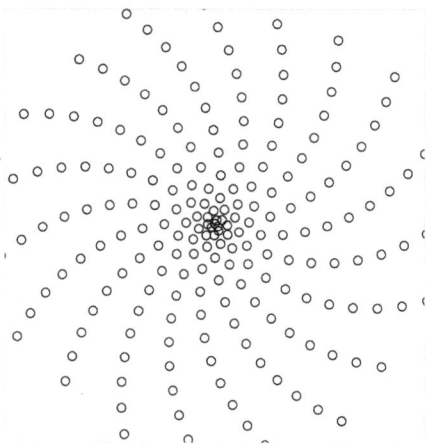

Figure 9.38: Phyllotactic spiral with a turning angle of $360°/e$.

new leaves will be placed. This figure is more realistic, however, when we consider where new growth mostly occurs in plants: at the tips of stems. On a real plant, the next leaf will appear near the center of the spiral, at some (potentially sharp) angle relative to the previous, pushing existing leaves further down the stem. Thus, while plants add leaves from the outside in, our drawing process does the reverse.

To make the pattern clearer, we'll erase the lines by calling turtle_up() before turtle_forward(i/2), and turtle_down() after (code not shown, output in Figure 9.37).

For a real plant this turning angle would be inefficient, because leaves are occurring along lines and crowd each other, while space between the lines is wasted. This is because 126° is a vary "rational" turning angle: over time, its repeated use produces cyclic patterns in leaf placement. Irrational numbers fare better; Figure 9.38 shows the result for turning by $360°/e \approx 132.436°$.

Even so, certain irrational numbers–or approximations of them– fare better than others. Famously, angles related to the golden ratio ϕ work very well. We last saw ϕ in Chapter 5, as the limit of the ratio of successive Fibonacci numbers:

$$\lim_{n \to \infty} \frac{fib(n+1)}{fib(n)} = \phi \approx 1.61803 \ .$$

The "golden angle" is $360°/\phi \approx 222.492°$, or its complement $360°/\phi^{-1} \approx 137.507°$. Figure 9.39 shows spirals provided by increasingly better approximations of ϕ provided by larger Fibonacci ratios.

In fact, botanists have discovered that many plants do not use the golden angle exactly, but some approximation provided by ratios of Fibonacci numbers! The reason for the appearance of ϕ and Fibonacci numbers specifically in phyllotaxis is still an open question.[1] ϕ does provide the mathematical property of being the "most irrational" number, in that it is hard to approximate with a small-denominator fraction. (For example, π is approximated to 5 decimal places by 355/113, while ϕ can be approximated to 5 places by $fib(15)/fib(14) = 610/377$.) The golden ratio is also easy to produce via simple processes (like honeybee generation sizes), and evolutionary pressure for efficient placement likely plays a significant role.

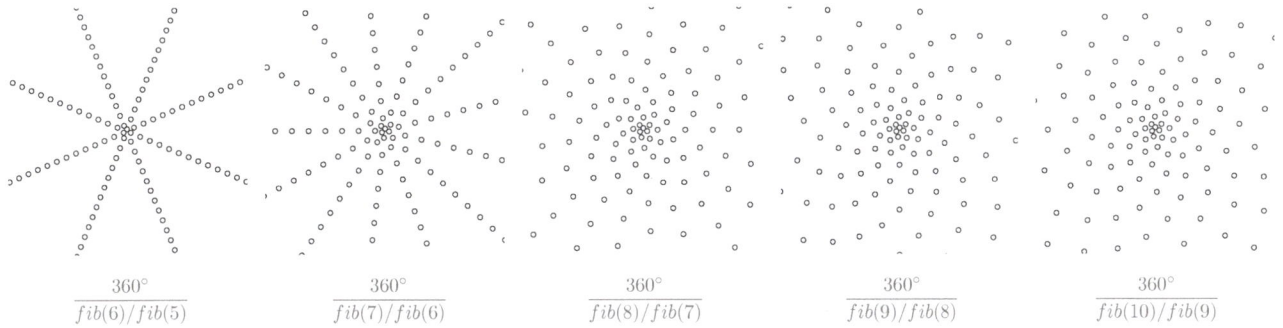

$$\frac{360°}{fib(6)/fib(5)} \qquad \frac{360°}{fib(7)/fib(6)} \qquad \frac{360°}{fib(8)/fib(7)} \qquad \frac{360°}{fib(9)/fib(8)} \qquad \frac{360°}{fib(10)/fib(9)}$$

Are phyllotaxis and recursion related? The approximations to ϕ provided by the Fibonacci numbers (recursively defined) and used in plant growth provide one such connection, though cryptic. Another is that plants frequently also produce phyllotactic spirals in self-similar patterns, where each "leaf" is itself a smaller spiral. Romanesco, a relative of cauliflower, provides a beautiful example in three dimensions (Figure 9.40). Unfortunately, as of this writing, I haven't yet produced a convincing recursive replica using R's TurtleGraphics library. Perhaps you can! In an effort to get one step closer, Figure 9.40 also shows a spiral with each leaf scaled by plotting turtle_circle(sqrt(i/2.5)) instead of turtle_circle(2).

Figure 9.39: Phyllotactic spirals produced by increasingly accurate approximations of the golden angle.

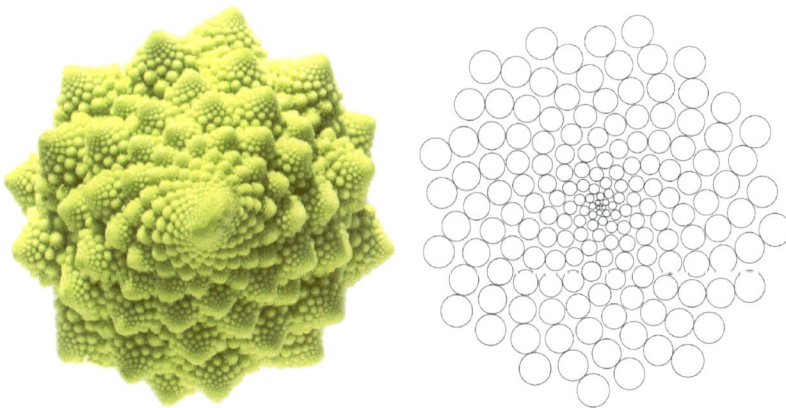

Figure 9.40: A romanesco plant, and a phyllotactic spiral with scaled leaf sizes.

Exercises

1. A line like status <- turtle_status() sets status to be a list describing various properties of the turtle, including the current drawing color (in status$DisplayOptions$col) and drawing line width (in status$DisplayOptions$lwd). The function turtle_lwd() sets the line width (where 1.0 is the default) and turtle_col() sets the drawing color (default "black"). Modify the turtle_getstate() and turtle_setstate() functions to also

save and restore the current line width and color. Next, modify the `simple_tree()` function so that the line width of the "trunk" and "branches" are a percentage of the `size`, giving the effect of narrowing branches toward the leaves of the tree.

2. Try adjusting the angles and sizes (or even number of branches) used in the `simple_tree()` function. What sorts of tree types can you create? Further, try using random sizes or angles; for example, `runif(1,30,35)` will return a random number uniformly from 30 to 35.

3. Write a `leaf()` function that draws a leaf-like shape–this could be as easy as a circle (drawn with `turtle_circle()`) or as complex as a pair or triplet of Koch curves. Rather than simply returning if `size` is too small in the `simple_tree()` function, call your `leaf()` function.

4. Write a function `draw_nested_list()` that illustrates the contents of nested lists from Chapter 2.

5. Write a function `illustrate_quicksort()` that implements the quicksort algorithm from Chapter 3 (page 50) and illustrates the call tree.

9.2 Lindenmayer Systems

Let's return to the honeybee family tree we studied in Chapter 4. Recall that in the family tree, male bees have a single female parent, but female bees have both a female and male parent. To recreate the tree, we could run these rules backward, such that a male bee "produces" his female parent and a female bee "produces" her male and female parents. Repeatedly applied, these *production rules*–

$$M \rightarrow F$$
$$F \rightarrow MF$$

–would produce the ancestry of the bee, as in Figure 9.41. We should specify that we are starting with a single male;

start: M

and if we want to be very rigorous we could further define all of the "symbols" that we are using:

symbols: M, F

These three components, the "start string," the "production rules," and the "symbols table" are the basic elements for a Lindenmayer System, or L-System: a system for iterative (though quite

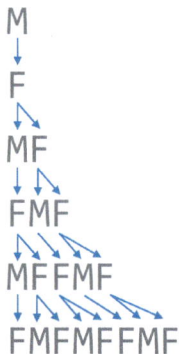

Figure 9.41: Generating the family history of a male bee (reverse through time) by applying a set of generating rules.

recursive and self-similar) generation of strings. They were first studied by the Botanist Aristid Lindenmayer in 1968.

We can devise a Lindenmayer system in code without too much trouble. For example, a sentence could just be a character vector, and the production rules could easily be encoded in a hash table (Figure 9.42).

```
sentence <- c("M")
rules <- hash()
rules[["M"]] <- c("F")
rules[["F"]] <- c("M", "F")
```

Figure 9.42: Implementing an L-System with character vectors and a hash table.

Applying the rules to a sentence to produce a new sentence is probably best encapsulated in a function. We'll construct the new sentence one symbol at a time, based on the rules, using a for-loop. If there doesn't happen to be a rule for a given symbol of a sentence, that symbol is simply copied over instead of replaced (Figure 9.43).

```
lproduce <- function(sentence, rules) {
  newsentence <- c()
  for(symbol in sentence) {
    if(has.key(symbol, rules)) {
      newsentence <- c(newsentence, rules[[symbol]])
    } else {
      newsentence <- c(newsentence, symbol)
    }
  }
  return(newsentence)
}
```

Figure 9.43: A function to generate successive L-System sentences from a current sentence and a ruleset. While appending to a vector with c() is slow in R, we won't worry about that here. If we did want to make this function more efficient, we could create the new sentence as an rstack, or as a nested list from Chapter 2.

Now, from our original sentence, we can produce successive ones (Figure 9.44).

```
print(sentence)    # "M"
sentence <- lproduce(sentence, rules)
print(sentence)    # "F"
sentence <- lproduce(sentence, rules)
print(sentence)    # "M" "F"
sentence <- lproduce(sentence, rules)
print(sentence)    # "F" "M" "F"
sentence <- lproduce(sentence, rules)
print(sentence)    # "M" "F" "F" "M" "F"
```

Figure 9.44: An example use of the lproduce() function to generate a male bee's family history.

Notice that each sentence has a length equal to the nth Fibonacci number. These will get long fast!

L-Systems are a game for symbol shuffling, but we usually add some interpretation to the symbols and sentences. In this case we've interpreted "M" to represent a male bee and "F" to represent a female bee in the ancestry tree.

A common interpretation of the symbols in an L-System are as *movements for a turtle* (the virtual, graphical kind). For example, we can consider another set of steps for drawing a simple tree in Figure 9.45. We can encode this sequence with the following symbols and their meanings:

F: Forward

+: Turn right

-: Turn left

[: Remember state

]: Return to state

1: Forward
2: Remember state α
3: Turn left
4: Forward
5: Return to state α
6: Forward
7: Remember state β
8: Turn right
9: Forward
10: Return to state β
11: Forward

Figure 9.45: Steps for creating an alternative simple tree.

With these symbols and interpretation, the tree in Figure 9.45 can be described by the sentence F[-F]F[+F]F. In a moment, we'll write a function that takes such a sentence as input, and directs our turtle accordingly. A difficulty will arise, though, for more complex shapes where more than one state needs to be remembered simultaneously (Figure 9.46).

Notice that in this case, however, we're always returning to the most recently stored state–just as in the earlier recursive drawing, where the states to return to were stored on the call stack (Figure 9.25). In fact, we can indeed keep the states that are being remembered on a stack! Thus, we'll reinterpret [and]:

[: Store current state on a stack

]: Return to the top state in the stack; remove it from stack

1: Forward
2: Remember state α
3: Turn left
4: Forward
5: Remember state β
6: Turn left
7: Forward
8: Return to state β
9: Turn Right
10: Forward
11: Return to state α
12: Turn right
...

Figure 9.46: Steps for drawing a tree where more than one state needs to be remembered simultaneously.

With these modified rules, the tree in Figure 9.46 can be described by the sentence F[-F[-F]+F]+F[-F]+F.

Now we can write our function that interprets such a sentence as instructions for a turtle (Figure 9.48). What sentences of this type don't specify is how *far* to move forward given an F symbol, or how far to turn left or right given - or + symbols. It makes sense then that we give these as parameters to the interpreting function. Finally, if the sentence contains any symbol not in the symbol set above (F, +, -, [, or]), then we'll simply instruct the turtle to draw that symbol as text at his current location. Figures 9.49 and 9.50 illustrate an example.

$$F[-F[-F]+F]+F[-F]+F$$
$$\uparrow \quad \uparrow \quad \uparrow \quad \uparrow \quad \uparrow \quad \uparrow$$
$$+\alpha \quad +\beta \quad -\beta \quad -\alpha \quad +\delta \quad -\delta$$

Figure 9.47: Sentence for drawing the tree described in Figure 9.46.

```
draw_sentence <- function(sentence, size, langle, rangle) {
  pos_stack <- rstack()
  for(symbol in sentence) {
    if(symbol == "F") {
      turtle_forward(size)
    } else if(symbol == "+") {
      turtle_right(rangle)
    } else if(symbol == "-") {
      turtle_left(langle)
    } else if(symbol == "[") {
      pos_stack <- insert_top(pos_stack,
                                turtle_getstate())
    } else if(symbol == "]") {
      turtle_setstate(peek_top(pos_stack))
      pos_stack <- without_top(pos_stack)
    } else {
      turtle_text(symbol)
    }
  }
}
```

Figure 9.48: A function interpreting a sentence of symbols as instructions for drawing.

```
turtle_init(mode = "clip")
turtle_hide()

turtle_setstate(c(50, 20, 0))
sentence <- char_vec("F[-F]F[+F]F") # aka c("F", "[", "-", ...
draw_sentence(sentence, 10, 30, 30)
```

Figure 9.49: Using the draw_sentence() function. The char_vec() function is from Figure 6.7 on page 89; it transforms a character vector containing a single string into a longer vector of single character strings.

THUS FAR, we've only talked about the graphical interpretation of L-System sentences, not any production rules. Here's an interesting rule to go along with the sentence drawn previously:

$$F \rightarrow F[-F]F[+F]F$$

This replacement rule replaces every instance of F with a copy of the original sentence! Graphically, each segment of the tree will be replaced with a copy of the overall structure (Figure 9.51).

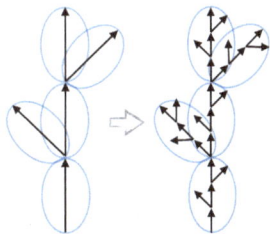

Figure 9.51: Interpreted result of applying one iteration of the rule F → F[-F]F[+F]F to the sentence F[-F]F[+F]F.

Thus, we can start with a sentence containing just "F" and apply the rule multiple times to generate ever-more complex sentences. One complication is that as the sentence grows, the drawn structure gets larger, so as we draw it with draw_sentence() we need to decrease the size used for each F instruction (Figure 9.52, output in Figures 9.53 and 9.54).

Figure 9.50: Displayed output for Figure 9.49.

Figure 9.52: Generating a complex L-System sentence and interpreting it with the draw_sentence() function.

```
rules <- hash()
rules[["F"]] <- char_vec("F[-F]F[+F]F")

sentence <- c("F")
sentence <- lproduce(sentence, rules)
sentence <- lproduce(sentence, rules)
print(unvec_char(sentence))

turtle_init(mode = "clip")
turtle_hide()

turtle_setstate(c(50, 20, 0))
draw_sentence(sentence, 6, 30, 30)
```

```
[1] "F[-F]F[+F]F[-F-F]F[+F]F]F[-F]F[+F]F
[+F-F]F[+F]F]F[-F]F[+F]F"
```

Figure 9.53: Printed output for Figure 9.52, showing the sentence used to draw Figure 9.54.

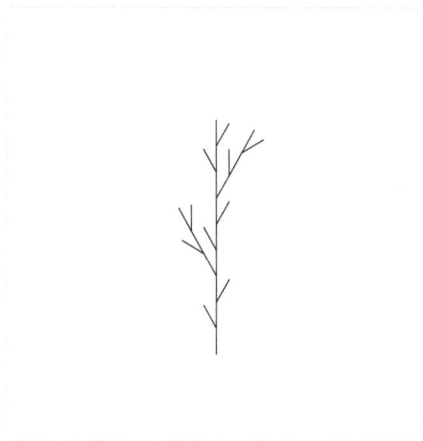

Figure 9.54: Displayed output for Figure 9.52.

Perhaps the most remarkable property of L-Systems is their flexibility: they provide almost endless opportunities for creativity. We could easily envision using random choices for sizes or angles (like runif(1, min = size / 2, max = size * 2)); these types of modifications often produce more life-like images.

For another example, rather than draw the entire structure smaller to fit all of the F moves in the turtle's drawing window, we could specify that each jump into a substructure (indicated by an addition to the state stack with a [character) could reduce the current size by 1/3, while each jump out (removal with a] character) reverses the adjustment. Other potential strategies include reducing the size at each F symbol encountered, setting the size according to the current size of the state stack, or increasing the symbol set with explicit "smaller" and "larger" symbols.

Figure 9.55: Potential adjustments for the draw_sentence() function (Figure 9.48), incorporating specific symbols for "smaller" and "larger."

```
  # ...
  } else if(symbol == "]") {
    turtle_setstate(peek_top(pos_stack))
    pos_stack <- without_top(pos_stack)
  } else if(symbol == "s") {
    size <- size * (2/3)
  } else if(symbol == "l") {
    size <- size / (2/3)
  } else {
  # ...
```

Figures 9.55, 9.56 and 9.57 show an example of the latter, a modification of the earlier L-System where s is interpreted as size <- size * (2/3) and l is interpreted as size <- size / (2/3) in the draw_sentence() function. (Note that since we've specified no replacement rules for s and l, the lproduce() function simply copies existing instances of them into each successive generation.)

```r
rules <- hash()
rules[["F"]] <- char_vec("Fs[l-Fs]F[l+Fs]Fl")

sentence <- c("F")
for(i in seq(1,4)) {
  sentence <- lproduce(sentence, rules)
}

turtle_init(mode = "clip")
turtle_hide()

turtle_setstate(c(50, 10, 0))
draw_sentence(sentence, 2.5, 30, 30)
```

Figure 9.56: Drawing a more sophisticated L-System including s and l symbols interpreted as in Figure 9.55.

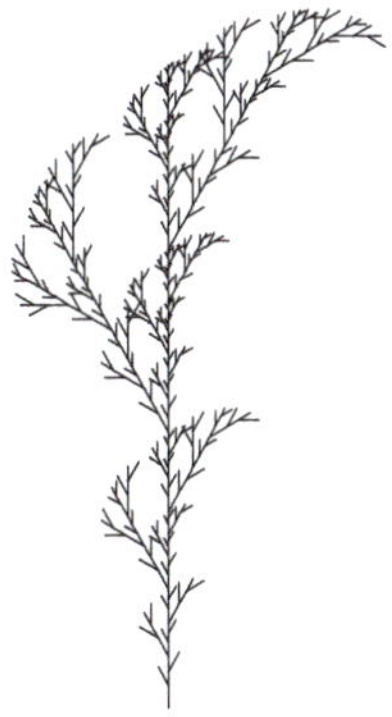

Figure 9.57: Displayed output for Figure 9.56.

```
[1] "Fs[l-Fs]F[l+Fs]Fls[l-Fs[l-Fs]F[l+Fs]Fls]Fs[l-Fs]F[l+Fs]Fl[l+Fs[l-Fs]F
[l+Fs]Fls]Fs[l-Fs]F[l+Fs]Flls[l-Fs[l-Fs]F[l+Fs]Fls[l-Fs[l-Fs]F[l+Fs]Fls]Fs
[l-Fs]F[l+Fs]Fl[l+Fs[l-Fs]F[l+Fs]Fls]Fs[l-Fs]F[l+Fs]Flls]Fs[l-Fs]F[l+Fs]Fl
s[l-Fs[l-Fs]F[l+Fs]Fls]Fs[l-Fs]F[l+Fs]Fl[l+Fs[l-Fs]F[l+Fs]Fls]Fs[l-Fs]F[l+
Fs]Fll[l+Fs[l-Fs]F[l+Fs]Fls[l-Fs[l-Fs]F[l+Fs]Fls]Fs[l-Fs]F[l+Fs]Fl[l+Fs[l-
Fs]F[l+Fs]Fls]Fs[l-Fs]F[l+Fs]Flls]Fs[l-Fs]F[l+Fs]Fls[l-Fs[l-Fs]F[l+Fs]Fls]
Fs[l-Fs]F[l+Fs]Fl[l+Fs[l-Fs]F[l+Fs]Fls]Fs[l-Fs]F[l+Fs]Flls[l-Fs[l-Fs]F[l+
Fs]Fls[l-Fs[l-Fs]F[l+Fs]Fls]Fs[l-Fs]F[l+Fs]Fl[l+Fs[l-Fs]F[l+Fs]Fls]Fs[l-Fs
]F[l+Fs]Flls[l-Fs[l-Fs]F[l+Fs]Fls[l-Fs[l-Fs]F[l+Fs]Fls]Fs[l-Fs]F[l+Fs]Fl[l
+Fs[l-Fs]F[l+Fs]Fls]Fs[l-Fs]F[l+Fs]Flls]Fs[l-Fs]F[l+Fs]Fls[l-Fs[l-Fs]F[l+F
s]Fls]Fs[l-Fs]F[l+Fs]Fl[l+Fs[l-Fs]F[l+Fs]Fls]Fs[l-Fs]F[l+Fs]Fll[l+Fs[l-Fs]
F[l+Fs]Fls[l-Fs[l-Fs]F[l+Fs]Fls]Fs[l-Fs]F[l+Fs]Fl[l+Fs[l-Fs]F[l+Fs]Fls]Fs[
l-Fs]F[l+Fs]Flls]Fs[l-Fs]F[l+Fs]Fls[l-Fs[l-Fs]F[l+Fs]Fls]Fs[l-Fs]F[l+Fs]Fl
[l+Fs[l-Fs]F[l+Fs]Fls]Fs[l-Fs]F[l+Fs]Flls]Fs[l-Fs]F[l+Fs]Fls[l-Fs[l-Fs]F[
l+Fs]Fls]Fs[l-Fs]F[l+Fs]Fl[l+Fs[l-Fs]F[l+Fs]Fls]Fs[l-Fs]F[l+Fs]Flls[l-Fs[l
-Fs]F[l+Fs]Fls[l-Fs[l-Fs]F[l+Fs]Fls]Fs[l-Fs]F[l+Fs]Fl[l+Fs[l-Fs]F[l+Fs]Fls
]Fs[l-Fs]F[l+Fs]Flls]Fs[l-Fs]F[l+Fs]Fls[l-Fs[l-Fs]F[l+Fs]Fls]Fs[l-Fs]F[l+F
s]Fl[l+Fs[l-Fs]F[l+Fs]Fls]Fs[l-Fs]F[l+Fs]Fll[l+Fs[l-Fs]F[l+Fs]Fls[l-Fs[l-F
s]F[l+Fs]Fls]Fs[l-Fs]F[l+Fs]Fl[l+Fs[l-Fs]F[l+Fs]Fls]Fs[l-Fs]F[l+Fs]Flls]Fs
[l-Fs]F[l+Fs]Fls[l-Fs[l-Fs]F[l+Fs]Fls]Fs[l-Fs]F[l+Fs]Fl[l+Fs[l-Fs]F[l+Fs]F
ls]Fs[l-Fs]F[l+Fs]Flll[l+Fs[l-Fs]F[l+Fs]Fls[l-Fs[l-Fs]F[l+Fs]Fls]Fs[l-Fs]F
[l+Fs]Fl[l+Fs[l-Fs]F[l+Fs]Fls]Fs[l-Fs]F[l+Fs]Flls[l-Fs[l-Fs]F[l+Fs]Fls[l-F
s[l-Fs]F[l+Fs]Fls]Fs[l-Fs]F[l+Fs]Fl[l+Fs[l-Fs]F[l+Fs]Fls]Fs[l-Fs]F[l+Fs]Fl
ls]Fs[l-Fs]F[l+Fs]Fls[l-Fs[l-Fs]F[l+Fs]Fls]Fs[l-Fs]F[l+Fs]Fl[l+Fs[l-Fs]F[l
+Fs]Fls]Fs[l-Fs]F[l+Fs]Fll[l+Fs[l-Fs]F[l+Fs]Fls[l-Fs[l-Fs]F[l+Fs]Fls]Fs[l-
Fs]F[l+Fs]Fl[l+Fs[l-Fs]F[l+Fs]Fls]Fs[l-Fs]F[l+Fs]Flls]Fs[l-Fs]F[l+Fs]Fls[l
-Fs[l-Fs]F[l+Fs]Fls]Fs[l-Fs]F[l+Fs]Fl[l+Fs[l-Fs]F[l+Fs]Fls]Fs[l-Fs]F[l+Fs]
Fllls]Fs[l-Fs]F[l+Fs]Fls[l-Fs[l-Fs]F[l+Fs]Fls]Fs[l-Fs]F[l+Fs]Fl[l+Fs[l-Fs]
F[l+Fs]Fls]Fs[l-Fs]F[l+Fs]Flls[l-Fs[l-Fs]F[l+Fs]Fls[l-Fs[l-Fs]F[l+Fs]Fls]F
s[l-Fs]F[l+Fs]Fl[l+Fs[l-Fs]F[l+Fs]Fls]Fs[l-Fs]F[l+Fs]Flls]Fs[l-Fs]F[l+Fs]F
ls[l-Fs[l-Fs]F[l+Fs]Fls]Fs[l-Fs]F[l+Fs]Fl[l+Fs[l-Fs]F[l+Fs]Fls]Fs[l-Fs]F[l
+Fs]Fll[l+Fs[l-Fs]F[l+Fs]Fls[l-Fs[l-Fs]F[l+Fs]Fls]Fs[l-Fs]F[l+Fs]Fl[l+Fs[l
-Fs]F[l+Fs]Fls]Fs[l-Fs]F[l+Fs]Flls]Fs[l-Fs]F[l+Fs]Fls[l-Fs[l-Fs]F[l+Fs]Fls
]Fs[l-Fs]F[l+Fs]Fl[l+Fs[l-Fs]F[l+Fs]Fls]Fs[l-Fs]F[l+Fs]Flll"
```

Figure 9.58: The sentence underlying Figure 9.57.

Parameterized L-Systems use symbols that encode additional information. For example `F(20)` might represent a forward movement of size 20, while `+(30)` might represent a right turn of 30°. Similarly, replacement rules could take this information into account; as in `F(n)` → `F(n/2)[+F(n/2)]-F(n/2)`. Such rules might be encoded as R lists (or our own nested lists) as in `s <- list(list("F", 20), list("+", 30), list("F", 20))`. Corresponding versions of `lproduce()` and `draw_sentence()` would need to be created to work with such lists-of-lists.

What about rules that are not deterministic? Perhaps with 25% probability we use the rule `F` → `F[+F]F` and with the remaining 75% probability we use `F` → `F[-F]F`. Symbols could be occasionally deleted (say, with 50% probability we neglect to put anything in the produced sentence for the symbol). "Context-sensitive" L-Systems take multiple symbols into account in sentence generation, as in `F+` → `F+F` and `F-` → `F-F`.

Finally, even basic L-Systems can include symbols that are completely ignored in drawing but are used in the sentence generation process. Consider the following L-System:

start: `X`

`X` → `F-[[X]+X]+F[+FX]-X`

`F` → `FF`

Figure 9.59 illustrates five iterations of `lproduce()`, where `X` is interpreted as "do nothing," left and right turns are 20° and 25°.

A vast array of geometric figures can be produced and drawn with L-Systems as well, including the Koch curve described by the rule `F` → `F-F++F-F` (with 60° turns). There are many resources to be found for L-Systems on the web. Excellent books that cover the topic include *The Nature of Code* by Daniel Shiffman and *The Algorithmic Beautify of Plants* by Przemyslaw Prusinkiewicz and Aristid Lindenmayer, both available for free online.

Figure 9.59: Drawing for an L-System with start symbol X and rules X → F-[[X]+X]+F[+FX]-X, F → FF.

Exercises

1. Consider the L-System sentence F[-Fc]F[+Fc]Fc, where c is interpreted as "draw a small circle." This would add circular "leaves" to Figure 9.50. Create a modified substitution rule such that after each sentence generation, leaves are present at the ends of all branches (but not at internal branching points).

2. Add randomness to the draw_sentence() function, such that each F, +, or - is interpreted and drawn slightly differently.

3. Research some of the properties of "space-filling curves," and implement one (such as the Hilbert curve) as an L-System.

4. See if you can implement a parameterized L-System, with "symbols" made up of 2-element lists and sentences as lists of symbols (e.g. list(list("F", 10), list("+", 36))). Rules will likely also need to be stored as lists; in fact, they could store *anonymous functions* (functions not given a name). For example, the rule $F(n) \rightarrow F(n/2)$ might be encoded as rules[["F"]] <- function(value) { return(value/2) }. Using the rule would require first extracting the function, with something like if(symbol[[1]] == "F") { func <- rules[["F"]] } and then calling it with something like newsymbol <- list("F", func(symbol[[2]])).

Epilogue

THIS BOOK IS AN OUTGROWTH OF A SHORT CLASS I taught at
Oregon State University through the Center for Genome Research
and Biocomputing, "Recursion and Dynamic Programming for
Sequence Analysis." My goal for the class was to introduce the
beauty of computer science to life scientists, via the algorithms
and tools they encounter frequently. Too often (in my opinion) are
methods in bioinformatics reduced to mechanistic table-filling,
when fundamental ideas about computing and mathematics lie so
close at hand.

This audience drove the use of R; in the first offering of the
class, R was a comfortable language for most, whereas other more
common choices (like Python) would have required additional
background. Soon what was a pedagogical challenge became an
opportunity, as R's flexible graphical utilities allowed us to explore
the internals of these algorithms in ways I had not previously. Additionally, I discovered that R's nature as a functional language with
procedural capabilities worked well with the recursion → memoization → dynamic programming exposition I prefer. Indeed, my
own experiments in R for this work have helped me explore the
fascinating interface between functional and procedural paradigms.

A secondary goal for this book was to produce an homage to
these topics I love so much, as an artifact of elegance itself worthy
of display. Hopefully my few skills in typesetting and design (with
the help of some excellent LATEX packages) have been up to the
challenge. I apologize that in some sections the reader must play
"hunt the figure," a consequence of the LATEX layout engine in figure-
dense regions.

With respect to content, in a few ways the current edition is
over-complete, and in others under-complete. Some of the material
in Chapters 3 and 4 was not included in the original class and is
tangential to the main topics. Yet, for example, it felt irresponsible
to cover stacks and depth-first-search in trees, but not depth- and
breadth-first search in graphs. In the future I'd like to add some
discussion of phylogenetic trees. I also think context-free-grammars,

the CYK dynamic programming algorithm, and their application to RNA secondary structure prediction would be a nice followup (or precursor) to L-Systems.

THIS BOOK WAS TYPESET with the excellent Tufte-LaTeX package, with Palatino and Helvetica typefaces for the main text, and Inconsolata for code. Other packages of note include `minted` for styling code blocks (with a custom scheme for R code), `epigraph` for chapter epigraphs, `wrapfig` for placing text-wrapping figures, and `subfloat` for numbering of sub-figures. Most figures were produced either as R output, or with Apple Keynote. The cover image is courtesy Wikimedia Commons. This work is self-published, and copyright Shawn T. O'Neil 2017.

Index